KANT AND THEOLOGY

WAS KANT A CLOSET THEOLOGIAN?

ELIZABETH CAMERON GALBRAITH

International Scholars Publications
San Francisco - London - Bethesda
1996

Library of Congress Cataloging-in-Publication Data

Galbraith, Elizabeth Cameron, 1965-
Kant and theology : was Kant a closet theologian? / Elizabeth Cameron Galbraith.
p. cm.
Includes bibliographical references (p.) and index.
ISBN 1-57309-075-1 (cloth : alk. paper). -- ISBN 1-57309-074-3 (pbk. : alk. paper)
1. Kant, Immanuel, 1724-1804--Religion. 2. Theology--History--18th century. I. Title.
B2799.R4G35 1996
230'.092--dc20 96-9255
CIP

Editorial Inquiries:
International Scholars Publications
7831 Woodmont Avenue #345
Bethesda,MD 20814

To order: (800) 55-PUBLISH

KANT AND THEOLOGY

DEDICATION

For my parents, whose unstinting love never ceases to amaze me.

TABLE OF CONTENTS

FOREWORD

Immanuel Kant, the renowned philosopher of the eighteenth century, is often thought of as the great sceptic of religion. His onslaught against the traditional arguments for the existence of God in the *Critique of Pure Reason* is considered decisive evidence of his efforts to destroy theology. In Chapter I of this work I argue that such an interpretation is mistaken. When Kant attacks the traditional arguments for the existence of God, he is doing so in order to clear the ground, as it were, in anticipation of a more convincing, moral apologetic. Chapters I and II illustrate that Kant's moral apologetic includes: a justification of the existence of God in face of the fact of evil, a positive appraisal of theological doctrines such as revelation, grace, and the kingdom of God, and what Kant considers to be an appropriate conception of salvation.

In Chapter III the sincerity of Kant's theological position is demonstrated by comparing it with the theology of well-known religious figures. Kant's personal theological outlook is found to bear striking resemblance to that of the fifteenth century Catholic theologian, Erasmus of Rotterdam. This is a rather surprising discovery, in light of the general assumption that Kant's philosophy has its roots in the Protestant tradition and has sometimes been linked to Martin Luther.

Hostility towards the association of Kant with theology often comes from those anxious to defend Christianity from possible threats. It is therefore of value to theology in general, and to Christian theology in particular, to clarify the areas in which Kant's perspective differs from the Christian faith. In chapter IV I show that Kant's theology does not have Christ at its centre. According to Kant, Jesus is neither redeemer, nor saviour, in the traditional understanding of these terms. Nevertheless, the understanding of Jesus' role offered by Kant presents exciting possibilities for modern alternatives to traditional Christian theology.

I thought it appropriate to conclude this book with a brief examination of Kant's final treatise, the *Opus Postumum*. In this work Kant is preoccupied with the central concerns of theology, namely God, humankind and the world, in an effort to develop a 'system of transcendental philosophy.' In particular, God, who is already the ground of the unity of nature, morality and end-purpose in Kant's system of theology, now becomes the key to his entire philosophy. This is taken to be a clear indication of Kant's recognition that the goal which he has spent his entire life working towards is grounded in theism. As a result, I argue that the theology that has always been present in Kant's writings, if in certain cases less apparent, finally comes to the fore.

ACKNOWLEDGEMENTS

Thanks are due, first and foremost, to John Heywood-Thomas, and Terrence Wilkerson, the two people who introduced me to Kant when I was an undergraduate at Nottingham University. I am indebted to Brian Hebblethwaite and to Don Cupitt for steering me through this project during my graduate years at Cambridge University. To Ann Loades, who became not only my most constructive critic, but also my greatest advocate, I shall be eternally grateful. It was her confidence in and encouragement of me that made the difference.

Elizabeth Cameron Galbraith
May 1996

NOTE

Versions of some of the material presented in this book appear as publications in the following journals:

"Kant and Religious Doctrines," Enlight*enment and Dissent*, 1992.

"Was Kant a Closet Theologian," *Theology*, 1992.

"Kant and Erasmus," Scottish Journal of *Theology*, 1993.

"Kant and a Catholic Theology of Hope," *Philosophy and Theology*, 1996.

***

The references to the German text of Kant's works are to Kant's gesammelte Schriften, edited by der königlich Preußischen Akademie der Wissenschaften, Berlin, Reimer, 1905 onwards. These are indicated in the footnotes as KW, with volume, and page number, after which the reference to the English translation, where available, follows.

***

The English translations of Kant's works used in this book are as follows:

Pre-critical

1755— "Nova Dilucidatio," transl. F.E. England in *Kant's Conception of God*. George Allen and Unwin, 1929.

1759— "Some Reflections on Optimism," transl. G. Rabel in *Kant: A Study*, O.U.P., 1963.

1763— "The Only Possible Argument for a Demonstration of the Existence of God," transl. G. Rabel in *Kant: A Study*, O.U.P., 1963.

Critical

1781—*Critique of Pure Reason*, transl. N. Kemp Smith, Macmillan and Co., 1990 edition. References to this work are to the paragraphs of the first (A) and second (B) editions.

1783—*Prolegomena to Any Future Metaphysics*, transl. L.W. Beck in *Kant Selections*, Macmillan and Co., 1988.

1785—*Groundwork of the Metaphysic of Morals*, transl. H.J. Paton, Harper and Row, 1964.

1786—"What is Orientation in Thinking," transl. L.W. Beck in the *Critique of Practical Reason and Other Writings in Moral Philosophy*, Garland, 1976.

1788—*Critique of Practical Reason*, transl. L.W. Beck, Macmillan and Co., 1985 edition.

1790—*Critique of Judgement*, transl. J.C. Meredith, Clarendon Press, 1985 edition.

1791—"On the Failure of All Attempted Philosophical Theodicies," transl. M. Despland in *Kant on History and Religion*, McGill U.P., 1973.

1793—*Religion Within the Limits of Reason Alone,* transl. T.M. Greene and H.H. Hudson, Harper and Row, 1960.

1794—"The End of All Things," transl. R.E. Anchor, in *Kant on History*, ed., L.W. Beck, Bobbs-Merrill, 1963.

1795—*Perpetual Peace*, transl, and intro. N.M. Butler, Columbia U. P.,1939.

1798—*The Conflict of the Faculties,* transl. and intro. M.J. Gregor, Abaris, 1979.

1797—*Metaphysic of Morals*, transl. and intro. T.K.Abbott, in *Kant's Critique of Practical Reason and Other works on the Theory of Ethics*, Longmans, 1883 edition; *The Metaphysical Elements of Justice, Part One of the Metaphysic of Morals*, transl. and intro. by J. Ladd, Bobbs-Merrill Co., 1965.

1800—*Kant's Introduction to Logic and His Essay on the Mistaken Subtilty of the Four Figures* (1762), transl. T.K. Abbott, Vision Press Ltd., 1963.

Posthumous

Lectures on Ethics, transl. L. Infield, Methuen and Co., 1930, as taken from the German text, *Eine Vorlesung Kants über Ethik,* compiled by P.Mentzer, 1924.

Lectures on Philosophical Theology, transl. A.W. Wood and G.M. Clark, Cornell U.P., 1978, as taken from the German text, *Vorlesungen über die philosophische Religionslehre,* compiled by Pölitz, 1830 edition.

PREFACE

Kant is often referred to as the great sceptic of religion. His onslaught against the traditional arguments for the existence of God in his *Critique of Pure Reason*[1] is considered decisive evidence of his efforts to destroy theology. Yet, for those who have the patience to read as far as Kant's *Critique of Practical Reason*, and even beyond that to his *Critique of Judgement*, there is the surprising revelation that Kant, the great sceptic, offers not only one, but two versions of his own argument for the existence of God. Is this a contradiction? How, after all, can Kant be the great philosophical sceptic of religion, and also offer his own version of an argument for the existence of God?

It was my own encounter with the apparent contradiction outlined above that led me to an investigation of Kant's treatment of religion. Of course, after very little analysis of the text it became clear that the situation was not contradictory. One can offer one's own argument for the existence of God as against other arguments which one believes to be invalid. However, the fact that Kant wants to offer a better, more convincing, argument for the existence of God than the ones previously on offer, is not always pointed out. Kant is shown to be the great sceptic, full stop. The fact that when Kant attacks the traditional arguments he is doing so in order to clear the ground, as it were, in anticipation of a more convincing apologetic, is very often neglected. On the other hand, for many who do come into contact with Kant's moral argument for the existence of God, no reference is made to Kant's great onslaught upon the traditional arguments in his earlier work. Kant is simply seen as one among many, who attempt to justify belief in God.

In an effort to change such one-sided presentations, my research on Kant began. What was to be revealed through that research was both surprising and enlightening. It became clear to me that the preoccupation of the great philosopher of the eighteenth century with belief in God went far beyond his moral argument. Kant was actively engaging in theology, to the extent that he propounded his own version of central theological doctrines such as revelation and grace.

The value of Kant's work for theology has never been denied, nor his influence upon the kind of theology which was to result from the eighteenth century. However, to say that what Kant wrote has value for theology is quite different from the claim that Kant actively engaged in theology. Therefore, it is worth considering what it means to say that Kant is engaging in theology. To begin with, it is necessary to point out that the theology with which this study is concerned is that which has taken place in the Christian tradition. Such theology is normally understood to be the study which treats of God, God's nature and attributes, and God's relation with humankind and the universe. It is normally an exercise from within faith, that is, a rational enquiry into the nature of God, as well as the formation of dogma concerning God. Philosophical theology denotes the attempt to give rational expression to belief in God and Christian doctrines. The aim of philosophical theology has traditionally been to underpin faith with rational argument in order to show how, as a rational person, one can profess belief in God. So far as the philosophical theologian explains the reasonableness of Christian belief, she is considered an apologist. Philosophical theology has often been associated with the quest to do something in order to prevent the spread of irrationalism in theology and even the decay of Christian faith among the more thoughtful elements of society. From the philosophical theologian's point of view, to say that faith and theology do not need rational justification, is to ignore faith's claim to be meaningful and true. Philosophical theology differs from the philosophy of religion, which tries to appraise the theologian's standard of evidence, such as her handling of concepts like faith and doubt, in order to test their validity and coherence.

Over the years theology has become more of an academic study, with the result that it has developed into a generic term for a number of interrelated disciplines, such as biblical, systematic, and moral theology. As theology comes to be increasingly identified with the academic discipline, it becomes less identifiable as a discipline carried out solely from within faith. In fact, some theologians have even fought against the idea that we should associate theology with commitment to the Christian faith. In 1955 for instance, Flew and MacIntyre claimed that the word 'theology' ought not to be identified with 'believing in God', so that the expression 'atheist theologian' ought not to be considered self-contradictory. Otherwise, we would be left with the paradox that 'those who reach opposite conclusions about certain questions must be regarded as having thereby shown themselves to have been engaged in different disciplines.'[2] Therefore, today it is no longer the case that to call someone a theologian is to associate that person with belief in God, be it either the God of the Christian tradition or any other.

It will be the aim of this thesis to demonstrate that Kant is not just a philosopher of religion, if we mean by this someone who simply scrutinises the claims of religion, but rather, advocating his own theology. With regard to Kant's theology two things can be said. First, at the time of Kant it was not acceptable to associate theology with anything other than belief in God. Secondly, Kant's treatment of religion suggests that he is an apologist for belief in God. The reader will note as this study progresses that I make use of less well known works by Kant in my efforts to illustrate his theology. I think it is vital to do this in order that these works are recognized for the valuable contribution they make to one's understanding of Kant's theology.

ENDNOTES

[1] Hereafter to be referred to as 'first *Critique*.' I shall use 'second *Critique*' to refer to the *Critique of Practical Reason*, and 'third *Critique*' to refer to the *Critique of Judgement.* I shall use the 'three *Critiques*' to refer to all three of the *Critique of Pure Reason*, *Critique of Practical Reason* and *Critique of Judgement.*

[2] *New Essays in Philosophical Theology*, ed. A. Flew and A. MacIntyre, S.C.M., 1955, p.x: 'The paradox that whereas St.Thomas' presentation of the quinque viae is a piece of (Natural or Philosophical) Theology, Hume's *Dialogues Concerning Natural Religion* must belong to some other and nameless discipline.'

FIRST COMMENDATORY PREFACE

Elizabeth Galbraith's book has much to offer in overcoming the lamentable neglect of Kant by theologians. It is not just that she gets us to attend to dimensions of the three great *Critiques* too frequently ignored or misread, and directs her readers also to significant shorter essays by Kant. Having shifted various boulders in the way, Kant, she argues, advances a form of theology which can be discerned to be both meaningful and true by a theological realist. She is herself an admirable exegete, but more than that, she does her own fair share of scrapping misapprehension by aligning Kant with Erasmus, rather than with Luther as a predecessor. This gives us a refreshing perspective on Kant, and makes it possible for us to get on the inside of what he has to offer in laying hold of a life of faith. Ignorant of God (and necessarily so) Kant yet makes some sense of 'inner revelation', of 'grace', of trust in divine justice and hence of 'hope'—he is a theologian of a kind whilst, notoriously, without a grain of ecclesiastical sensitivity so far as one can see. What he's up to is far more important either than the labels he used for his own activity or those which prevent us from 'reading' him.

Since John Hick has himself explicitly appealed to Kant's 'Copernican revolution' as provocation for his own re-evaluation of the human and historical Jesus, Elizabeth Galbraith's critical comparison of Kant with Hick is very illuminating. Her book is provocative of argument not merely about Kant's texts, but about his value for theology both now and for the future. He was not a voice stifled by 'the dead hand of the past', and however much we agree to disagree with him, his very distinctive position in evaluating Christianity has been given new life in Elizabeth Galbraith's book.

Ann Loades
University of Durham

SECOND COMMENDATORY PREFACE

Elizabeth Cameron Galbraith's study of Kant as theologian exemplifies many of the traits which have marked the best of recent English language scholarship on Kant: a careful analysis of Kant's texts; sensitivity to the historical context in which Kant did his work; attentiveness to the shifts and developments that took place within Kant's thinking, balanced by a probing search for previously unnoticed continuities between his pre-critical and critical writings; and a well-informed critical engagement of the interpretations which have held sway among prior generations of Kant scholars. These features have helped bring about significant reassessment of a number of elements in the interpretations of Kant's philosophy which, for much of the current century, have been taken as standard within much of the Anglo-American philosophical community. Kant's treatment of religion within his critical project is one element for which some major reassessment—in this case, long overdue—has already started to take place.

Within the context of this reassessment of Kant's thought on religion, the arguments and evidence which Professor Galbraith offers in this volume to support the claim that Kant was: "actively engaged in theology" rather than what we have come to call "philosophy of religion" should be the locus of much instructive discussion. This claim moves at least one step beyond the work of scholars such as James Collins, Michael Despland, Gordon Michalson, and Allen Wood who have done much to correct the almost exclusive emphasis that much previous scholarship placed upon Kant as "the great skeptic" of religion." Their work has pointed out positive and constructive features which are just as essential to Kant's treatment of religion as the more well-known negative strictures he places on church dogma and practice. Professor Galbraith does not, however, see Kant as simply placing these positive and negative elements in balance with one another—a balance, which Michalson has argued, seems uneasy and may ultimately be unstable. She argues instead that Kant's critical work as a whole advances a positive theological program in that it articulates a generally sympathetic, albeit heterodox, account of a crucial set of Christian doctrines (revelation, salvation, grace, and incarnation). This account, moreover, is one which she claims can be instructively mapped out in reference to other thinkers, both before and after Kant, who have explicitly framed their accounts of these doctrines in the context of Christian theological tradition. She thus provides illuminating comparisons between Kant and Erasmus on the topics of sin, grace and freedom, and between Kant and John Hick on the topics of incarnation and the possibility of a universal religion.

Professor Galbraith's book adds an important new dimension to the current scholarly reassessment of Kant's treatment of religion, which has made it increasingly implausible to consider it as simply an exemplar of the secularizing currents of Enlightenment thought and culture. Kant's thought on these matters is complex, subtle, and supple—and Professor Galbraith has done it justice in her work.

Philip Rossi, S.J.
Marquette University

I: KANT'S COPERNICAN REVOLUTION IN THEOLOGY

INTRODUCTION

In order to understand Kant's theology, it is necessary first to examine the way in which it develops. I shall consider Kant's pre-critical stance, and then examine the scepticism concerning traditional religious metaphysics which results from the revolution in his thought. It is only by considering the kind of criticism Kant was offering that one can truly appreciate the apologetic he then goes on to offer. The very fact that Kant has an apologetic to offer also needs to be demonstrated. Therefore, the next task will be to defend the very idea that Kant is engaging in apologetics, before outlining the main features of that moral apologetic, which is given in an attempt to replace traditional theology with what Kant considers a more plausible alternative, namely, moral theology. I shall then defend Kant's project as an exercise in theology, and summarise the main features of his critical theology as compared with his pre-critical theology. Finally, I shall demonstrate Kant's Copernican revolution at work in his essay on theodicy. To summarise, in this chapter I shall do four things:

I) Examine the development in Kant's thought which led him to his scepticism concerning traditional religious metaphysics, as well as the main features of the critique resulting from his scepticism.

II) Demonstrate the fact that Kant's critique is nothing other than a preliminary to the positive moral theology with which he seeks to replace traditional theology, and then outline his moral theology.

III) Defend Kant's exercise in his three *Critiques* as an exercise in theology, and highlight the distinct features of what I shall call Kant's Copernican revolution in theology.

IV) Demonstrate Kant's theology at work in his essay on theodicy.

I: REJECTION OF TRADITIONAL THEOLOGY[1]

Critique of Pure Reason

Most people who know anything about Kant identify him with what has been called the Copernican revolution in philosophy.[2] In this study I am more concerned with theology than philosophy,[3] but not surprisingly, Kant's revolution in philosophy also has repercussions for his attitude towards theology. Kant initiates what I shall call a Copernican revolution in theology as well as in philosophy. In order to assess Kant's Copernican revolution in theology, it will be necessary to begin with an account of the development from the pre-critical period through to the critical period in Kant's religious thought.

Before his critical revolution, which occurred in the 1770's, Kant's stance on religion was informed by a preoccupation with the theological concept of creation: the universe had a beginning and depended upon a Creator. Kant thought that arguments from the beauty and perfect arrangement of the world were sufficient to establish the existence of a supreme, wise Creator, but personally he preferred to start with arguments drawn from the analysis of physics. In 1755 he wrote of the certainty of all events which are determined 'by ever preceding grounds in a concatenated nexus until the first condition of the world which directly displays God as Creator is as it were a fountain and gushing spring from which all things take their downward course by an infallible necessity.'[4]

Kant's theological outlook was very close to that of Leibniz. His essay of 1759, "Some reflections on Optimism,"[5] shows an unambiguous re-affirmation of the optimism of Leibniz. Kant followed Leibniz in the belief that this is the best of all possible worlds, and that there is a moral necessity determining God's choice of this world. Leibniz had maintained that God's benevolence could be known by reason, and that a person's rationality was a reflection of God's. In his own way, Kant followed Leibniz in his claim that the deity was to be adored for the very rationality of human beings, a rationality which enabled them to govern themselves justly.

It is important to realise that even in what is usually referred to as his pre-critical stage, Kant was not entirely happy with the Ontological and Cosmological arguments for the existence of God as they were traditionally presented.[6] He offered instead, his own version of an Ontological argument in "The Only Possible Argument For A Demonstration of the Existence of God."[7] However, he ended this essay with the statement that 'it is absolutely necessary to convince oneself of the existence of God, but not as necessary that one should demonstrate it.'[8] This is a marked pointer to his later stance.

All of this confidence concerning our knowledge of the goodness of God and our ability to prove God's existence was to change. It was Hume who awoke Kant from his dogmatic slumbers on the bounds and capacities of reason. Kant tells us this in the *Prolegomena to any future Metaphysics.*[9] This work, which is a re-write of the first *Critique* in simpler and more concise language, was produced in response to criticisms of the first *Critique* and in order to overcome misunder-standings of the arguments offered therein. Waking from dogmatic slumbers meant wakening to the reality that human reason cannot prove as much as tradi-tional theology had claimed that it could. The influence of Hume led Kant to question his own contemplative optimism. He came to re-examine his own under-standing of the role of the theistic proofs in making it possible to affirm the existence of God. The result of this self-critical exercise was that Kant eventually abandoned the claim that it is possible to ascend to knowledge of the deity by means of theoretical reason. By the 1770's Kant was of the opinion that the human intellect could not gain knowledge of a transcendent deity as Leibniz had thought. Far from advocating traditional rational theology, Kant now felt com-pelled to attack the dogmatism of such theology and of ecclesiastical claims to the possession of revealed truth. Inevitably this meant that he had to reject any theol-ogy which was dependent on the Ontological argument as a rigourous demonstra-tion of the existence of God. Kant now saw that theology could not be defended in this way. He also became convinced that a responsible affirmation of faith in God could not depend philosophically upon the traditional causal maxims. This change was the result of his realization, thanks perhaps to Hume, that human beings are not equipped to give an account of the being of the deity as Leibniz had proposed.

The move from Kant's pre-critical to his critical stance on theology amounted to the move from the conviction that traditional rational theology could prove the existence of God to the critical claim that it could not. Having decided that the kind of theology which he himself had previously advocated could not prove the existence of God, Kant set out to show why it could not. I shall not go into the details of Kant's criticism of the three traditional arguments for the existence of

God for two reasons. First, this area of Kant's work has already been given much attention. Secondly, my main concern is to examine Kant's approach to theology rather than to examine the kind of theology he rejects. However, it is relevant to an understanding of Kant's approach to theology to explain the grounds upon which he rejects traditional rational theology. In order to do this I shall turn to Kant's Copernican revolution as outlined in his first *Critique.*

Kant's Copernican revolution amounts to a change in view about how one comes to have knowledge of the world. Instead of the traditional view, which assumed that knowledge is passive conformity to an object, Kant came to believe that the human mind also had a part to play in the reception and formation of knowledge. According to Kant, knowledge requires a synthesis of a relevant concept with a relevant intuition. The world provides the intuition, the mind the concept, and then the intuition is synthesized to give knowledge.

The results of this change in opinion for Kant's attitude towards theology are significant. It leads Kant to rule out what he considers to be traditional metaphysics,[10] namely alleged knowledge of supersensible and unconditional reality. Traditional rational theology, which claimed to be able to prove the existence of God by means of theoretical argument, had originally been an aspect of such metaphysics. Thus, part of Kant's rejection of traditional metaphysics is his rejection of traditional rational theology.

In the place of such metaphysics Kant seeks to establish a new metaphysics, which is a system of *a priori* knowledge from mere concepts. This new metaphysics has two parts: a metaphysics of nature, consisting of all *a priori* principles of all that is, and a metaphysics of morals, comprising all *a priori* principles of what ought to be. Kant is attempting to replace what he considers invalid metaphysics with valid metaphysics. It will later be shown how this attempt includes his effort to replace what he considers invalid theology with valid theology. For the moment, it is enough to point out why Kant considers traditional theology to be invalid.

Traditional rational theology claimed to be a legitimate route to knowledge of God, and in particular, to knowledge of God's existence. Kant's new theory of knowledge means that he has to deny this claim. If knowledge requires a concept and an intuition working together, then there can be no knowledge of God, since it is not possible to have an intuition of God. God is not an object of possible experience. In their attempt to prove the existence of God the traditional arguments had been using a concept of God without a corresponding intuition. Therefore, traditional rational theology is invalid as a means of proving the existence of God. Moreover, since the Ontological, the Cosmological, and the Physico-theological arguments for the existence of God all attempt to overstep the bounds of theoretical reason, they are also invalid as forms of metaphysics.

From the above it may appear that Kant has become convinced of Humean scepticism concerning belief in God, and thus seeks to reject theology totally. Fortunately, this is not the case. In a section of the first *Critique* entitled "The Impossibility of a Sceptical Satisfaction of Pure Reason in its Internal Conflicts,"[11] Kant makes it clear that his aim in the first *Critique* has been to find an approach to metaphysics which lies between dogmatism and scepticism. The result of this is that Kant attempts to find an approach to theology which also lies between traditional rational theology and Humean scepticism. The way in which Kant does this is hinted at in his famous statement 'I have found it necessary to deny knowledge in order to make room for faith.'[12] Kant found it necessary to close off theology from the domain of scientific investigation, in order to safeguard it from Humean scepticism. The way in which he does this is by using the concept of two worlds, a world of appearances and a world of things in themselves. Previous theories of knowledge assumed that the world one comes to know is the world as it is in itself. However, Kant now argues that since the mind has such an active part to play in the reception of knowledge, it is appropriate to assume that we only come to know the world as it is for us, not as it is in itself. Therefore beyond the world as we know it, the world of appearances, there is the world of things in themselves, or as Kant refers to it, the world of noumena. In ruling out the possibility of knowledge of God, Kant is not ruling out God altogether. Rather, he argues that God belongs to the world of things in themselves, as distinct from the world of appearances. From the theoretical point of view Kant will only allow noumena a negative role:

> If, however, we have in mind only objects of nonsensible intuition, in respect of which our categories are admittedly not valid, and of which therefore we can never have any knowledge whatsoever (neither intuition nor concept), noumena in this purely negative sense must indeed be admitted.[13]

Thus, one can have no theoretical knowledge of noumena,[14] indeed their role seems, from the theoretical point of view, to be no more than that of preventing us from outreaching the bounds of theoretical knowledge. Nevertheless, Kant insists that this does not mean that the concept of God can be ruled out entirely. Although Kant's first *Critique* is often seen as a negative exercise with regard to traditional rational theology, Kant's aim is in fact to answer Humean scepticism with regard to metaphysics and theology.

But where does Kant stand if he has been sceptical enough to reject the traditional approach to demonstrating belief in God, but has not latched hold of complete scepticism. By simply offering Kant's critique of traditional theology one gains no great insight into his own perspective. Yet, an outline of Kant's rejection of the traditional theological approach is as far as many studies go, in spite of the fact that there is a great deal of information in the first *Critique* which reveals Kant's own theological outlook. Such information has been highlighted in the works of Donald MacKinnon,[15] which have proven valuable as an insight into Kant's stance. The points which can be gathered concerning Kant and theology from a reading of MacKinnon will now be considered.

MacKinnon acknowledges the importance of Kant's distinction between the world of appearances and the world of things in themselves. The world of appearances is the world of scientific knowledge, the world of things in themselves is that which lies beyond the world of science. We can know nothing about the world of things in themselves. The attempt of traditional rational theology to represent God is an attempt to represent the unrepresentable,[16] since the concepts we use are inadequate to lay hold of the reality of God.[17] In claiming that traditional rational theology, or metaphysics, cannot prove the existence of God, Kant is seeking to place God beyond the means of scientific proof. There is a sense in which Kant is safeguarding God, by cutting off our access to God. God lies outside the frontiers of intelligible referential and descriptive statement.[18] God is simply beyond the reach of representation.[19] In his denial of traditional metaphysics Kant is setting out the limits of conceptual adequacy with regard to the transcendent and thereby any limitations we might seek to impose upon God. Nicholas Lash has referred to a particular kind of agnosticism which he describes as 'a theological policy aimed at insistently reminding the believer of the limits of his language and theoretical understanding.'[20] MacKinnon would say that Kant professes an agnosticism of this kind, namely a metaphysical agnosticism which is not damaging to theology.[21]

MacKinnon also recognises that the whole of Kant's attack upon speculative metaphysics is in order to safeguard against the danger of anthropomorphism,[22] which in MacKinnon's view is more idolatrous than an honest agnosticism.[23] Kant hints at this idea in the first *Critique*,[24] but makes it more explicit in his *Prolegomena*.[25] He points to the danger of using finite concepts to refer to God, since any such finite concepts would be anthropomorphic. He also offers a replacement for what he calls dogmatic anthropomorphism,[26] advocating instead of this anthropomorphism, a kind of 'symbolic anthropomorphism,' according to which:

> We then do not attribute to the Supreme Being any of the properties in themselves by which we represent objects of experience, and we thereby avoid dogmatic anthropomorphism; but we attribute them to the relation of this Being to the world and allow ourselves a symbolic anthropomorphism, which in fact concerns language only and not the object itself.[27]

Symbolic anthropomorphism, which Kant also refers to as 'a concept of the Supreme Being sufficiently determined for us, though we have left out everything that could determine it absolutely or in itself,'[28] is a means for Kant to retain reference to God, but without claiming to be able to say anything about God as God is in God's self. It allows for a distinction between the way in which we conceive of God, and the true nature of God, which is beyond our conceptual capacities. It is important to realise that Kant does not throw out all reference to the transcendent, but rather rejects dogmatic anthropomorphism, which attributes to the Supreme being certain finite characteristics as if they belonged to such a being in itself. His approach is therefore significantly different from that of Logical Positivism, which denies the possibility of transcendent assertion.[29] Ann Loades compares Kant's symbolic anthropomorphism with Jaspers' 'ciphers of transcendence' which are pointers to the transcendent that are not literally translatable.[30] They are rational concepts which transcend all experience, gaining certainty through approximation. These ciphers determine God as God is for us, not as God is in God's self. Kant is willing to refer to God only in ways which do not bring God down to the human level. There is nothing here to suggest that symbolic anthropomorphism involves the rejection of belief in a transcendent God. Kant rejects only dogmatic anthropomorphism, which mistakes authentic belief for literal truth.[31]

MacKinnon's exposition suggests that although Kant's rejection of the traditional arguments for the existence of God seems to be ruling out all access to God, it actually safeguards God, by claiming that God belongs to a realm beyond the mere limits of scientific, or human, knowledge. Kant's first *Critique*, in which he rejects traditional rational theology, is both setting certain limits to the exercise of theology, and at the same time is a theological discipline advocating the use of symbolic anthropomorphism, in an attempt to speak responsibly about God. Kant is trying to prevent us from straining after the unattainable. He is also trying to purify the concepts we use to refer to God from anthropomorphism. Kant's agnosticism is, as MacKinnon sees it, a habit of mind to be cultivated.[32] Kant is pointing out what our limited kind of experience alone makes possible. The rejection of traditional theology is not meant to detract from belief in God, since according to Kant 'the inscrutable wisdom through which we exist is not less worthy of veneration in respect to what it denies us than in what it has granted.' One might even go so far as to say that, from MacKinnon's point of view, our very inability to know God is itself an indirect or negative witness to the transcendent.[33] Finally, in MacKinnon's opinion it seems appropriate to align Kant with the tradition of Negative Theology: 'It is with the tradition of negative theology that in the end Kant,...comes to rest.'[34]

In my opinion MacKinnon is entirely correct in his interpretation of Kant, who does not deny that the world belongs to a Supreme being, but does claim that theoretical knowledge of God is not possible for us. The existence of God is not something we can prove, or disprove for that matter, because the reality of God transcends all human reason. It is better to admit what we don't know than to make presumptuous claims about God. Theoretical attempts to prove the existence of God, or to encompass God within empirical boundaries do not work. But to say this is not to limit God, rather it is to suggest that God is beyond the limitations of empirical knowledge. The tradition of negative theology does, therefore, appear a suitable framework within which to place Kant's position.

It is also worth noting that although Kant rejects all attempts to prove the existence of God by means of traditional theology, he nevertheless maintains that traditional theology is still 'of great importance in its negative employment, and serves as a permanent censor of our reason.' By this Kant means that traditional theology teaches how one ought to conceive of God, namely as the most perfect Being. It thus denies the appropriation of any limitation to God. Such theology is:

> Of very great utility in *correcting* any knowledge of this being which may be derived from other sources, in making it consistent with itself...and in freeing it from everything incompatible with the conception of an original being and from all admixture of empirical limitations.[35]

Kant makes this idea much clearer in his *Lectures on Philosophical Theology*. These lectures were composed over the same period of time as the three *Critiques*. Yet they have gained remarkably little attention in Kant scholarship. Therefore, although the three *Critiques* will be the main texts used to analyse Kant's moral theology in this chapter, I shall also use the *Lectures on Philosophical Theology*,[36] as well as other less well-known works, to supplement and often clarify suggestions made in the *Critiques*. In these lectures Kant says that traditional theology 'puts us in a position to remove from our concept of God everything sensible inhering in our concepts.'[37] Therefore, traditional theology can also help to purify our conception of God as long as we use it to tell us how we ought to think of God, and how we cannot think of God, instead of using it to tell us that God exists. This is a very important point. It hints at a kind of negative knowledge, a knowledge of what God is not, and could never be conceived to be, whilst at the same time informing us of what our concept of God must include.

Now it would have been quite plausible for Kant to have left the matter of theology and that of metaphysics here. Having rejected the traditional arguments for the existence of God, and having given his reasons why, he could have simply washed his hands of theology. And having replaced dogmatic metaphysics with a sound metaphysics of experience, he could have ended his concern with metaphysics. But, he does not. There is a double edge to Kant's rejection of traditional theology, namely, the attempt to retain the notion of God for use in the moral sphere, and thereby in relation to his metaphysic of morals. Kant wants to change the domain in which the notion of God is made available to us from that of theoretical speculation to that of moral practice. Correspondingly, he wants to change the whole definition of theology from being a theoretical enterprise, to being a practical exercise. He will attempt to do this by distinguishing between theoretical and practical uses of reason. In the preface to the second edition Kant states that the first Critique is concerned with setting limits to empirical enquiry, but in doing so it has a positive value in that it narrows the domain of theoretical knowledge, thus making way for a realm beyond, and for the work of practical reason in that realm:

> On a cursory view of the present work it may seem that its results are merely *negative*, warning us that we must never venture with speculative reason beyond the limits of experience. Such is in fact its primary use. But, such teaching at once acquires a *positive* value when we recognise that the principles with which speculative reason ventures out beyond its proper limits do not in effect *extend* the employment of reason, but, as we find on closer scrutiny, inevitably *narrow* it...So far, therefore, as our Critique limits speculative reason, it is indeed *negative*: but since it thereby removes an obstacle which stands in the way of the employment of practical reason, nay threatens to destroy it, it has in reality a *positive* and very important use.[38]

The obstacle which needs to be removed is that of theoretical knowledge. When this has been done the positive use referred to above can be employed regarding 'the concept of God.'[39] By this Kant means that we can acknowledge the possibility of practical rather than theoretical arguments in favour of belief in God. However, doing so points beyond the purposes of the first Cr*itique*, which consists in the demarcation between the realm of knowledge and that which is beyond, towards the purposes of the second *Critique*, which is concerned with the employment of practical reason in that realm which is beyond theoretical knowledge. It thus points us in the direction of Kant's moral approach to theology.

II: MORAL THEOLOGY

Part i: *Critique of Practical Reason*

I have shown that Kant was driven to reject theoretical proofs of the existence of God. I have also pointed to the fact that in doing so Kant was making way for the analysis of an area of concern which is beyond the demarcations of theoretical knowledge, and which is to become the realm of true theological preoccupation. Kant will attempt to offer a moral approach to the question of the existence of God, in place of the theoretical approach of traditional theology. He will therefore be attempting to give a practical answer to traditional metaphysical questions.[40] However, since many people might question the claim that Kant intends to offer an alternative kind of theology to that which he had shown to be invalid, it will be useful to begin with claims made by Kant in the first *Critique* which demonstrate his intention. Kant maintains that it is not possible to make progress in metaphysics without a previous critique of pure reason.[41] This implies that the same is the case for theology, given that the kind of theology with which Kant is concerned has traditionally been a part of metaphysics. Kant also suggests that we can only do justice to morality and the concept of God once the limits of empirical enquiry have been marked out.[42] By offering a critique of pure reason he claims to be able to silence all objections to morality and religion, by the clearest proof, 'of the ignorance of the objectors.'[43] He considers a theoretical approach to the existence of God to be damaging to morality,[44] which, as will become clear in this chapter, is the true realm of theological concern.[45] He then goes on to say that:

> When all progress in the field of the supersensible has thus been denied to speculative reason, it is still open to us to enquire whether, in the practical knowledge of reason, data may not be found sufficient to determine reason's transcendent concept of the unconditioned, and so to enable us, in accordance with the wish of metaphysics and by means of knowledge that is possible *a priori*, though only from a practical point of view, to pass beyond the limits of possible experience. Speculative reason has thus at least made room for such an extension; and if it must at the same time leave it empty, yet none the less we are at liberty, indeed we are summoned, to take occupation of it, if we can, by practical data of reason.[46]

When theoretical reason has achieved as much as it can in demarcating between the realm of knowledge and that beyond, it leaves ready for practical reason the role of entering that vacant realm beyond, which was denied to theoretical knowledge. In fact, it is essential that practical reason do so, since 'we are convinced that there is an absolutely necessary *practical* employment of pure reason—the *moral*—in which it inevitably goes beyond the limits of sensibility.'[47] Moreover, this realm is the realm of authentic metaphysical concern because, as I shall show, by the occupation of this sphere, practical reason will be able to postulate the existence of God.

It is now possible to set Kant's first *Critique* in its true perspective with regard to theology. The critique of traditional metaphysics is offered as a preliminary to Kant's presentation of valid metaphysics in what he considers to be its two divisions, as well as a preliminary to his presentation of valid theology which he claims belongs to only one of these two divisions. In the first *Critique* Kant intends to remove all invalid metaphysical arguments. He also attempts to show that there are two forms of valid metaphysics, a metaphysic of experience and a metaphysic of morals. The first *Critique* deals with the metaphysic of experience, and aims to show that theology does not belong within this area of metaphysical concern, which has as its goal theoretical knowledge. However, Kant is also preparing the way for the examination of the realm in which theology can perform its proper function. That realm is the realm of morality, which also happens to be the second division of valid metaphysics. Kant thus points to the concerns of his second *Critique*.

It was largely due to his concern with morality that Kant could not give in to the absolute scepticism of Hume and reject metaphysics entirely. Kant's attempt in the first *Critique* must be viewed as both an attack upon the traditional metaphysics advocated by Leibniz, and Wolff, and as a defence against the reduction of morality and ethics to a natural phenomenon which is to be explained away, by Hume. Kant felt that Hume had omitted some of the most important characteristics both of rationality and of morality from the facts which were to be explained. It is interesting to consider how this concern with morality, which is essential to Kant's moral theology, arose.

Just as it was through Hume that Kant found traditional metaphysics, and with it traditional theology, to be invalid, so it was through Rousseau that Kant discovered that true theological reflection had its being within the moral realm. There was no longer to be any toying with the intellectual in and for itself. Any theology which represented a purely intellectual ideal was to be subordinate to moral principles. The analysis of human morality was to take precedence over rational satisfaction at the spectacle of the world. As a result, preoccupation with the theoretical was replaced by a preoccupation with the practical. Inevitably this change directly affected Kant's entire concept of God, as well as his approach to the question of God's existence. Kant turned to the realm of morality to explore the adequacy of the concept of deity, rather than relying, as he had done in his pre-critical days, upon speculation about the Divine being. He began to think of God in practical terms, solely in relation to the moral law. He claimed that our very conception of God was determined by the requirements of morality. And, as a result, he came to believe that the only way in which we could begin to justify belief in God was by offering moral grounds for God's existence. In his second *Critique* Kant embarked upon what he later referred to as the moral argument for the existence of God.[48] We shall now examine this argument, which counts as evidence for Kant's moral approach to theology and metaphysics.

Although Kant maintains that traditional rational theology cannot prove the existence of God, he does think that it is possible rationally to justify belief in God.[49] He claims that the ability to do so rests upon a distinction between pure reason, that is theoretical reason, which guides and organises our search for knowledge, and practical reason, which guides intentional behaviour. Kant suggests that the existence of God can be established only by practical reason. Thus, he attempts to give a practical rather than a theoretical answer to the problems of speculative metaphysics, at the same time doing so without, in his opinion, breaching the theoretical limits that he has set up in the first *Critique*.[50]

Kant replaces the traditional arguments for God's existence with his moral argument. He argues that any argument for the existence of God must be a moral one, for a non-moral argument would yield a non-moral God. He then goes on to infer God's existence as a necessary postulate of morality.[51] In doing so he is not maintaining that morality is derived from God, but rather that morality is dependent upon the assumption of God's existence for its rationality. The reasons for this are as follows:

1) Morality is essentially rational, it derives from the faculty of reason, and applies to all rational agents, whose duty it is to strive towards moral perfection.

2) However, doing one's duty does not necessarily result in happiness, the virtuous person often forsakes happiness for the sake of duty.

3) But it is rational to assume that virtue ought to be matched to happiness.

4) Therefore, we must postulate a Supreme being, who matches virtue to happiness by rewarding the virtuous and punishing the wicked.

As stated in points 1) to 4), Kant claims in his moral argument that it is rational to believe in God, who is conceived of as the ground of the harmony of virtue with happiness required by the moral law. This argument, which is based on the assumption that moral obligation demands a belief in the conditions without which it cannot be rationally fulfilled, offers us an excellent insight into Kant's new approach to theology. First of all Kant makes it clear that morality is not derived from God's will. This reflects his belief that morality must be autonomous rather than heteronomous. If we obeyed the moral law because it was God's will, then we would be acting heteronomously. We must do our duty because it is our duty, not because God wills it. Kant's conception of valid theology is entirely in moral terms. His argument also displays a belief in divine justice: virtue must ultimately be matched to happiness. Most significantly, however, he cannot avoid belief and faith in God, as indispensable to the moral life. It will add to the understanding of Kant's moral theology to consider briefly how he defines belief and faith in God.

Kant's notion of religious belief is not theoretical. He makes this clear when he distinguishes between doctrinal and moral belief in the first *Critique*.[52] Religious belief is not a theoretical affair, because there can be no theoretical knowledge of God. In connection with the idea of God Kant endorses what he calls moral belief, one which is achieved on a practical, and ultimately personal basis. Thus, one must not say '*It is* morally certain that there is a God,' but '*I am* morally certain.'[53] It is a subjective, rather than objective claim. Kant also distinguishes moral from pragmatic belief. When he refers to practical belief this is not pragmatic belief, but a belief which is bound to our moral obligation and is therefore absolutely necessary.[54] Although indefensible by theoretical argument this kind of belief is no less certain in terms of conviction. Kant himself says 'I inevitably believe in the existence of God..., and I am certain that none can shake this belief, since my moral principles would thereby be themselves overthrown, and I cannot disclaim them without becoming abhorrent in my own eyes.'[55] Moreover, the fact that we cannot prove that God exists theoretically does not mean that God has no reality, for Kant maintains that 'in the practical sphere reason has rights of possession, of which it does not require to offer proof, and of which, in fact, it could not supply proof.'[56] It would appear that the belief that there is a God is a possession of practical reason for which no theoretical proof is required.

Kant's treatment of faith is similar to his treatment of belief. Even though he claims to have established the existence of God as necessary to morality, this amounts to a rational faith in God's existence, as distinct from a theoretical knowledge of God's existence. It is extremely important to understand this distinction between faith and knowledge, which in Kant's opinion is vital to his own proclamation not to be overstepping the bounds of theoretical reason. He advocates what he calls 'moral faith.' In *Philosophical Theology* he has a whole section devoted to "The Nature and Certainty of Moral Faith"[57] in which he argues not only in favour of faith in God, but points out why faith is better than knowledge:

> Hence our faith is not scientific knowledge, and thank heaven it is not! For God's wisdom is apparent in the very fact that we do not *know* that God exists, but should *believe* that God exists. For suppose we could attain to scientific knowledge of God's existence, through our experience or in some other way...And suppose further that we could really reach as much certainty through this knowledge as we do in intuition. Then in this case, all our morality would break down. In this very action, man would represent God to himself as a rewarder or avenger. This image would force itself involuntarily on his soul, and his hope for reward and fear of punishment would take the place of moral values. Man would be virtuous out of sensuous impulses.[58]

In the second *Critique* Kant refers to faith as a pure rational faith, 'because pure reason alone (by its theoretical as well as practical employment) is the source from which it springs.'[59] This, like moral belief, does not amount to scientific knowledge, but rather, the assent to the proposition that there is a God through practical reason. Kant also points out that such faith cannot be commanded.[60]

Allen Wood has called Kant's notion of moral faith a kind of moral blik,[61] by which he means a way of interpreting the world which cannot be justified by empirical demonstration, but which forms part of the outlook of the moral person. According to Wood, moral faith is the attitude of the rational person who has chosen not to succumb to moral despair, who has chosen hope rather than despair.[62] This kind of moral hope has something in common with the New Testament claim that 'faith is the substance of things hoped for, the evidence of things not seen.'[63] The source of such an outlook is a belief that the world is a moral world in co-operation with God's moral volition. But moral faith is also the moral person's trust in God, it is not a matter of wishful thinking or will to believe, but rather, that moral people must assume a trust in God if they are to continue in their moral endeavours. This feature of trust, as embraced within Kant's attitude of faith, also determines his notion of belief. Belief in God is a belief that there is a being in whom we can place our trust, a being who rules the world justly. Thus a belief in God involves trust in God.

Kant does maintain that religion is a matter of faith, not knowledge, but it would be wrong to see this claim as a derogation of religion in comparison, for instance, with science. It is more appropriate to put him alongside S.T. Coleridge, who in the nineteenth century claimed that religion 'could not be intellectually more evident without becoming morally less effective.'[64] It may be that in voiding religious language of descriptive and referential import, and in advocating a moral faith which is distinct from theoretical knowledge, Kant is attempting to preserve the true essentials of religion. As far as he is concerned, God's existence has not been proven as a matter of theoretical knowledge, but rather as a matter of faith. Therefore his moral argument does not claim anything which was ruled out by the first *Critique*. He insists that the assurance which a person arrives at concerning God's existence is not cognitive or scientific, but moral, it is not an objective, but a subjective assurance. And, even given that a person may be certain that God exists, he or she still has no knowledge of what God is in God's self.

It is also interesting to consider what kind of a concept of God the moral argument provides us with. In the second *Critique* Kant argues that the concept of God is one belonging to morality rather than to scientific investigation. He points out that traditional metaphysics could never provide an adequate concept of God, but practical reason can. It is again worth quoting Kant at length:

> In the unavoidable task of directing the will to the highest good, there is...shown an exactly defined concept of this being, something completely lacking in the progress of reason in the path of nature......This being must be omniscient, in order to be able to know my conduct even to the most intimate parts of my intention...In order to allot fitting consequences to it, He must be omnipotent, and similarly for omnipresence, eternity etc. Thus the moral law...defines the concept of the First Being as that of a Supreme Being. This cannot be accomplished by...any speculative procedure of reason. Therefore, the concept of God is one which belongs originally not to physics, ie., to speculative reason, but to morals.[65]

In Kant's opinion, by using moral, practical reason, one can arrive at a perfectly adequate, all fulfilling, moral concept of God. His approach to belief in God appears to commit him to some kind of moral theism, which is described in detail in a section in *Philosophical Theology*.[66] He claims that from the point of view of moral theism the traditional proofs of God's existence are insufficient. The moral theist asserts that it is impossible for speculative reason to demonstrate the existence of God. But, the moral theist is convinced of God's existence and has a faith beyond doubt from practical grounds. The foundation of faith is morality, and the moral theist therefore needs no speculative proof of God's existence, as one can be convinced of God's existence with absolute certainty on moral grounds. It is also worth noting Kant's explicit claim that theology also arises from morality. That is, valid theology results from practical presuppositions rather than from theoretical speculation, from faith rather than scientific knowledge. According to moral theism, God is thought of as the author of our moral laws. And this is real theology.[67]

Having outlined Kant's moral argument and what it tells us about God, I now turn to the reception which this argument has received. There have been many criticisms of Kant's argument, on the grounds that it is reductionist. There is something to be gained by considering some of these criticisms, in the hope of defending Kant, and in doing so, being able to draw out some more valuable features of his new approach to theology not appealed to directly in the moral argument itself. Therefore, I shall now attempt to answer some of the criticisms made of Kant's argument.

To begin with, it has been claimed that Kant's moral argument proves no more than that the idea of God is a guiding principle, used to encourage us in our moral endeavours. It is not surprising to find this interpretation of Kant's notion of God, when Kant himself says as much in the section on the 'Regulative Employment of the Ideas of Pure Reason' in the first *Critique*.[68] The view expressed results from Kant's distinction between constitutive and regulative concepts. According to Kant a constitutive concept is one which helps to constitute our knowledge of the world. The concept of God, because it does not refer to an object of possible intuition, cannot help to constitute knowledge. Rather, the concept of God, as a concept of pure reason, is a regulative concept, aimed at directing the understanding to a certain theoretical goal, namely, that of unifying experience. Those who argue that for Kant the idea of God is merely a guiding principle assume that what Kant says about regulative concepts in the first *Critique* also applies to his moral argument which appears in the second *Critique*. They conclude, therefore, that in the moral argument the idea of God is no more than a guiding ideal which functions as a focus for our moral life. However, to take such a view is to miss two vital points. First, the whole distinction between constitutive and regulative concepts in the first *Critique* was offered as an attempt to safeguard theology and ethics from Hume's scepticism. Kant recognized that if Hume's strict criteria of knowledge was accepted, then ethics and theology as areas of rational discourse were ruled out. Kant's aim was not to suggest that the concept of God was 'no more than an idea' because it was not constitutive. By 'regulative' he meant 'not constitutive of theoretical knowledge' only so as to point out that 'God' cannot possibly be an object of empirical knowledge. He wanted to show that in the speculative proofs the notion 'God' was misused. Such misuse consisted in its spurious application to alleged objects of experience. Far from being reductionist, the claim that the concept of God is regulative acts as a basis upon which Kant attempts to build a new and firmer foundation for theology, one based on practical rather than theoretical reason. Secondly, and more significantly, in his moral approach to theology Kant points to the reality of God. Ideas which were insupportable in the speculative domain now take on *objective reality.*[69] Thus, 'through the practical law which requires the existence of the highest good possible in the world, there is postulated the possibility of those objects of pure speculative reason whose objective reality could not be assured by speculative reason.'[70]

Kant even suggests that the concept of God and the other regulative concepts of freedom and immortality 'become immanent and constitutive,'[71] and that there is a knowledge of God, though for practical purposes only.[72] Exactly what Kant means by these claims is not clear. They do seem to contradict his earlier suggestions in the first *Critique*, to the effect that the concept of God is a regulative concept, and that no knowledge of God is possible. But they perhaps do so only if one persists in applying theoretical terminology to practical presuppositions. This is what the reductionist often tends to do. Kant makes it clear that nothing can be made of these claims from a theoretical point of view, no extension of knowledge for theoretical purposes is achieved.[73] By this he probably means that no objective certainty can ever be gained, so that when he talks about 'knowledge for practical purposes' what he means is a subjective moral certainty of the existence of God. Consider, for instance, the often mentioned religious claim to know that God exists. Such a claim is, as Kant seeks to show, a quite different claim from any kind of scientific knowledge, but it has its own validity in terms of personal conviction.

Therefore, Kant's claims to the effect that the concept of God becomes immanent and constitutive, and that we can have a knowledge of God, deny the very foundation upon which the idea of God as a mere guiding principle is based, unless one wants to argue that constitutive concepts are also only guiding principles. Practical reason can, as far as Kant is concerned, give us a practical knowledge of God, of God's moral nature, and of God's will, for moral beings.

It has also been suggested that Kant's moral argument implies that we must view the world *as-if* God exists to match virtue to happiness, even though we know in reality that such a being does not exist. It would be futile to deny that Kant uses the notion *'as-if'* in connection with the idea of God. In the first *Critique* he suggests that we should act *'as-if'* the world were ruled by an omnipotent being.[74] And this does conjure up the thought of an illusory, albeit, useful device. However, Kant never says that God does not exist, and, if one bears in mind that he denied ever asserting what he did not believe,[75] then his notion of *'as-if'* would appear quite dishonest if it positively advocated what he knew was a fiction. Far from implying that God is nothing but a fictional idea invented by the human mind, Kant claims that we are assured of the reality of the conceptions which are required for the Summum Bonum.[76] Since one of these conceptions is that of God, it follows that we are assured of the reality of God. Kant also implies that if people are to think consistently about the implications of their attempt to act morally, then they must either admit to the existence of God, or admit that morality is an irrational form of activity.[77] It is also worth noting that Kant uses the notion *'as-if'* in connection with the idea of freedom, which he certainly believes, and actually states to be a reality.[78]

Given these facts, it is more plausible to assume that when Kant uses the notion of *'as-if'* in connection with the idea of God, what he means is that we must indeed act *'as-if'* God exists, even though we cannot prove God's existence theoretically. Such an *'as-if'* is an assumption to the effect that, although the transcendental limits of experience make it impossible to have a theoretical knowledge of God's existence, I do have very good (moral) reasons for believing that God exists. The objects of religious belief cannot be illusory projections because rational moral activity requires their reality for its coherence and completion.

Kant's moral argument has also been considered to be entirely pragmatic. The belief in God which it entertains is used, not because it has some intrinsic value, but rather because of its serviceability. This view is often expressed as follows: Kant advocates a moral faith according to which belief in God is essential as a practical postulate of morality. That is, without belief in God morality would be irrational. However, morality takes priority over faith, since these religious beliefs are advocated only because they are necessary to morality. Therefore the belief in God is no more than a useful means of support to the moral life. Against this claim I would reply that Kant's 'moral faith' simply does not dissolve into pragmatism. Admittedly, Kant does imply that in the theoretical domain religious beliefs can be used pragmatically. But, as far as he is concerned, there is a huge difference between the theoretical and the moral domain. It is perhaps in failing to recognise Kant's distinction between the theoretical and the practical domain that his concept of God is found to be pragmatic only. The use of the notion of God may be pragmatic as far as scientific investigation is concerned, but it cannot be pragmatic when used in connection with morality. As far as moral purposes are concerned, the belief in a moral God, the ground of the matching of virtue to happiness, cannot be pragmatic. In fact it is hard to understand why Kant's 'moral faith' is so often assumed to be pragmatic, when Kant continually distinguishes between the moral and the pragmatic. He states that a history, for instance, is composed pragmatically when it teaches prudence, ie. instructs the world on how it can provide for its interests better. As such it is concerned with general welfare. Morality, in contrast, pays no attention to the attainment of what is, in general, most advantageous.[79] In the first *Critique* Kant describes the concept of pragmatic belief as a 'contingent belief which yet forms the ground for the actual employment of means to certain ends.'[80] This implies that pragmatic beliefs are contingent, and lead to acts which are determined by certain ends. For a more detailed account of the distinction between pragmatic and moral belief it is useful to refer to Kant's *Lectures on Ethics*. According to this work, which is composed of students notes taken from Kant's lectures and published posthumously, moral beliefs are absolutely necessary, and are not determined by ends,[81] because if they were morality would be heteronomous. Both in the first *Critique* and in the *Lectures on Ethics*[82] Kant distinguishes between pragmatism which is governed by the concerns of prudence, and practical morality which dictates regardless of ends in view.

Another criticism of Kant's argument begins with the claim that it is clear from the first *Critique* that noumena have no positive role whatsoever. They have only a negative and limiting role in the sense that they limit our preoccupation with ideas that extend beyond the boundaries of knowledge. Therefore the concept of God as used in the moral argument, because it is a noumenal as distinct from a phenomenal concept, has no positive, or meaningful connotation. In reply, I would point out that whereas it is right to say that noumena have a negative role in the first *Critique*,[83] the same does not apply to the second *Critique*. The first *Critique* can speak positively only of phenomena, the second *Critique* can speak positively of noumena. For instance, according to Kant, noumenal freedom cannot be explained theoretically in its positive role because the freedom of a person as a being of the intelligible world (ie, as a noumenal being) cannot be defined theoretically. But in the second *Critique* noumenal freedom takes on a positive role in connection with morality. People must think of themselves as noumenon.[84] Also, noumenal freedom can be explained practically in its positive role because the postulation of human freedom in the moral sphere is both possible and necessary. If this is so for freedom, then the same can be said for the notion of God which takes on a positive and meaningful role in the moral argument. The tendency to think of noumena in negative terms only, results from carrying over the negative status attributed to noumena from the first *Critique,* to the second *Critique*.

It should have become clear from the above that a positive interpretation of Kant's argument is possible, given a wider awareness of the facts as Kant presents them. However, I have not yet dealt with what is perhaps the most popular criticism of Kant's moral argument, and also the most severe, namely, that through the moral argument Kant reduces religion to morality. A complete answer to this claim would require extensive treatment of the relationship between morality and religion in Kant's theology, and in the progression of this study that relationship will become clearer. For the present, it is possible to offer an initial response to this interpretation by pointing out that it is unfair to Kant, who, contrary to popular opinion, makes a clear distinction between morality and religion.[85] Those who suggest that Kant reduces religion to morality usually make use of his claim that whereas morality is the concern with moral duty, religion is the recognition of all duties as divine commands. And on the face of it, there does seem to be little difference between duties, and duties considered as Divine commands. However, Kant also says that morality is the doctrine of how to make ourselves worthy of happiness, namely, by obeying the moral law. Religion, by contrast, is concerned with the hope of achieving the happiness which morality bids us to make ourselves worthy of. In fact, it is 'only if religion is added,' that the hope of someday participating in happiness arises. In other words, the hope of attaining happiness arises with religion. The point here is to distinguish between morality which is a matter of obligation, and religion, which is a matter of hope. If we think of religion as a matter of hope, as well as trust, we can better understand the full implication of statements made by Kant concerning morality and religion. For instance, in the first *Critique* he suggests that we cannot, for the sake of morality itself, discard belief in God. Morality ultimately involves belief in God, which 'is so interwoven with my moral sentiment that as there is little danger of my losing the latter, there is equally little cause for fear that the former can ever be taken from me.'[86] Kant maintains that 'I am certain that nothing can shake this belief, since my moral principles would thereby be themselves overthrown, and I cannot disclaim them without becoming abhorrent in my own eyes.'[87] When one considers statements such as these in the light of the notions of hope and trust in God, it appears that far from reducing religious beliefs to moral assertions, or evaluating religious credenda as aids to living well, Kant is asserting that God's existence, and the relation of the world to God, cannot be left out of account if the moral life itself is to make sense.

In the exposition offered above, I have shown that the reductionist interpretations of Kant's moral argument for the existence of God are incorrect. It would be quite easy to leave Kant's moral theology at this point. After all, most studies of Kant deal with the moral argument, with criticisms of it, and then consider the matter closed. However, in my opinion, a treatment of Kant's moral argument in itself is simply not enough to give a full impression of his moral theology. There is much more in Kant's second *Critique* to enhance the conception of his moral approach to belief in God. And, once again, the works of D.M. MacKinnon have proven valuable in highlighting Kant's stance.

MacKinnon thinks that Kant's criticism of metaphysics simply prepares the way for his assertion of the primacy of practical reason.[88] He points out that as far as Kant is concerned 'metaphysical agnosticism safeguards the transcendent character of morality.'[89] Not only will it do this but it will also 'thrust us back on the road that we must follow.'[90] That road is the road of morality, since according to MacKinnon, 'we are all the time thrust ...outside those frontiers (of theoretical knowledge), precipitated beyond them by a moral experience.'[91]

Central to Kant's concern with morality is the unconditional nature of moral obligation. He says that we are bound 'completely to actions unconditionally conformable to the law,' and that 'the pure moral law inexorably binds every man as a command.'[92] Morality places an unconditional command upon us. Whereas the theoretical person is concerned only with the conditioned, the practical person is faced with the categorical nature of moral obligation, which has the quality of the unconditioned. Human beings are always morally committed, and are therefore involved unceasingly with the unconditioned. In MacKinnon's view, Kant insists that it is in the moral life that we enjoy commerce with the unconditioned. Kant states, for instance, that the moral law 'allows us a view into the realm of the supersensible, though only a glimpse.'[93] Thus, according to MacKinnon, in acknowledging the moral law within us we are 'all the time enjoying commerce with the unconditioned.'[94] MacKinnon thinks that in Kant's moral theory:

> There is a haunting sense that the notion of the transcendent, and the relation of the transcendent to the familiar, breaks in upon us at the level of practical life, and...we are projected into commerce with the ultimate, even if our relation to it resists altogether intelligible representation.[95]

This suggests that moral experience may be legitimately regarded as an experience of the Divine. The absoluteness of moral obligation implies for MacKinnon a relation between the person obligated and an objective reality capable of evoking the sense of duty which all people apparently possess. Comments, such as those above, seem to suggest that when we act in unconditional conformity to the moral law,[96] we are going beyond the bounds of phenomenal reality and in some way entering into the world of the noumenal, and with it into commerce with the Supreme reality. And, if this is the case, then Kant is not reducing religion to morality, rather, he is assuming access to God, who is the subject of traditional metaphysics, through the moral life. It is in morality that we come to experience the reality of God.

MacKinnon thinks that Kant's preoccupation with the unconditional character of morality is his way of dealing with the very problem of metaphysics. Kant presented the problem of metaphysics with a new depth, in that he recognised that a proper ethical seriousness makes people unsatisfied with scepticism, yet at the same time it prohibits them from accepting traditional theological approaches to God.[97] For Kant, recognition of the reality of God can only be found in relation to the practical life, and he establishes the indispensability of God for the proper orientation of that life.[98] Kant therefore made possible 'a deepened understanding of the metaphysical impulse,'[99] because for him 'the moral universe is the universe with which the transcendent metaphysician, if he understands his job aright, is really concerned.'[100] MacKinnon seems to be suggesting that for Kant, morality is metaphysical discovery. The disclosure of the moral order is itself the fundamental metaphysical discovery.[101]

MacKinnon thus emphasises the way in which Kant's ethics play the role of metaphysics. He suggests that for Kant the unconditional nature of moral obligation amounts to commerce with the unconditioned. Unfortunately however, for MacKinnon, such commerce with the unconditioned in the moral, or supersensible realm, implies an overstepping of the limits laid down for theology in Kant's first *Critique*. Thus:

> No modern philosopher raises more acutely than Kant, the problem of the representation of the unrepresentable, the problem of assuming to the full the disciplines of *theologia negativa*, and then, as it were, seeking to escape from them.[102]

MacKinnon claims that Kant himself may be described as a speculative metaphysician,[103] since in his ethical approach to metaphysics he has finally jumped out of his own cognitive skin.[104]

Although I entirely agree with MacKinnon's valuable account of the moral order as the realm of true metaphysical discovery for Kant, I am led to a different conclusion from him with regard to whether Kant's moral approach to metaphysics oversteps the limits he placed before metaphysical enquiry in the first *Critique*. I shall now attempt to explain why, by analysing Kant's own suggestions in this respect.

Kant claims to be offering a metaphysic of morals. By this he means the *a priori* laws that inform our moral judgements and are then applied to moral experience. However, the preoccupation with the unconditioned in morality connects *a priori* metaphysics with that which traditional metaphysical reflection had sought to comprehend. It does this in the sense that the moral law establishes to some extent the nature of the supersensible reality. It may appear as if Kant has abandoned the concept of God in the first *Critique* and brought God back in in the second. But it only looks as if he has done this if one considers the first *Critique* as a whole system in itself, instead of as part of a system, with regard to which the second *Critique* is the second half. As has already been argued, Kant does not negate God entirely in the first *Critique*. Rather, he has limited our affirmation of God, in order to proceed to a more compelling affirmation in the second *Critique*. However, Kant is still not allowing any theoretical insight into God's nature. We still cannot intuit God. Theoretical knowledge gains nothing by what is established in the second *Critique*. It can make no additional use of the concepts established in the second *Critique* as necessary for practical reason, other than its regulative use. Thus, the moral argument does not jump the walls built by theoretical reason between what we can and cannot know. In the dialectic of practical reason in the second *Critique* Kant actually shows that he is still restraining dogmatism and fanaticism in the same way that he had done in the first *Critique*. Only this time it is of a moral kind, which claims on moral grounds to have an insight into ultimate metaphysical reality. And in *Philosophical Theology* Kant makes it clear that his moral theology does not contradict the critique established in the first *Critique*:

> At the conclusion of moral theology it should be remarked that the three articles of faith, *God, freedom* of the human will, and a *moral world*, are the only articles in which it is permissible for us to transport ourselves in thought beyond all experience and out of the sensible world; only here may we assume and believe something from a practical point of view for which we otherwise have no adequate speculative grounds. But however necessary and dependable this procedure may be for the purposes of our morality, we are in no way justified in admitting ourselves further into this idea, and venturing to go with our speculation to a region with which only our practical interest is concerned. If we do so we are *fanatics*. For at this point the limits of our reason are clearly indicated, and whoever dares to transcend them will be punished by reason itself for his boldness with both pain and error. But if we remain within these boundaries, then our reward will be to become wise and good men.[105]

What motivates Kant's moral theology is not simply scepticism concerning religion, but his own conviction that true metaphysical concern is informed by, takes place within, and gains its validity through the sphere of morality. He retains an ultimate respect for religion due to his confidence in the transcendent import of moral experience. Yet even though moral theology is concerned with the moral experience itself and with what that experience tells us about God, it is still far from a supersensible insight into God's nature. Kant's moral theology does not, therefore, overstep the limits set out in the first *Critique*.

In the above, I have shown that although Kant's entire religious perspective is moulded by his preoccupation with morality, his moral theology is more than the reduction of religion to morality. Faith and morality are quite different, but at the same time inseparable. Hopefully, I have also shown that Kant's moral argument for belief in God involves more than using the idea of God's existence as a reason for fulfilling our moral obligations. If this is not yet clear, consideration of a further development of Kant's moral approach to theology, which appears in his third *Critique*, ought to prove more convincing. It is to an examination of this development that I now turn.

Part ii: *Critique of Judgement*

Most people associate Kant's third *Critique* with aesthetics, the study of art. However, the third *Critique* also contains an appendix in which Kant further develops his moral theology.[106] In the second half of the third *Critique*, which is entitled the 'Analytic of Teleological Judgement,' Kant is concerned with teleology. In particular he is concerned with the question of whether one can observe a final purpose in nature. In the appendix Kant argues that one cannot establish a final purpose in nature by means of physical teleology, that is, by an examination of nature itself. And it follows from this that physico-theology, which infers a supreme cause of nature from the purposes of nature, is bound to fail. As Kant has already shown in the first *Critique*, the physico-theological argument leads only to a first cause, not to the God of theism. But there is the added implication here that physical nature is no evidence of either a final purpose or a first cause of that purpose. Therefore, it would appear to be almost impossible even to start the inference from purpose in nature to a Supreme Being. Physico-theology seems to be no more than a misunderstood physical teleology.[107]

According to Kant, it is in so far as the physico-theological argument looks to nature and not to the moral purposes of human beings in the natural world that it is mislead. It is only when we look for moral purposes in nature that we can establish a final purpose, and a moral God to explain the existence of such purpose. The argument[108] Kant offers in support of this claim is as follows:

1) Moral teleology finds purpose in the moral endeavours of rational beings.[109]
2) The purpose at work in the endeavours of these moral beings is the highest good, the Summum Bonum.

In the second *Critique* Kant has already established that a moral God is needed to make the achievement of the Summum Bonum possible. Here he argues slightly differently, that:

3) Since there is a moral end for humans, namely the highest good, there must be a cause of the moral purpose connected with that end.
4) The only cause appropriate to such an end is a Supreme Moral Being.
5) In order to meet the requirements of creation in accordance with moral purposes, this being must be a legislator in the kingdom of moral purposes.

It may appear from the above that Kant is simply reiterating the moral argument of the second *Critique*. But in fact Kant is adding something quite new to his moral argument here. He is saying, as in the second *Critique*, that there is a moral purpose, and that God is necessary to its attainment. But, in addition, in point three, he is saying that God is necessary to explain the very existence of the moral purpose in nature. The difference is between arguing that God is needed to join happiness to virtue, and arguing that God is needed to explain the existence of moral teleology in the world. In Kant's opinion we have a moral ground for thinking in the world a final purpose of creation. This claim includes both end purpose and creation, and thus points to the being who matches virtue to happiness, but also to the Creator. The difference is a subtle, but important one. It is the theme of a teleological order of the world as a creation of God which forms the main part of the argument in the third *Critique*.

Having added a new dimension to the moral argument in this way, Kant then goes on, as with the moral argument of the second *Critique*, to determine the attributes applicable to the concept of the Supreme moral Being. At the same time he points out that they are only the attributes we conceive in such a Being,[110] thus retaining his concept of symbolic anthropomorphism as distinct from dogmatic anthropomorphism.

In similar fashion to the second *Critique*, Kant also argues in the third *Critique*

Kant's three *Critiques*, but concentrate this time upon Kant's specific claims concerning theology.

In the first *Critique*, the passage in which Kant criticises the traditional arguments for the existence of God is called, "Critique of all *theology* based upon speculative principles of reason."[117] This whole passage is concerned with Kant's distinction between good and bad theology. He makes it clear what he thinks of as theology, namely, "knowledge of the original being."[118] Such theology, he suggests, is based either solely upon reason (rational theology) or upon revelation (revelation theology). Rational theology starts with concepts, in which case it is transcendental theology, or nature, in which case it is natural theology. When transcendental theology attempts to prove the existence of God from experience in general, it is cosmo-theology, when from concepts alone without any experience whatsoever, it is onto-theology. Natural theology, when inferring the existence of God from the order of the natural world, is physico-theology, when from the moral world, is moral theology.

After having defined the different approaches to theology in this way, Kant goes on to explain which approaches are invalid, which valid. He suggests that 'all attempts to construct a theology through purely speculative reason, by means of a transcendental procedure, are without result.'[119] From the above it would appear that by this Kant means only the Ontological and Cosmological arguments, but from his critique it is clear that he also thinks that the Physico-theological argument falls back upon transcendental concepts for its proof.[120] Therefore, he is ruling out all three of the traditional arguments for the existence of God. As far as he is concerned, the concept of God reached through traditional theology is at the very most deistic.[121] The traditional arguments for the existence of God cannot provide the God of theism, who must be omnipotent, omniscient, omnipresent, and eternal. The only kind of theology that can provide such a God is moral theology:

> This moral theology has the peculiar advantage over traditional theology in that it inevitably leads to the concept of a sole, all-perfect, and rational being, to which traditional theology does not, on objective grounds, even so much as point the way.[122]

Therefore, in Kant's opinion, 'the only theology of reason which is possible is that which is based upon moral laws or seeks guidance from them.'[123] The details of such a moral theology are left until the second *Critique*, but Kant does hint at the fact that he will offer an argument for the existence of God using such a moral approach: 'at some future time we shall show that the moral laws do not merely presuppose the existence of a supreme being, but also...justify us in postulating it, though, indeed, only from a practical point of view.'[124] And, as was referred to earlier, whilst ruling out traditional theology as a means of acquiring knowledge of God, Kant retains the transcendental conception of God as a permanent means of censoring reason's efforts to overstep its boundaries:

> If then there should be a moral theology that can make good this deficiency, transcendental theology, which before was problematic only, will prove indispensable in determining the concept of this supreme being and in constantly testing reason.[125]

Kant adds that the predicates we use to refer to God, such as necessity, eternity, and infinity, are transcendental, and 'for this reason the purified concepts of them, which every theology finds so indispensable, are only to be obtained from transcendental theology.'[126] Therefore the usefulness of transcendental theology is acknowledged at the same time as its ability to prove the existence of God is ruled out.

In the first *Critique,* Kant rejects any theology but a moral one. The full details of that moral theology, only hinted at in this work,[127] find their completion in the second and third *Critiques*.

In the second *Critique* Kant tells us that what he did in the first *Critique* was entirely fruitful for theology and morals.[128] He thinks that he is doing theology a service, since moral theology is the only kind which can provide an adequate concept of the God of theism. And it is by means of the moral argument for the existence of God that Kant shows the way in which moral theology achieves this. The second *Critique* also points the way to the development of Kant's moral theology in the third *Critique*. Kant says that 'if we enquire into God's final end in creating the world, we must name not the happiness of rational beings in the world but the highest good.'[129] Although the emphasis here is upon the highest good as a final end, it offers an insight into what will be a central feature of Kant's argument in the third *Critique*, namely Divine creation of purpose in moral nature. However, this does not imply that by the time of the third *Critique* Kant had decided that purpose in creation was more important then the final end of that creation, namely, the highest good. The point is rather to show that in the second and third *Critiques* different emphasis is given within the moral argument itself.

Earlier, I outlined Kant's argument that physico-theology needed morality to get anywhere near to an appropriate concept of God as the moral author of the world. As a corollary of this, Kant claims that physico-theology needs morality to become theology. There are long passages of the third *Critique* devoted to the argument that physico-theology, which is concerned with teleology in nature, is only a preliminary to theology proper.[130] It cannot prove the God required; the most it can give is a first cause, the God of the deists.[131] The conception of a supreme cause is not enough for theology.[132] The kind of purpose or end in existence which teleology looks for can only be given in moral teleology because moral teleology alone can furnish the conception of a unique Author of the world suitable for a theology.[133] It is in assuming this moral Author that one enters into theology, and thus reaches what alone for Kant amounts to a theological conception of God.[134] That conception is the one outlined earlier, a moral legislator in the kingdom of ends, concerning whom we can establish certain attributes by means of symbolic anthropomorphism. Thus moral teleology leads ultimately to a moral theology, which is the only valid kind of theology. It is worth quoting Kant himself in defence of the possibility of moral theology:

> A knowledge of God and of His existence, that is to say a theology, is possible by means of attributes and determinations of this causality merely conceived in Him according to analogy, and this knowledge has all requisite reality in relation to morality...An ethical theology is therefore possible.[135]

Admittedly it is Kant's preoccupation with morality which moulds his conception of theology. Yet in adopting the notions of creative purpose in the world and a final end, Kant has gone beyond pure morality and entered into what for him is theology proper.[136] The most important claim as evidence of this view is as follows:

> For while morality without theology may certainly carry on with its own rule, it cannot do so with the final purpose which this rule enjoins, unless it throws reason to the winds as regards this purpose.[137]

This statement reinforces the fact that God is essential to Kant's whole moral outlook, and therefore ultimately, that morality needs theology.

I am now in a position to remark upon the central tenets of Kant's Copernican revolution in theology, which can best be arrived at by a comparison with his pre-critical stance. First of all, Kant had believed that his own version of traditional theology could demonstrate the existence of God. What is now clear is that the critical Kant still believes that the existence of God can be established, but by means of a different approach than that of theoretical proof, and by means of a different certainty than objective certainty. Kant believes in the moral argument for the existence of God,[138] which amounts to a subjective certainty on the part of the moral individual. He objects to traditional theology, and replaces it with moral theology. But, his theology is still rational theology. It is a natural, moral, rational theology, as distinct from a transcendental rational theology. The reasoning involved is practical, not theoretical.

Secondly, before the revolution in his thought Kant endorsed the notion of Divine creation. This very notion, far from being thrown out, returns with added force in his third *Critique*, although the approach is again somewhat different. It is through moral reflection, rather than reflection upon physical nature itself that the notion of Divine creation may be defended.

Thirdly, the Leibnizian optimism of Kant was a distinct feature of his pre-critical phase. Many have assumed that the critical Kant has lost all such optimism. However, what is more representative of Kant's critical attitude is a redefined optimism. That is, Kant's optimism is no longer contemplative, but rather practical. His optimism is now based upon moral purpose and trust in God. His optimism issues in a moral and rational faith, the details of which are also considered in a section of the third Crit*ique* entitled "The Type of Assurance Produced by a Practical Faith."[139]

It should be clear from the above that the most significant change in Kant's attitude towards theology since the critical revolution in his thought, is that theology must be moral and practical. Theology can no longer exist or justify itself as a theoretical, contemplative, preoccupation. The practical undertone which supports such a change in Kant's thought is the very crux of his new, moral theology.

IV: KANT'S THEOLOGY AT WORK

I have named the change in Kant's thought from his pre-critical to his critical period a 'Copernican revolution in theology.' My examination of Kant's revolution in theology began with his first *Critique*. This implied that the revolution in his thought commenced prior to the writing of the first *Critique*. Although there is no doubt that this was the case, I shall now examine an area of Kant's thought in which the full consequences of his revolution take time to emerge. The area in question is Kant's attitude towards theodicy. In 1783-4, two to three years after the first *Critique*, Kant is still using an approach to theodicy which he later realises is totally at odds with his new approach to theology. By 1791 the full implications of Kant's Copernican revolution in theology can be identified in his treatment of the notion of theodicy. Not only is this the case, but an acquaintance with the moral theology that issues from Kant's Copernican revolution is, by 1791, essential to comprehension of his attitude towards theodicy.

In line with the approach taken in the examination of Kant's Copernican revolution in theology, I shall begin with Kant's pre-critical period,[140] before examining in detail the kind of theodicy that Kant advocates in 1791.

Leibniz appears to have coined the term 'theodicy,' which is made up of the compound of the Greek words for God (theos) and justice (diké). A theodicy is a defence of the righteousness of God in the face of the fact of evil. In his work of that name, Leibniz sets out to show that God's permitting and even facilitating the evil in the world can be justified as being for the sake of the greater harmony of the world. Leibniz explains evil itself as a privation,[141] thus following the Augustinian tradition which sees evil as a defection from good. Physical suffering is a penalty imposed by God against those who commit moral evil,[142] and innocent suffering is justified on the grounds that it 'prepares for us a greater happiness.'[143]

In the 1750's Kant's thought on theodicy was very close to that of Leibniz. In an essay called "Nova Dilucidatio" of 1755, Kant claims that:

> in undertaking the primordial affairs of the universe, God started a series which includes, in a fixed nexus of reasons bound together intimately and interconnectedly, even moral evils, and corresponding to these, physical evils.[144]

This suggests that God has chosen to create a world which includes evil. However, according to Kant, it does not follow from this that God can be held responsible for evil. It is rather that God allows evil to exist for the sake of the greater perfection of the world as a whole. He also suggests that it is appropriate that those who commit evil acts be punished for doing so. At the same time, God compensates for the evil in the world by 'bringing back those addicted to evils..to the better course.'[145] Kant thus follows Leibniz in embracing a theodicy which includes the divine permission of evils, the interpretation of natural evil as punishment for moral evils, and God's providential rule for the ultimate good of creatures.[146]

In his essay of 1759 called "Some Reflections on Optimism," Kant also followed Leibniz in the belief that this is the best of all possible worlds.[147] Like Leibniz, he is convinced that if God chooses, God only chooses the best. He professes:

> I am happy to see myself as a citizen in a world which could not be better. Having been selected as an insignificant member, unworthy in itself, to serve in the most perfect of all possible schemes, I appreciate my existence so much the more. I call out to all creatures who do not render themselves unworthy of being so described: Hail to us—we are! And the Creator is well pleased.[148]

Kant's position in these early days displays a somewhat innocent optimism concerning the ability to interpret God's relationship to the evil in the world, and a committed faith in the justice of God's ways.

By 1781, and the publication of his first *Critique*, Kant had come to the opinion, contrary to the thought of Leibniz, that there could be no knowledge of God. It is therefore interesting that in his *Philosophical Theology*, which was composed between 1783 and 1784,[149] he is still offering Leibnizian-like arguments in defence of God's righteousness in the face of evil. At this stage Kant has not yet shaken off all of his pre-critical tendencies.

However, all of this optimism concerning the ability to defend God's relation to evil was soon to change. It seems plausible that it was Hume who awoke Kant from his dogmatic slumbers concerning theodicy, as well as on the bounds and capacities of reason. Hume had no time for Leibnizian theodicy, because in his opinion reason was unfit to describe or comment on God's relation to, or responsibility for, the evil in the world. In light of the critical revolution in his thought it was inevitable that Kant should, like Hume, come to the conclusion that we can have no knowledge of God's relation to the evil in the world. He began to question the adequacy of traditional attempts at theodicy. In particular, he became critical of the Leibnizian assumption that the goodness of God could be defended by theoretical reasoning from the natural world. One might expect therefore, that together with Hume, Kant would reject theodicies outright. But, as with his position on the arguments for the existence of God, Kant eventually takes a line which falls somewhere between those of Leibniz and Hume. That is, rather than ruling out theodicy altogether, Kant goes on to advocate a different kind of theodicy from that of the Leibnizian tradition. However, it is not until ten years after the first *Critique* that he is in a position to do so.

In 1791 Kant published an essay called "On The Failure Of All Attempted Philosophical Theodicies."[150] The title itself hints at the fact that Kant is going to attack all arguments offered in defence of the righteousness of God in face of the fact of evil, and this is exactly what he does. He first outlines the defence given, and then offers a counter assertion to disqualify it. I do not intend to consider the kinds of theodicy that Kant rejects, but it is important to understand why it is that he now feels he must reject them. At the very outset of his essay Kant hints at the reason why these theodicies do not work, namely, because they all make a plea for reason which 'presumptuously ignores its own limits in these matters.'[151] Each defence steps beyond the limits of valid reasoning. Throughout his exposition Kant also hints at the difference between a defence offered on theoretical grounds in connection with the examination of the world of nature, which is what each of the traditional theodicies does, and a moral approach which looks beyond the world of experience. According to Kant no theodicy proposed so far has managed to justify the moral wisdom at work in the government of the world against the doubts raised by the experience of evil. This is as much as to say that the theodicies offered do not justify a moral God because they argue from the world of nature, which points at most to divine wisdom, as distinct from moral wisdom. Kant does hint at the possibility of a better justification of the wisdom at work in the world,[152] but at the same time warns that 'all further attempts of "human wisdom" to fathom the ways of the divine wisdom must be abandoned.'[153] This suggests that it is a mistake to try and explain the ways of God. Theodicies fail because they ignore the limits of human reason which is not in a position to work out the ways of the divine, and because the defence they offer does not justify a moral God. Thus far, Kant sounds as if he is ruling out theodicy completely.

However, he goes on to say that:

> we are capable at least of a negative wisdom. We can understand the necessary limits of our reflections on the subjects which are beyond our reach. This can easily be demonstrated, and will put an end *once and for all* to the trial.[154]

Kant's efforts to demonstrate such 'negative wisdom' occupy the rest of his essay on theodicy, to which I now turn.

Kant distinguishes between what he calls artistic wisdom manifested in the arrangement of the world, which issues in physical theology by means of theoretical reason, and moral wisdom which is a concept of practical reason and makes sense only on the supposition of the highest possible good in the moral world. He does so in an effort to reinforce his earlier point about the kind of wisdom that can and cannot be defended by appeal to the world of experience. The concept of moral wisdom is not achieved by appeal to experience alone. This distinction between artistic and moral wisdom is also the key to Kant's distinction between what he calls doctrinal and authentic theodicy. Doctrinal theodicy, or theodicy in its traditional sense, refers to attempts to read the ultimate intention of God from the world of experience. In Kant's opinion, however, the world is always a closed book when we attempt to interpret the 'moral' intentions of God from the world of nature. In contrast to traditional theodicies, authentic theodicy is based upon the 'moral' conception of God arrived at by reason before all experience:

> God, through our reason, becomes the interpreter of his will as manifested in creation. And this interpretation we can call authentic theodicy. This is not an interpretation set forth by *ratiocinating* (speculative) reason, but by an *authoritative* practical reason, which having in itself authority to legislate can be considered to be the immediate expositor and voice of God in charge of the interpretation of the book of creation.[155]

According to this passage one can have a moral conception of God and of God's will independent of all experience of the world. Such a conception is obtained by the revealing of God's will to us through our moral reason. This implies that whereas traditional theodicy claims that the world is a manifestation of God's will, authentic theodicy claims that our reason is a manifestation of God's will. The interpretation of God's will so mediated results in authentic theodicy. The reason at work in this case is practical, not theoretical. By this Kant means it is a reason informed by moral considerations rather than by reflection upon human experience of the world. What is surprising however, is that to give an example of the authentic theodicy to which he refers, Kant uses a book of the Old Testament: 'such an authentic interpretation I find expressed allegorically in an old scripture.'[156] The Scripture referred to is the book of Job, to which Kant next turns to further exemplify his distinction between authentic and traditional theodicy.[157]

Job is Kant's model for his answer to the good person confronted by evil. Job was a man who lived in the best circumstances, being rich, healthy, and free. However, all his blessings were suddenly removed from him by a series of misfortunes, and he soon began to complain. His friends who came to comfort him proposed their own theodicy to explain Job's misfortune. According to them all woes were punishments for crimes committed, and they maintained this despite the fact that they could not name any crimes that Job had committed. In contrast to them, Job claimed that he could not accept such a theodicy, because according to his own conscience he was not guilty of any crime. Job could only conclude, with regard to his own affliction, that 'God is unique' and 'does what he wills.'[158] In other words, he could give no reason as to why God had allowed him to suffer as he had.

The difference between the reaction of Job and that of his friends is very important to Kant's interpretation of authentic theodicy. According to Kant, Job spoke 'as he thought, as he felt, and as every man in his position would feel.'[159] His friends spoke 'as if they were overheard by the Almighty, whose behaviour they were judging, as if they cared more for willing his favour by passing the right judgement than for saying the truth.'[160] Kant's attitude towards the reaction of Job's friends is apparent in the following:

> The dishonesty with which they affirmed things of which they should have confessed that they had no knowledge and with which they feigned convictions which in fact they did not have, contrasts with Job's free and sincere outspokeness, which is so removed from lying flattery that it almost borders on temerity...'Do you want,' asked Job, 'to defend God with unjust arguments.'[161]

Kant's sympathy clearly lies with Job. Job's friends claimed that Job was suffering because he had sinned. They assumed Job's guilt in order to justify their theodicy. But it was not true that Job had sinned, and Job's reluctance to accept their explanation is in a sense a defence of God against false interpretations.

The unravelling of the story supports Job's stance as against that of his friends:

> God honoured Job by showing him the wisdom of his creation and its unfathomable nature. He let him see the beautiful side of creation, where man can see in an indubitable light (and understand) the purposes of the Creator and his wise providence. But he also showed the horrible side, including things which do not seem to agree with the idea of a plan established with wisdom and goodness.[162]

This passage hints at the fact that the natural order simply is no guide to the wisdom or otherwise of the divine creation. The result of God's revealing to Job the two sides of nature is that 'Job confessed not that he had spoken sacrilegiously for he was sure of his good faith, but only that he had spoken unwisely about things that were above his reach and which he did not understand.'[163] Thus Job, who before his own suffering had held opinions on theodicy similar to those of his friends, now acknowledges that human reason cannot fathom the ways of the divine. Not only is nature no pointer to the goodness or otherwise of God, but also, reasoning from our experience to God is inadequate.

Through Kant's presentation of this story one is encouraged to think that Job has done well to admit his ignorance. All the more interesting then, when Kant suggests that if one were to examine the positions of Job and his friends, then that of the friends would probably appear more reasonable to speculative reason and would seem to exhibit more pious humility. According to Kant: 'If Job were to appear before some tribunal of dogmatic theologians,... he probably would have met with a worse fate.'[164] Yet, and this is the crucial point, in the end God prefers Job to his friends who, in their efforts to gain an insight into the ways of God, whilst ignoring what they really know, persist in developing totally inadequate doctrinal theodicies.

Kant's criticism of traditional theodicies in the passage above is explicit. Traditional theodicies prefer theoretical justifications to admissions of human limitation in relation to the divine. Still referring to Job, Kant goes on to say that 'the faith which arose...simply out of the conviction of his ignorance could arise only in the soul of a man who in the midst of his most serious doubts could say 'until the hour of my death I will hold fast to my piety.'[165] This implies the determination of the person of faith to persevere no matter what; it means persevering in one's commitment to the goodness of God. Kant claims that such resolution on Job's part demonstrates that he based his faith on morality, not his morality on his faith. Job's faith is a better faith, because he is unwilling to relinquish it even when faced with personal, innocent suffering.

Kant begins his conclusion to this story by claiming that:

> theodicy is not a task of science but is a matter of faith. The authentic theodicy has taught us that what matters in such affairs is not reasoning but honesty in the avowal of the powerlessness of our reason and sincerity in the expression of our thoughts (a sincerity that never lends itself to a lie, however pious it might be).[166]

This statement insists that theodicy is a matter of faith, which for Kant amounts to a practical, or moral faith, as distinct from a theoretical assertion. This is the most important point for Kant, who wants to replace the notion of theodicy as a theoretical defence with a practical theodicy which amounts to a personal commitment issuing in a moral way of life. In light of this conclusion, one can also understand what Kant meant at the beginning of his story when he suggested that, although we could not fathom the ways of God, a 'negative wisdom' was possible. The story of Job is evidence of the limits of the human intellect in relation to the ways of the divine. Our wisdom is negative in the sense that we must acknowledge that we do not know God or the ways of God, which are beyond us. But, such negative wisdom has as its positive side the fact that we should hold fast to our faith, which for Kant is moral faith, regardless of our experience of evil and the fact that we cannot explain it.

Kant's analysis of the story of Job, as outlined above, is his way of comparing and contrasting his own moral, or authentic, theodicy with the kind of theodicy that he himself, even as late as 1784, had still to some extent maintained. Although not all traditional versions of theodicy have attempted to explain human suffering in terms of divine punishment for wrongs committed, most traditional versions of theodicy have rested upon theoretical arguments, which attempt to offer an insight into God's relationship to, or allowance of the evil in the world. It is the theoretical attempt to explain away evil in claims such as these, that Kant now objects to. Such attempts always claim an insight into the ways of God which is not possible.

Having given an outline of Kant's treatment of the story of Job, I am now in a position to demonstrate that Kant's attitude towards theodicy in 1791 fully reflects his Copernican revolution in theology. Kant's rejection of all previous theodicies coheres with his rejection of the theoretical arguments for the existence of God in the first *Critique*. His notion of authentic theodicy coheres with his insistence in the second *Critique* that the only adequate argument for the existence of God is a moral argument, and with his preference for moral over physical theology as evidence of a moral God in the third *Critique*. In order to demonstrate more precisely that this is the case, I shall now go back through Kant's version of the story of Job, highlighting as I do so, those features which illustrate the Copernican revolution in theology attributed to Kant earlier in this chapter.

Kant's criticism of traditional theodicies echoes his criticism of theoretical arguments for the existence of God in his first *Critique*. Traditional theodicy lacks a sense of the limits of our reason. The 'negative wisdom' that Kant suggests is possible for us, ought to remind one of the 'negative theology' attributed to him in the analysis of his position in the first *Critique*. In both instances the emphasis is upon the limits of human knowledge with regard to God. The distinction Kant goes on to make between artistic wisdom and moral wisdom, which then becomes central to his distinction between traditional and authentic theodicy, quite clearly parallels that between physico-theology and 'ethico,' or moral theology, initially mentioned in the first *Critique*. It is the distinction between a concept of God arrived at by reflection upon nature itself, and a concept of God arrived at by means of moral reflection. The suggestion following this distinction between artistic and moral wisdom, namely, that only a moral concept of God issues in authentic theodicy, is entirely in line with Kant's second *Critique,* in which he argues that we can provide practical, though not theoretical, justification of belief in God. The story of Job is then offered as a means of establishing a moral, as distinct from a traditional theoretical, theodicy. Kant does this by using the experience of Job to reinforce the points already made. Thus, Job's refusal to accept the theodicies offered by his comforters is a rejection of theoretical theodicies.

The idea that God shows Job both the good and the bad side of nature is once again a rejection of physico-theology. We are reminded specifically of Kant's critical opinion in the third *Critique*, namely, that physical teleology cannot establish a moral God. This view differs markedly from Kant's pre-critical attitude, according to which, from the beauty of the world we could deduce the goodness of God. The confession given by Job demonstrates Kant's view that people do not have the acquaintance with God's ways that they sometimes claim to possess. Even to charge God with injustice is to claim knowledge, and so Job acknowledges his fault, that he had spoken beyond his limits. However, Job's reluctance to abandon his faith in God is evidence that he based his faith on his morality. If one bears in mind Kant's own moral conception of God which results from his critical revolution, together with the claim he made earlier in this essay, that any authentic theodicy must begin with a moral conception of God, it becomes evident that the realm which Kant demarcates for his authentic theodicy is morality, not theoretical speculation. This adheres with his insistence, as a result of his Copernican revolution, that authentic theology is moral theology. Kant's conclusion that theodicy is not a task of science, but is a matter of faith, holds the key to his new attitude towards theodicy. This statement reflects his claim in the first Critique to the effect that he must 'deny knowledge in order to make room for faith.' By saying that theodicy is a matter of faith rather than knowledge, Kant is taking leave of Leibniz, who attempted to establish theodicy as a form of knowledge of God and of God's ways. Theodicy becomes authentic only when it issues in a practical lived faith, as distinct from a philosophical deduction. This is an important point, considering the standard identification of Kant with philosophy rather than theology. Kant is pointing out that theodicy does not belong to the realm of philosophical reflection. In his opinion, theodicy belongs to the practical life of faith, or moral theology. However, Kant is also taking leave of Hume, who thought that faith, and theodicy also, could not be defended rationally. In cutting theodicy off from philosophical reflection, Kant is not cutting theodicy off from the rational. Rather, by basing theodicy upon a moral reason, as distinct form theoretical reason, Kant has been able to retain a form of rational theodicy which counters the scepticism of Hume. Thus, Kant's treatment of the story of Job contains within it the main elements of his Copernican revolution in theology.

In the above I hope to have established that Kant's essay on theodicy bears the marks of his Copernican revolution in theology. There are, however, a number of difficulties which ought to be considered. First of all, it is not at all clear what Kant's authentic theodicy amounts to. In fact, Kant may be criticised for ruling out traditional theodicies, without replacing them with any substantial alternative. Secondly, Kant claims that Job bases his faith upon his morality without clearly explaining why he assumes this to be the case, or exactly what this involves.

Thirdly, Kant's whole treatment of the story of Job is concerned with innocent suffering. He gives no attention whatsoever to the fact of human, or what might be called moral evil, and therefore only deals with half of the problem of theodicy. In order to reply to each of these criticisms in defence of Kant, it is necessary to appeal to the details of his moral theology, which help to explain the kind of theodicy he is advocating.

From a first reading of Kant's essay, the force of the first criticism must be acknowledged. For one is left with the uneasy feeling that according to Kant, God cannot be defended in face of the fact of evil. In Kant's opinion we are too limited to be able to understand God's position with regard to evil. And if we cannot understand God's ways, then there is no point in trying to defend God's relation to evil. As Job himself suggests when he says that 'God is unique and does what he wills,' there is no clear-cut theoretical theodicy enabling us either to explain away evil or say why God acts in a certain way. Nor is nature evidence in favour of either a good or evil deity. We cannot therefore positively justify God's ways, and it is simply no good trying to defend God with unacceptable arguments. In fact, what appears to be more important from Kant's point of view, is sincerity in the expression of one's doubts. This theme is taken up at length by Kant in his conclusion. His appeal for sincerity, which is 'the main requirement in matters of faith,' illustrates the depth of his concern with confessions of belief which people make without real sincerity, and the dishonesty involved in doing so. God prefers Job because Job refrains from feigned convictions that he really does not feel, in this way remaining true to his conscience, which is the only guide in matters of faith. He also shows uprightness of heart, by giving a sincere and undisguised confession of his doubts. Job does not accept the advice of his friends because it is false to the conviction of his integrity. In a letter to a friend Kant states that 'in the final moment, only the purest candour concerning our most hidden inner convictions can stand the test,' and that like Job, he 'takes it to be a sin to flatter God and make inner confessions, perhaps forced out by fear, that fail to agree with what we freely think.'[167] This implies that beliefs cannot be held at the cost of sincerity. A lack of sincerity in admitting what we cannot believe turns us into inward hypocrites.

If the above were all that Kant had to say about theodicy, then the critic of Kant would appear to be absolutely right. Kant seems to be saying either that no theodicy whatsoever is possible, or assuming that it is not necessary. And what is more important than creating arguments to defend God, appears to be actually voicing one's doubts. Yet, if Kant favoured a total rejection of theodicy, as this interpretation implies, then he would not claim to be presenting an authentic theodicy. It is unfortunate that the allusions Kant makes to this so-called authentic theodicy are so vague that it is hard to establish anything substantial from them. However, this can perhaps be explained by the idea that Kant assumes that readers of his essay on theodicy will be acquainted with his earlier works. For, as I shall now show, by appeal to Kant's moral theology as outlined earlier in this chapter, it is possible to identify the main features of Kant's authentic theodicy, and thereby to verify that Kant is ruling out one kind of theodicy, and replacing it with another.

Kant's moral argument for the existence of God is based on the idea that we have an obligation to fulfil the moral law. However, the moral obligation itself demands a belief in the conditions without which it cannot be rationally justified. According to Kant, a Supreme being must exist in order to match the virtue of moral persons to their ultimate happiness. The moral life we lead makes a difference to the happiness we will receive. This is as much as to say that morality makes a difference, and divine justice must prevail. It is this belief in divine justice which lies implicit in Kant's essay on theodicy. The assumption is that in the end justice will prevail. The belief that there is a divine Judge who will eventually assess the moral life we have led, enables the moral person to persevere with the moral life in spite of personal hardship. Although Job cannot at present comprehend the apparent injustice in his life, he will finally be vindicated for his upright life. In Kant's essay, there is a sense of a non-understanding commitment of faith to the goodness of God, and to the justice of God's ways. This explains why, although Kant claims to have disproved earlier theodicies, he does not claim either to have disproved the fact of God's wisdom or the righteousness of God in the face of the fact of evil.[168] Instead, he claims to be establishing the only valid way in which that justice and righteousness can be maintained, namely, by his moral approach to theodicy. And it is also by appeal to Kant's moral theology that one can best appreciate what a moral approach to theodicy implies. Kant claims that authentic theodicy is based upon practical, as distinct from theoretical reason. By this he means that authentic theodicy is theodicy derived from presuppositions about God attained through moral reasoning. What makes Job's continuing commitment to the goodness of God possible is the fact that his conception of God is one formed by the requirements of the moral life. Authentic theodicy must be based upon a moral conception of God: God is the moral judge. This also explains why one's concept of God must be arrived at separately from reflection upon the world, because it is a concept arrived at by reflection upon the *a priori* requirements of morality independent of experience. By basing our conception of God upon the requirements of the moral life, we are led to the conclusion that morality must make a difference, divine justice must prevail. But, and this is the most important point, the belief in a moral God, who assures that justice will prevail, is as much as authentic theodicy can claim. Kant makes no effort to defend God's ways by reflection upon the physical world, or to suggest that we know if, why, or how, God acts. In other words, theoretical reasoning is ruled out by the authentic theodicy which bases itself upon moral assumptions.

It should also now be clear, in answer to the second criticism, what Kant means by saying that Job bases his faith upon morality. Implicit to Job's reluctance to abandon his faith is the belief that morality must make a difference. Job is a morally upright man whose faith testifies to trust in a moral God, whose ways are just. Morality and divine justice are the two most distinct features of Kant's authentic theodicy. It is the morality of Job, and his belief in a just God, that makes theodicy possible. Until the moral basis of Job's faith and the trust in divine justice, which makes such a faith possible, are recognised, neither the purpose of such a theodicy nor Job's persistence in his faith will be fully understood. At the very basis of both Job's moral life, and the concept of the God in whom he believes, is the belief in divine justice.

Ann Loades has recognised the significance of the idea of divine justice to Kant's authentic theodicy.[169] She suggests that divine justice is the most crucial feature of Kant's authentic theodicy.[170] Most significantly, Loades points out that this preoccupation with divine justice shows a change from Kant's pre-critical stance. Whereas in the 1750's Kant had relied on the idea of divine goodness, by the 1790's divine goodness has become for him the presupposition of divine justice, and it is divine justice upon which he has come to rely.[171] The theme of divine justice takes us to the very heart of Kant's theodicy, which does not amount to an objective justification of God by means of attack and defence.

However, and perhaps much more significantly, there is a sense in which God is vindicated in the heart of the person of faith, who believes that divine justice must prevail.[172] Even though his own honesty leads Job to argue with, and question God, it is a faith in divine justice which prevents him from despairing. For Kant, we cannot explain God's ways, yet we remain in quiet trust in God's justice. This interpretation of Kant's position is supported by the following episode recorded from his last days:

> When Kant had discovered that in a bad summer swallows threw some of their own young out of the nest in order to keep the others alive, he said: 'My intelligence stood still. There was nothing to do but to fall on one's knees and worship.'

We can compare this reaction with Job's refusal to abandon his faith in spite of the suffering which had fallen upon him. According to Rabel, this is the person who is silenced by the deity's self-manifestation in the natural order. But it is also the person who, despite a total failure to comprehend the way in which justice prevails, makes an unreserved commitment, in the quiet hope that it must.

My answers to the first two criticisms ought to be sufficient to establish Kant's moral theodicy as an alternative to traditional theodicies. But, as the third criticism suggests, Kant's theodicy can still be found lacking because it fails to deal with moral evil. In reply to this criticism I would argue that although Kant does not specifically deal with the question of moral evil, he does allude to something which would be a contender for human vice, namely, the lies told by Job's so-called comforters in order to maintain their traditional theodicies. In the conclusion to his essay Kant contrasts 'sincerity' with 'the disposition to falseness and deception,' which is the 'main vice found in human nature.' Since making 'false' assertions and engaging in 'deceit' is exactly what Job's comforters do, it seems plausible to assume that on Kant's interpretation of vice, one can attribute at least a tendency to moral evil to Job's comforters. Furthermore, at the very end of the conclusion Kant also makes a reference to 'a disposition to subtle duplicity' in human nature. By 'subtle duplicity' he means vice, or what might otherwise be referred to as moral evil. Therefore, Kant seems to be implying that there is a disposition to evil in human nature. In the passage concerned he is relating the story of a traveller who 'after his belief in man's selfless inclination to help the fellow man had been shaken by experience' had come to the conclusion that:

> man, when it comes to benevolence, is good enough (little wonder! for this rests on an innate inclination of which God is the author), but there exists in him a disposition to subtle duplicity! (This also should cause no wonder, for the repression of the vice rests upon the human character, which man himself must build.)[173]

This statement does not explicitly say that the tendency to evil in human nature is the fault of humankind, whereas it does say that God is the author of the tendency to benevolent behaviour in human nature. However, it does imply that the responsibility for overcoming the vice which lies in human nature lies with humankind, not with God. In a moment I shall attempt to show how this responsibility for overcoming the evil in our nature might find its place in Kant's authentic theodicy. But first it is worth noting that the very implication that there is a 'disposition' to evil in human nature displays a marked divergence not only from Kant's pre-critical stance, but from his treatment of evil in *Philosophical Theology*. In these lectures Kant, like Leibniz before him, interpreted evil as a negation which consisted 'only in a limitation of what is good.'[174] He claimed that we have a predisposition to goodness, a seed placed in us by God, whereas 'a special seed for evil' was 'unthinkable.' Evil was 'nothing but the incomplete development of the seed of goodness out of its uncultivated condition.'[175] Therefore for Kant now, in his essay on theodicy, to be suggesting that there is a 'disposition' to evil in human nature, is to be throwing out all of his earlier assumptions about evil as a defect of goodness, rather than a disposition in itself. In the examination of Kant's later works in Chapters II and III, the full consequences of this break with the Leibnizian conception of evil will be demonstrated. For the moment, it is sufficient to acknowledge that yet another break from the Leibnizian tradition has been made.

I can now return to the fact that Kant ends his essay on theodicy with this rather vague hint at human evil, which does suggest a concern with the evil disposition in humankind.[176] Unfortunately, Kant does not expand upon this issue, and offers no further explanation, other than to end with the subtle suggestion that everyone has a propensity to such 'duplicity' within them. He gives no explanation as to why the disposition to evil in human nature exists, nor does he make such a bold assumption as to claim outright that God is not responsible for this human fault. Such a position is entirely in line with his authentic theodicy, which simply acknowledges the limits of human reason with regard to these matters.

However, what does need to be accounted for is the claim that human beings are responsible for overcoming their disposition to evil, and whether this claim coheres with Kant's authentic theodicy. Although no clarification is offered by Kant, his desire to stress human responsibility for the overcoming of evil tendencies can be explained in terms of his authentic theodicy and the moral theology which underpins it, as I shall now demonstrate.

From Kant's moral argument for the existence of God it is clear that responsibility for the moral life lies in our own hands. Such responsibility involves improving ourselves morally. In fact the notion of a Supreme being proportioning virtue to happiness would make little sense if persons were not responsible for their failure to follow the moral life, or their improvement morally. From Kant's treatment of the story of Job one can assume that improving oneself morally includes telling less lies and being less deceitful, amongst other things. If moral integrity and uprightness make one worthy of God's favour, as the story of Job suggests, then it follows from this that those persons who are lacking in moral integrity will not receive God's favour. This would explain the fact that Job's comforters do not receive God's favour at the end of the story, since they defend God with unjust arguments, are dishonest, and display no moral integrity. Kant's position with regard to moral evil would thus be that those who do not display moral integrity, honesty and sincerity, as well as those who do not take on the responsibility to improve themselves morally, or make little effort in doing so, will be judged unfavourably. However unappealing this version of moral failure and divine justice may sound, it does fit with Kant's position. Therefore, if one accepts that duplicity and falseness are moral evils, then Kant's authentic theodicy can be applied to moral evil as well as to innocent suffering.

In the above I have been able to overcome the difficulties with Kant's essay on theodicy by appeal to features of his moral theology. However, Kant's critics might still find a point of query with his theodicy. Ultimately, it has been argued, Kant's authentic theodicy depends upon the assumption of divine justice. But the notion of divine justice is exactly what traditional theodicies are trying to defend. Therefore, despite Kant's claims to be offering something different, his approach to theodicy actually falls back upon the same kind of defence as traditional theodicies. There is something to be said for this claim, but in reply it must be pointed out that even the way in which Kant's theodicy depends upon divine justice differs from traditional theodicies. Kant's theodicy is not so much an effort to establish the goodness of God in the face of evil by rational argument here and now. Rather, Kant's theodicy is based upon the assumption that morality demands that God's justice will finally prevail, even though we are at present unable to establish God's goodness by rational argument. Kant's theodicy is, in this sense, a deferred moral theodicy. According to Kant's presentation, the story of Job can be read in either of two ways: it can be read as an abandonment of the very effort to comprehend God's justice on the basis that human beings cannot ask God to render account, or it can be read as showing, not that God is unjust or beyond justice, but that we are unprepared here and now to fathom God's righteous ways. And this latter interpretation leaves open the possibility of God ultimately being vindicated. Those who see only a rejection of theodicy in Kant's essay are misinterpreting the assumption that the vindication of the justice of God must be deferred, for the assumption that no theodicy is possible. Moreover, there is even evidence in Kant's text in favour of deferred theodicy. In the passage where Kant suggests that God honoured Job by displaying both the good and bad side of nature to him, he adds:

> Even through these things, God showed to Job an ordering of the whole which manifests a wise Creator, although his ways remain inscrutable for us, already in the physical ordering of things but even more in the connection between this order and the moral one(which is even more unfathomable to our reason).[177]

This suggests that God is in control of nature, regardless of how things may appear to the human eye. And the result is not that Job attempts, in spite of his suffering, to defend God's control over nature. Rather, Job chooses to deny that the mystery of suffering can be fully understood. Likewise, Kant chooses to defer comprehension of evil, trusting instead in God's ultimate justice, as commitment to the moral life obliges him to do. It would be a mistake however, to misinterpret Kant's support for deferred theodicy as support for the idea that God's justice is different from ours. Believing that God's justice is different from ours would place God beyond moral accountability, something Kant's moral theology would not entertain. If there was no question of morally justifying God, then there would be no real theodicy. The assumption must therefore be that God's justice will ultimately be vindicated. Faith for Kant is not belief in a God beyond justice, but a belief that God's justice will finally be vindicated.

Kant's deferred theodicy is not therefore an explanation of experience as is often the case with traditional theodicies, but the conviction that despite the experience of evil, goodness and righteousness will triumph. It might otherwise be described in terms of a faith and trust in divine justice. Such faith and trust is partly lived out in the story of Job. Loss and suffering do not finally detach Job from God. Nor is Job abandoned by God. Far form God abandoning Job, the latter is victorious, through holding fast to his piety and not losing his trust in God. Therefore, Job's faith is vindicated, though not as far as an explanation of evil is concerned. Rather, Job is vindicated in being shown God's favour. This displays once again, that it is rational moral faith which wins through, rather than philosophical reasoning. Perhaps the most significant element of Kant's theodicy rests in the fact that it is a matter of faith, or a practical exercise in theology, rather than a philosophical enterprise which seeks to replace the unique quality of moral faith with theoretical justification.

As has been shown in the above, Kant's Copernican revolution in theology leads him to a rejection of all previous theodicies. He offers instead his own authentic theodicy, which has its place within the sphere of morality. Kant does not offer an explicit vindication of God by showing that God is justified in the face of the fact of evil. Rather, as Collins points out, Kant's treatment of the story of Job transfers all attention entirely from preoccupation with the justification of God, to the experienced manner in which the religious person endures evil. Job is an example of the fact that the only resolution of the problem of evil is in the realm of personal commitment, or moral faith. This amounts to a commitment to the moral way of life. But this would not be possible without faith and trust in the justice of the moral God, whose existence is fundamental to the rationale of the moral life itself. In this way Job demonstrates what true theodicy requires.

I have identified the development in Kant's attitude towards theodicy in terms of a break with Leibnizian theodicy, and eventually in terms of a different theodicy. The limitations of our knowledge mean that we can no longer claim to be able to demonstrate that this world is the best of all possible worlds. However, there is a fundamental feature of Leibnizian theodicy which survives the Copernican revolution in Kant's thought. We can best identify this feature by comparing Kant's treatment of the story of Job with that of his contemporaries. According to Johann G. Hamann 'reason discovers nothing more for us than what Job saw, the misery of our birth—the advantage of the grave—the uselessness and inadequacy of human life.' Voltaire had come to the same conclusion on his reading of the book of Job. Kant's exposition of Job shows that he comes to a conclusion different from those of Hamann and Voltaire. He remains convinced that divine justice will prevail. This conviction reflects a basic optimism which has remained with Kant throughout his Copernican revolution in theology. Admittedly, his optimism is now different from the kind which claimed to be able to explain away God's ways—an optimism which Hume had found so abominable. It is now a moral optimism directed towards divine justice, which presupposes divine goodness, rather than an innocent optimism in divine goodness. Therefore Kant, the previously over-optimistic believer, is still a believer, even if he formulates that belief differently. The main features of that continuing belief, however radically reformulated, are apparent in Kant's authentic theodicy, which exemplifies a moral faith and trust in the divine justice of God in the face of the fact of evil.

CONCLUSION

From the analysis carried out in this chapter it should be clear that Kant's opposition to speculative metaphysics in his first *Critique* is not an attempt to discredit belief in God. Kant is quite different from other opponents of metaphysics and religion, since he attempts to discredit atheists and deists, as well as anthropomorphic conceptions of God.[178] However, Kant is convinced that God's existence cannot be theoretically known by humankind, and his critique of traditional theism is a critique of the supposition that it can.

Even though with regard to theoretical knowledge of God Kant's attitude is very close to the tradition of negative theology, he still offers a positive metaphysic resulting in the moral argument for the existence of God. Kant's conception of God is entirely in moral terms, and God's relation to humankind is through the moral law. As a result, Kant's theology is clearly demarcated as one within the bounds of reason and morality. But it is, nevertheless, a theology.

Kant's moral argument for the existence of God in his second *Critique*, and what he has to say about rational faith, suggests a kind of moral theism, that is, a belief in a living God,[179] who must be conceived of in terms of moral concepts.[180] Kant also argues, i) for the primacy of practical reason over theoretical,[181] ii) that what practical reason establishes, the speculative must accept,[182] and iii) that only in practical employment is reason complete,[183] and thus makes it clear that the moral argument for the existence of God is superior to previously attempted theoretical proofs.

Although Kant is critical of the traditional arguments for the existence of God, there is evidence in his third *Critique* to suggest that he at the same time endorses the beliefs which motivate such theories.[184] He argues that 'faith is the moral attitude of reason in its assurance of the truth of what is beyond the reach of theoretical knowledge.'[185] Elsewhere he protests that 'that man is morally unbelieving if he does not accept that which though impossible to know, is morally necessary to suppose.'[186] It is clear from claims such as these that in Kant's opinion, even though the theoretical arguments for God's existence are unsatisfactory, we cannot reject their conclusion.[187]

Thus, from a closer reading of Kant's three *Critiques*, it becomes clear that as far as Kant was concerned, theology could no longer present itself as a factual science providing knowledge of God by theoretical argument. The only kind of theology he could allow was a practical or moral one, and he conceived of this theology in its most developed form as ethico-theology.[188] My examination of Kant's essay on theodicy has illustrated his moral theology at work in his analysis of the story of Job. But, it has also offered greater insight into Kant's theology. First, Kant's presentation of Job illustrates precisely the difference between moral and theoretical faith. Moral faith is a matter of practice, actually leading the life of faith. As such, it is far removed from theoretical assertions of belief. Secondly, Kant's moral theology is permeated by a belief in divine justice, something perhaps not immediately apparent in the moral argument itself, but implicit to it. Most significantly however, I have been able to establish not only that in his essay on theodicy Kant is actively engaging in theology as distinct form advocating a philosophical treatise, but also that he has demonstrated through the figure of Job how his own theology works in practice. Therefore, it seems appropriate to conclude from this chapter that Kant was a theist seeking to develop a practical, moral, approach to theology.

ENDNOTES

1 I shall use the general title 'traditional theology' for what Kant refers to on different occasions as speculative, rational, or dogmatic theology.

2 That is because he initiated a revolution in philosophical conceptions about how knowledge is gained, similar to Copernicus' revolution concerning the status of the sun in relation to the earth.

However, it would be more appropriate to refer to Kant's Copernican revolution in metaphysics.

[3] I shall not therefore be concentrating upon the connections between Kant's theory of transcendental idealism and his attitude towards theology.

[4] KW I, 403; "Nova Dilucidatio" p.236.

[5] KW II, 27-35; "Some reflections on Optimism" p.41.

[6] KW I, 396; "Nova Dilucidatio," pp.225-6.

[7] KW II, 70ff; "The Only Possible Argument For A Demonstration of the Existence of God," p.52ff.

[8] Ibid., 163; Ibid., p.58.

[9] KW IV, 260; *Prolegomena to any Future Metaphysics,* p.159. Hereafter to be referred to as *Prolegomena.*

[10] KW IV, vii-xii; First *Critique*, Aii-Axii.

[11] KW III, 495; First *Critique*, A758 / B786.

[12] Ibid., 19; Ibid., Bxxx.

[13] Ibid., 230; Ibid., B342.

[14] See Ibid., 209-210; Ibid., B307.

[15] The principle works are:
A Study in Ethical Theory, Adam and Charles Black, 1957.
Borderlands of Theology, Lutterworth, 1968.
"Kant's Agnosticism," in *Blackfriars XXVIII,* 1947, pp.256-263.
Themes in Theology, T. and T. Clark, 1987.
The Problem of Metaphysics, C.U.P., 1974.

[16] *The Problem of Metaphysics*, p.69.

[17] *A Study in Ethical Theory*, p.241.

[18] *The Problem of Metaphysics*, p.57.

[19] Ibid., p.64.

[20] N. Lash, "Ideology, Metaphor and Analogy," in *The Philosophical Frontiers of Christian Theology*, ed. B.L. Hebblethwaite and S. Sutherland, C.U.P., 1982, p.83.

[21] See "Kant's Agnosticism," and *Themes in Theology*, pp.34-5.

[22] *Themes in Theology*, pp.34-35.

[23] Ibid., p.1. This point has been illustrated by L.W. Beck, who when speaking of Kant's attack upon speculative metaphysics claims that 'a false conception of God degrades rational conception into something anthropomorphic,' in *Six Secular Philosophers*, The Free Press, 1966, p.76.

[24] KW III, 425; First *Critique*, A640 / B668. Kant suggests that the rejection of speculative metaphysics is an attempt to free the concept of the Supreme being from anthropomorphic assertions.

[25] KW IV, 358; *Prolegomena,* p.223.

[26] MacKinnon points out that for Kant it is important to recognise the analogical character of the language we use to refer to God, and the unknown structure of that to which it points. See *Themes in Theology*, p.36.

[27] KW IV, 357; *Prolegomena*, p.222.

[28] Ibid., 358; Ibid., p.223.

[29] Logical positivism rejects transcendental metaphysics on the grounds that its assertions are meaningless, whereas Kant rejects only its claim to be a form of theoretical knowledge.

[30] A.L. Loades, *Kant and Job's Comforters*, Avero, 1985, p.122.

31 Cf. Lash, "Ideology Metaphor and Analogy," pp.77, 82.

32 *A Study in Ethical Theory*, p.219.

33 KW V, 148; Second *Critique*, I.II.II.ix., p.153.

34 This is the way in which Cupitt describes MacKinnon's view, in "Kant and the Negative Theology" in *The Philosophical Frontiers of Christian Theology*.

35 *Cf. Themes in Theology*, p.36, *The Problem of Metaphysics*, p.9.

36 KW III, 425; First *Critique*, A639 / B668.

37 Ibid.

38 Hereafter to be referred to as *Philosophical Theology*.

39 KW XXVIII 2.2, 1046; Cf. 1036-1037; *Philosophical Theology*, p.80. Cf. p.69.

40 KW III, 16; First *Critique*, Bxxv.

41 Ibid., 18; Ibid., Bxxix.

42 From a philosophical perspective many questions can be raised concerning the relationship between Kant's critical perspective in the first *Critique*, and his moral approach to metaphysics, in particular with regard to whether the two are compatible. Although such questions do not fit into the scope of this thesis, they do offer exciting possibilities for future research.

43 Ibid., 19; Ibid., Bxxx.

44 Ibid., 18; Ibid.

45 Ibid., 19; Ibid., Bxxxi.

46 Ibid., Ibid., Bxxx.

47 Ibid., 18-19; Ibid., Bxxix-Bxxxi.

48 Ibid., 14, Ibid., Bxxi-Bxxii.

49 Ibid., 16; Ibid., Bxxv.

50 KW V, 459; Third *Critique*, II, Appendix, p.130.

51 Ibid., 124ff; Second *Critique*, I.II.II.v., p.128ff.

52 Practical reason goes beyond experience, but because it is not concerned with theoretical knowledge, it is not breaching the limits of sensibility.

53 KW V, 125; Second *Critique*, I. II.II.v., p.130.

54 KW III, 534-537; First *Critique* , A825 / B853—A829 / B857.

55 Ibid., 537; Ibid., A829 / B 857.

56 Ibid.

57 Ibid., 536; Ibid., A828 / B856.

58 Ibid., 506; Ibid., A777 / B805.

59 KW XXVIII 2.2, 1082-1091; *Philosophical Theology*, pp.121-131.

60 Ibid., 1083-1084; Ibid., p.123.

61 KW V, 126; Second *Critique*, I.II.II.v., pp.130-131.

62 Ibid., 144; Ibid., I.II.II.viii., p.149.

63 A.W. Wood, *Kant's Moral Religion.*, Cornell U. P., 1970, p.176. See also, R.M. Hare, "Theology and Falsification, B," in *New Essays in Philosophical Theology*.

64 Ibid., p.160.

65 Paul's Epistle to the Hebrews, 11: 1.

66 See A.L. Loades, "Coleridge's Discovery of Kant's Authentic Theodicy," in *An Infinite Complexity*, ed. J.R.Watson, Edinburgh U. P., 1983.

67 KW V, 139-140; Cf. 131, note; Second *Critique*, I. II.II.vii., pp.144-145. Cf. p.135, note, in which Kant refers to God as the holy lawgiver (Creator), beneficent ruler (Sustainer), and just Judge.

68 KW XXXVIII 2.2, 1010-1012; *Philosophical Theology*, pp.40-42.

69 Ibid., 1002; Ibid., p.30.

70 KW III, 427; First *Critique*, A643 / B671.

71 KW V, 137-138; Second *Critique*, I.II.II, vii., pp.142-143. According to MacKinnon Kant claimed that 'where the moral universe was concerned we were free to use concepts in expounding the "postulates of pure practical reason," in ways free of the restrictions laid down in his first *Critique*.' See *Borderlands of Theology*, p.28.

72 Ibid., 134; Ibid., 1, II II. vii., p.139.

73 Ibid., 135; Ibid., p.140.

74 Ibid., 137; Ibid., p.142.

75 Ibid., 134; Ibid., p.139

76 KW III, 444; First *Critique*, A673 / B701.

77 KW X, 66; A. Zweig, ed., *Immanuel Kant: Philosophical Correspondence, 1759-1799*, Chicago U.P., 1967, p.54.

78 KW V, 134; Second *Critique*, 1, II. II. vii., p.139.

79 KW XXVIII 2.2, 1072; *Philosophical Theology*, pp.110-111.

80 KW VI, 221; "Introduction to the Metaphysic of Morals," iv., p.277: 'The concept of Freedom...proves its reality by practical principles.'

81 Ibid., 216; Ibid., ii., p.271.

82 KW III, 534; First *Critique* , A824 / B852.

83 *Lectures on Ethics*, p.5.

84 KW III, 534; First *Critique*, A824 / B852, *Lectures on Ethics*, pp.4, 34, 52.

85 See p.5.

86 KW V, 114; Second *Critique*, 1, II. II. ii., p.118.

87 Ibid., 129-130; Ibid., I. II. II.v., p.134.

88 KW III, 537; First *Critique*, A829 / B857.

89 Ibid., 536; Ibid., A828 / B 856.

90 *Borderlands of Theology*, p.212.

91 *A Study in Ethical Theory*, p.75.

92 *The Problem of Metaphysics*, p.147.

93 Ibid., p.57.

94 KW V, 143; Second *Critique*, I.II.II.viii, p.148.

95 *Borderlands of Theology*, p.28.

96 Ibid. p.153.

97 *A Study in Ethical Theory*, p.65.

98 *The Problem of Metaphysics*, p.62.

99 KW V, 143; Second *Critique*, I.II.II.viii., p.148.

100 *The Problem of Metaphysics*, p.60.

101 Ibid., p.67.

102 Ibid, p.59.

103 *A Study in Ethical Theory*, pp.235-6.

104 *The Problem of Metaphysics*, p.69.

105 Ibid., p.57.

106 Ibid., p.56.

107 MacKinnon referred earlier to Kant's criticism of those who attempt to jump out of their cognitive skins. Ibid., p.55.

108 KW XXVIII 2.2, 1091; *Philosophical Theology*, p.131.

109 KW V, 416ff; Third *Critique*, II, Appendix, p.75ff.

110 Ibid., 442; Ibid., p.108.

111 Ibid., 447-453; Ibid., pp.114-121.

112 According to Kant, man must be the final end of creation. Without man the whole of creation would be a wilderness: KW V, 445, 448-450; Third *Critique*, II, Appendix, pp.112, 116-118.

113 Ibid., 456-457. Cf. 484-5; Ibid., II. Appendix, pp.126-7, Cf. General Remark on Teleology, p.163.

114 Ibid., 474; Ibid., p.148.

115 Ibid.; Ibid., p.149.

116 Ibid., 456; Ibid., p.126.

117 Ibid., 478; Ibid., General Remark on Teleology, p.154.

118 Ibid., 447ff, 453ff.; Ibid., Part II, Appendix, pp. 114ff. and 122ff., where Kant refers to "The moral proof of the existence of God," and the "Limitation of the validity of the moral proof," respectively.

119 See p.3.

120 KW III, 420ff. Cf 423; First *Critique* , A631 / B659ff. Cf. A636 /B664.

121 Ibid., 258; Ibid., A 334 / B391.

122 Ibid., 424. Cf. 423; Ibid., A638 / B666. Cf. A 636 / B664.

123 The Physico-theological and Cosmological arguments are not transcendental in their starting points, but in order to reach their conclusion, each appeals to the transcendental theology of the Ontological argument. See "The Impossibility of a Cosmological Proof of the Existence of God," and "The Impossibility of the Physico-theological Proof": Ibid., 403ff. and 413ff.; Ibid., A603 / B 631ff. and A620 / B648ff., respectively.

124 Ibid., 445; Ibid., A675 / B703. The transcendental concept of God is no more than deistic, but what Kant wants, and in his view theology needs, is a living God. Only moral theology can supply this need.

125 Ibid., 528; Ibid., A815 / B842.

126 Ibid., 423; Ibid., A636 / B664.

127 Ibid., 422; Ibid., A634 / B662.

128 Ibid., 426; Ibid., A641 / B669.

129 Ibid., 426; Ibid., A641 / B669-670.

130 Ibid., 422. Cf. 426; Ibid., A 634 / B 662. Cf. A 641 / B 669.

131 KW V, 141; Second *Critique*, I.II.II. vii, p.146.

132 Ibid., 130; Ibid., I.II. II.v, p.135.

133 KW V, 442. Cf. 437. Third *Critique*, II, Appendix, p.108. Cf. p.102: 'Its attempt falls short of its proposed aim of affording a basis of theology.'

134 Ibid., 437. Cf. 440; Ibid., p.101-2. Cf. p.106.

135 Ibid. There is a hidden point in this claim which applies not only to physico-theology, but to each of the traditional arguments for the existence of God. The traditional arguments, which tried to prove God's existence by means of theoretical argument, were not really theological arguments at all,

because, what they proved was not the God of theism. They could not prove a God who had all the necessary qualities, such as omnipotence, omniscience, and omnipresence. In particular, they could not prove a moral God. One needs morality to reach theology. It is only when a moral God has been established that one has theology. It is not therefore that Kant is rejecting theology, but rather, that he is rejecting what he considers to be a theoretical preoccupation which claims the title of theology.

136 Ibid, 444; Ibid., pp.110-111.

137 Ibid., 446-7. Cf. 448; Ibid., pp.114, 116.

138 Ibid., 484-5; Ibid., II, General Remark on Teleology, p.163.

139 This highlights the fact that Kant does not reduce religion to morality.

140 KW V, 485; Third *Critique*, II, General Remark on Teleology, p.163.

141 Ibid., 447 and 453; Kant refers to his moral argument as the moral proof in the third *Critique*, II, Appendix, pp.114 and 122.

142 Ibid., 467; Ibid., II, Appendix, p.140.

143 I have argued that an examination of the development in Kant's thought from his pre-critical phase up to his scepticism concerning traditional theology helps one to understand the critique resulting from that scepticism. See p.1.

144 G.W.Leibniz, *Theodicy*, Routledge and Kegan Paul, 1951, Part I, par.33, p.142.

145 Ibid., III, 241., p.276.

146 Ibid.

147 KW I, 404; "Nova Dilucidatio," p.236.

148 Ibid.; Ibid., p.237.

149 See *Kant and Job's Comforters*, p.108, where Loades suggests that such features are also familiar to the Christian tradition.

150 KW II, 32; "Some Reflections on Optimism," p.41. Cf. *Theodicy*, II, 228-230, pp.271-2. Leibniz does not only maintain that this is the best of all possible worlds, but also that there is a moral necessity determining God's choice of this world.

151 Ibid., 34; Ibid.

152 See *Philosophical Theology*, translator's introduction, pp.14-5.

153 KW VIII, 253-271. This essay first appeared in the September 1791 edition of the *Berlinische Monatsschrift*.

154 Ibid., 255; "On The Failure Of All Attempted Philosophical Theodicies," p.283.

155 Ibid., 263; Ibid., p.290: 'Will it be possible in time to find better grounds of justification so that the supreme wisdom under attack will not be simply absolved on lack of evidence but will be positively vindicated?.'

156 Ibid.

157 Ibid.

158 Ibid., 264; Ibid., p.291.

159 Ibid.

160 For a recent philosophical treatment of the story of Job which refers to Kant's account, see Martin Warner, *Philosophical Finesse*, O.U.P., 1989, Chapter 4.

161 KW VIII, 265; "On The Failure Of All Attempted Philosophical Theodicies," p.292.

162 Ibid.

163 Ibid.

164 Ibid, 265-266; Ibid.

165 Ibid.

166 Ibid., Ibid., p.293.

167 Ibid.

168 Ibid, 267. Ibid.

169 Ibid.

170 Cf. the title of Kant's essay, which is concerned with the failure of 'philosophical' theodicies.

171 It is important to see these points about sincerity in the context in which they are given. Kant is voicing his objection to conditions in his day which demanded religious obedience, and prevented the free expression of thoughts held to be unorthodox. Religion for Kant, should never be a forced matter, but rather a free confession of belief, made in all honesty and sincerity. Such sincerity also means being honest about one's doubts. The story of Job illustrates this point well for Kant.

172 KW X, 168; Zweig, *Kant: Philosophical Correspondence*, p.80. (Letter to Lavater, April 28th, 1775)

173 VIII, 263; "On The Failure Of All Attempted Philosophical Theodicies," p.290: Kant says that in the light of 'the limits of our reason' doubts raised by the existence of evil cannot disprove moral wisdom.

174 *Kant and Job's Comforters,* esp. p.148.

175 See A.L. Loades, "Moral Sentiment and Belief in God,' *Studia Theologica* 35, 1981.

176 *Kant and Job's Comforters*, p.109.

177 Therefore I would argue that Kant's notion of theodicy does not simply stop at the recognition of the limits of human understanding and the retaining of one's integrity, as Warner seems to assume in *Philosophical Finesse*. Kant's account has within it an implicit appeal to the heart. But the rationale of the heart implicit in Kant's account is also somewhat different from the Pascalian appeal proposed by Warner.

178 G. Rabel, *Kant,* O.U.P., 1963, p.vii.

179 KW VIII, 271; "On The Failure Of All Attempted Philosophical Theodicies," p.297.

180 KW XXVIII, 2.2, 1078; *Philosophical Theology*, p.117.

181 Ibid.

182 In later writings, such as the *Religion Within The Limits Of Reason Alone*, Kant becomes preoccupied with human wickedness rather than with the human experience of natural evil. A more detailed examination of Kant's interpretation of human evil in the *Religion Within The Limits Of Reason Alone* is given in Chapter III. See pp.96ff. and 116ff.

183 KW VIII, 266; "On The Failure Of All Attempted Philosophical Theodicies," pp.292-293.

184 J. Collins, *The Emergence of the Philosophy of Religion*, Yale U. P., 1967, Chapter 3.

185 F.C. Beiser, *The Fate of Reason.*, Harvard U. P., 1987. p.31.

186 KW III, 425; First *Critique*, A 640 / B 668.

187 Ibid, 421: A 633 / B 661.

188 KW XXVIII 2.2, 1002. Cf. 1010-1012; *Philosophical Theology*, p.30. Cf. pp.40-42.

189 KW V, 121; Second *Critique*, I.II.II. iii, p.126.

190 Ibid., 120-121; Ibid., pp.125-126.

191 Ibid., 121; Ibid., p.126.

192 See pp.27-29.

193 KW V, 471; Third *Critique*, II, Appendix, p.145.

194 KW IX, 70; *Kant's Introduction to Logic*, p.60.

195 R.G.Collingwood claims that Kant never doubts God's existence. See "Reason is Faith Cultivating Itself," *The Hibbert Journal 26*, 1927.

196 KW V, 442-445; Third *Critique*, II., Appendix, pp.108-112.

II: THE RATIONALE OF KANT'S THEOLOGY

INTRODUCTION

I began Chapter I with an examination of the way in which Kant's theology developed up until, and including his three *Critiques*. It is now necessary to move beyond the three *Critiques* in order to illustrate Kant's continuing preoccupation with theology in his later works. However, in order that this can be done, I must first dispel the illusion that in his *Religion Within the Limits of Reason Alone*[1] Kant has moved from a concern with pure theology to a more general interest in religion, and has given up the idea of moral theology in favour of a somewhat divorced philosophy of religion. When I have shown that Kant continues to advance his own theology throughout the *Religion* and elsewhere, I shall move on to a more detailed treatment of Kant's theology. Part of my task will be to defend the idea that Kant advocates his own version of religious doctrines. I shall consider two of the religious doctrines peculiar to Kant's theology, namely revelation and grace. Therefore, in this chapter I shall do four things:

I) Illustrate Kant's continuing preoccupation with theology in the *Religion*.

II) De-construct Kant's role as that of philosopher of religion.

III) Defend and outline Kant's doctrine of revelation.

IV) Defend and outline Kant's doctrine of grace.

I: THEOLOGY OR RELIGION?

In Chapter I my efforts to show that Kant developed his own theology seemed to run fairly smoothly. After all, in my favour were numerous claims made by Kant as evidence of his attempt to develop a moral alternative to traditional theology. All the more surprising then, as I now turn from Kant's three *Critiques* to his *Religion,* written several years after the third *Critique*, in which it appears that far from developing his own theology, Kant offers an independent philosophical appraisal of religion.

Kant's *Religion,* which is generally considered to be his most direct treatment of religious themes such as the kingdom of God, revelation, grace, radical evil and salvation, has been almost unanimously accepted in the history of philosophy and theology as a classic example of the philosophy of religion.[2] The term 'philosophy of religion' refers to an investigation of religion from a philosophical standpoint. And it is difficult to deny that the title of Kant's work,[3] which suggests the study of religion as distinct from theology, and in particular, the study of only the rational content of religion, sounds like a philosophical investigation of religion. Therefore, readers cannot be blamed for assuming that by the time he came to writing the *Religion* Kant had given up the idea of a moral theology, and had decided instead, to simply examine religion in general from the stand-point of philosophy, in order to establish its rational content. Nor would I wish to deny that this is the initial impression that Kant's title gives. But there are two essential points which need to be considered. The first is that Kant has a specific understanding of the relationship between theology, morality and religion, according to which 'religion' presupposes the presence of 'theology.' Secondly, it is important to remember that the kind of reason which Kant associates with theology, and with religion also, is practical reason, ie. that concerned with moral obligations and practice.[4] In light of these two points it is possible that Kant has not turned away from moral theology in the *Religion,* but rather, incorporated it into his treatment of religion. In order to discover whether this is the case, I shall outline Kant's interpretation of the relationship between moral obligation, theology and religion, and then see if such a relationship is at work in the *Religion*.

At the end of my examination of Kant's three *Critiques,* I reached the conclusion that according to Kant, theology is necessary to morality. It may therefore appear strange that in the third *Critique* Kant also says that 'we need theology solely on behalf of religion.'[5] How can theology be required 'solely on behalf of religion' when it is also required on behalf of morality? One way of getting round this problem would be by identifying religion with morality. However, during my examination of Kant's second *Critique* I pointed out that Kant does not identify religion with morality. The reason for this was that religion was a matter of hope as well as moral obligation, whereas morality was only concerned with moral duty. It is in *Philosophical Theology* that the explanation is given as to how theology can be essential to both morality and religion. Religion, Kant says, is 'the application of theology to morality, that is, to a good disposition and a course of conduct well-pleasing to the highest Being.'[6] Elsewhere, Kant implies that theology and morality, when combined, give religion.[7] I shall now examine briefly the extent to which such a combination can be identified in Kant's treatment of the religious theme of the kingdom of God in the *Religion*.[8]

The title of the third book of the *Religion* is "The Victory of the Good over the Evil Principle and the Founding of a Kingdom of God on Earth."[9] According to Kant, the founding of the kingdom is a social endeavour, since 'the highest moral good cannot be achieved merely by the exertions of the single individual toward his own moral perfection, but requires rather a union of such individuals into a whole toward the same goal.'[10] In other words, Kant's preoccupation with moral obligations results in the idea of a social quest for moral perfection. This can, without doubt, be identified as the moral aspect of Kant's interpretation of the kingdom of God. However, not only does the pursuit of the highest good require a community working together, but also 'the presupposition of another idea, namely that of a higher moral Being through whose universal dispensation the forces of the separate individuals, insufficient in themselves, are united for a common end.'[11] This higher moral Being is 'one who knows the heart', and brings it about that 'each receives whatever his actions are worth.' This is because a perfect ethical commonwealth, or kingdom of God, would require more moral wisdom than humankind at present possesses. Therefore, it is nonsensical to say that 'men ought to found a kingdom of God.' Rather, 'God himself must be the founder of this kingdom.'[12] Although human moral achievement is essential to the realization of the kingdom, the final initiation of the kingdom can only be an act on God's part.[13] According to Kant it follows from this that 'an ethical commonwealth can be thought of only as a people under divine commands, ie., as a *people of God*, and indeed *under laws of virtue*.'[14] The idea that God is a necessary presupposition for the realization of the kingdom is reinforced by the claim that 'to found a people of God is therefore a task whose consummation can be looked for not from men but only from God Himself',[15] and the wish of all well-disposed people is 'that the Kingdom of God come, that His will be done on earth.'[16] This is unmistakably the theological element in Kant's account of the kingdom of God.

Unfortunately, according to Kant, one can never be sure of the realization of the kingdom of God. This is simply because its ultimate realization depends upon God, and we are not in a position to know 'what God may do directly to translate into actuality the idea of His kingdom.'[17] Therefore, we have no guarantee that God will initiate the kingdom. This does not, of course, prevent us from actively participating in what we conceive to be the goal of ethical perfection, but it does remove a false sense of certainty with regard to the kingdom. All that we can do is continue in our moral endeavours, and hope that God will supply what is lacking in us in order to realize the kingdom. It is with this notion of 'hope' that we meet with the truly religious perspective in regard to the kingdom of God.[18] We have a religious hope that human nature can strive towards moral perfection, but more significantly, that God will realize the kingdom.[19] This emphasis upon hope is quite different from, but at the same time supports Kant's conviction that God is necessary to the moral goal.

It should now be clear that, far from giving up his concern for moral theology in the *Religion*, Kant shows how morality and theology, when combined, lead to religion, and in particular to a religion of hope. He seeks to raise both morality and theology to a higher level of significance in the progression towards religion, a fact which has been neglected in a great deal of Kant scholarship. Therefore the *Religion* is not as independent an investigation of religion from a philosophical standpoint, as its title leads one to believe.

II: PHILOSOPHER OF RELIGION?

However, despite my efforts to show that Kant is still engaging in theology in the *Religion*, I cannot deny that he appears to be identifying his own role in writing the *Religion*, with that of a philosopher of religion. The title 'philosopher of religion' implies that one is first and foremost a philosopher and assesses the truth of religion from outside of religion.[20] In the *Religion*,[21] Kant certainly claims to be examining the doctrines of religion from the perspective of philosopher. But, as I shall presently demonstrate, it is possible to distinguish what Kant does from what he claims he is doing in the *Religion*. I will show that throughout the *Religion*

Kant continues to engage in theology, whilst claiming that he is engaging in philosophy. However, it is essential to point out that it is not my intention to suggest that Kant thought of himself as a theologian. Rather, Kant engaged in theology whilst acting under the title of philosopher. It is for this reason that I have chosen to call him a 'closet' theologian. And I shall now use exactly those areas in which he claims the role of philosopher in relation to religion to show this.

Apart from drawing upon his position as philosopher of religion, Kant actually uses the title 'philosophical theology' when referring to his intentions in the *Religion*.[22] The use of this title ought to remind one of his *Lectures on Philosophical theology,* already referred to in Chapter I.[23] As it is understood today, philosophical theology is first and foremost a theological exercise. It refers not so much to the investigation of religion from a philosophical standpoint, as does the philosophy of religion, but to the use of philosophical methods in the critical articulation of theology. The theological stand-point has priority. Of course, one might argue that Kant's use of the phrase 'philosophical theology' does not denote the same activity referred to by the title 'philosophical theology' today. In fact, Hebblethwaite has already pointed out[24] that *Lectures on Philosophical Theology* is a rather loose translation of the German title *Vorlesungen über philosophisches Religionslehre.* Hebblethwaite does have a point here. But it is worth bearing in mind that the lectures were published posthumously, and that the title Vorlesungen *über philosophisches Religionslehre* is the editor, Pölitz's choice, rather than Kant's own. The English translation is perhaps an attempt to closer identify the content of these lectures. As Wood, the translator says, 'the *Lectures on Philosophical Theology* are our main source for Kant's views on many of the traditional issues of philosophical theology: the nature and attributes of God, God's relation to the world, God's causality, creation, and divine providence.'[25] In addition, the text of these lectures in the Akademie edition of Kant's works appears under the heading "Rational Theology."

However, despite the discrepancy over the title of the lectures, there is no such ambiguity with regard to the *Religion*, in which Kant quite clearly uses the phrase 'philosophical theology' to refer to what he is doing. Of concern, however, is that Kant appears to make no distinction whatsoever between 'philosophical theology' and the 'philosophy of religion.' He uses both titles interchangeably. Furthermore, he also suggests that philosophical theology, which works within the limits of reason alone, belongs to the philosophy faculty.[26] Today, the philosophy of religion can be a discipline within both theology and philosophy departments. Therefore it would be no great surprise to hear that the *Religion* was an example of the philosophy of religion, and being taught in either a theology or a philosophy department. But it is much less common to hear of philosophical theology, given its theological priorities, being taught within philosophy faculties. Therefore, if I can now show that in the *Religion,* and elsewhere, Kant is not simply offering a divorced philosophical analysis, but rather engaging in something more akin to philosophical theology, as it is defined above, then I have grounds for placing his treatment of religion within the domain of theology rather than within philosophy, as he suggests. Moreover, if I can determine the circumstances according to which Kant places philosophical theology within the philosophy faculty, I will also have an explanation as to why Kant considers his role to be that of philosopher rather than theologian. In order to do this, it is helpful to consider a distinction which is important to Kant's own understanding of his role.

Kant appeals to his role as philosopher investigating religion when he is actually distinguishing between two different kinds of theology, namely, between what he calls rational theology, and biblical theology.[27] In fact, he assumes the role of philosopher in an effort to distinguish his role from any association with that of the biblical theologian and in order to advocate rational theology over biblical theology. This distinction between rational theology and biblical theology is even more apparent in the *Conflict of the Faculties*,[28] a work which, although almost entirely neglected in Kant scholarship, is vital to an appreciation of Kant's theology. This work is concerned with the positions and status of various University faculties. At the time of Kant's writing, theology had highest status in the University, and philosophy lowest. Of particular interest to this study, is the conflict which, according to Kant, takes place between the faculties of philosophy and theology over the use of reason in the interpretation of religion. Kant wants to defend the rational interpretation of religion, as a study belonging to the philosophy faculty, against authoritarian claims of priority of interpretation coming from biblical theologians in the theology faculty.

By 'biblical theologian' Kant means those theologians concerned entirely with Scripture, and its literal interpretation. Biblical theology, which draws its teaching from the Bible, is the church's own public teaching and is rightly subject to ecclesiastical control. The 'rational' theologian is one versed in reason, whereas a 'biblical theologian' is one versed in the Scriptures.[29] The rational assessment of Scripture implies that it cannot be interpreted literally, since its meaning must meet with the demands of reason. According to Kant, although literal interpretation may be important for scholarship, it does not promote the higher end of religious teaching.[30] This is partly because the higher end of religious teaching ought to be concerned with practical issues, that is, with religion rather than with dogma, whereas the biblical theologian is concerned primarily with theoretical biblical knowledge.[31] In Kant's opinion, the biblical theologian misinterprets the husk of religion, which includes scholarship concerned with the literal interpretation of Scripture as based on historical fact, for religion itself.[32] Rational theology deals only with the kernel of religion, which includes its moral rational content.

From the above it should now be clear that in both the *Religion* and the *Conflict* Kant is simply using the cover of philosophy in order to advocate his own rational theology over strictly biblical theology. Bruch was entirely correct when in *Kant: Lettres Sur La Morale et La Religion*[33] he suggested that the conflict with which Kant is so concerned is not so much that between philosophy and theology faculties, as a conflict within theology itself, namely between biblical and philosophical / rational theology. Moreover, in a revealing statement in the *Conflict,* [34] Kant suggests that it is not that the interpretation of religion offered by the philosopher is philosophical, but that the principles of interpretation are philosophical, and by this he means simply that they are based upon the dictation of practical reason. In other words, they are dictated by the requirements of rational theology. This claim, far from meeting the conditions of the philosophy of religion as it is defined above, actually meets with the conditions for philosophical theology, namely, the use of philosophical tools in the critical articulation of theology.[35]

One might even conclude from this that I now have grounds for calling Kant a philosophical theologian. But in my opinion there is already too great a significance given to the labels attached to people, as well as too much confusion concerning the various disciplines within both theology and philosophy, when it is the activity pursued which counts. And, as has been shown above, the activity being carried out in the *Religion* and in the *Conflict* is still a matter of theology. As the theologian Carl Friedrich Stäudlin[36] had pointed out as early as 1797,[37]

Kant's main point in the *Conflict* was that theology in general ought to make more use of reason, and less use of dogmatic assertion about Scripture and historical fact. This is exactly what Kant's rational moral theology attempts to do. In the *Religion* Kant says that the philosopher is concerned with the study of religion from pure reason, by which he means pure practical reason,[38] and that those studying biblical theology should be allowed to add to their study, 'a special course of lectures on the purely *philosophical* theory of religion.' Such a purely 'philosophical' theory, by which Kant means rational, practical theology, would today be a discipline within academic theology.

Thus, not only is Kant's role as philosopher investigating religion shown to break down under scrutiny, and his engagement in a theological conflict brought to light, but he has also been found to be further advancing his own version of theology throughout the *Religion* and the *Conflict*. Why is it, therefore, that Kant is so determined to retain the kind of theology he advocates for the philosophy faculty? First, Kant associated theology faculties with a kind of biblical theology which rested upon historical fact, and the literal interpretation of Scripture. The theology he wanted to advocate was so far removed from biblical theology as he understood it, that he thought the safest way of distinguishing it from biblical theology would be to distinguish it from the theology faculty altogether. Secondly, the period in which the *Religion* was produced, in contrast to the three *Critiques*, was one of strict scholarly censorship.[39] Anything thought to be diverging from the traditional interpretation of religion was liable to censorship. Therefore, as a means of defending his own version of theology against censorship, Kant defined it as a philosophical exercise.

Admittedly, the kind of theology Kant favours is heavily moralistic and rationalistic. It would be pointless to deny this. It would also be pointless to deny that so far Kant's theology seems rather shallow. But my purpose up until now has been to show that Kant continues to advocate a certain kind of theology in the *Religion*, not to critically evaluate the theology advocated. Having done this, I can now turn to the specific details of Kant's rational theology. I shall demonstrate that contrary to popular opinion, Kant's theology amounts to more than just a preference for the moral life and the rational belief in God which such a life entails. In particular, I shall defend Kant's theology against the criticism that it is lacking in doctrinal content, by showing that despite the fact that he has little sympathy for institutional religion, Kant does propound positive interpretations of doctrines such as revelation and grace. Yet, and this is a crucial point for anyone wishing to take Kant's theology seriously, a true appreciation of Kant's theology will not be possible if one limits oneself to the *Religion.* Although even to the present day this work is assumed to be Kant's main thesis on religion, we can no longer concentrate upon it alone, whilst ignoring the wealth of insight into Kant's theology to be gained from other works. Therefore, as well as basing my analysis of Kant's doctrines of revelation and grace upon the standard text of Kant's *Religion,* I will also make greater use of the *Conflict* [40] in particular, but also of other less well-known works by Kant.

III: KANT'S DOCTRINE OF REVELATION

Little has been said so far about the fact that the religious context of Kant's theology is that of the Christian tradition. In particular it is that of Lutheran Christianity in the eighteenth century. This becomes more relevant now as I begin to deal with Kant's treatment of specifically Christian doctrines. Kant's attitude towards revelation is in many respects determined by his view of the shortcomings of ecclesiastical Lutheranism. Kant saw the church as endorsing the view that divine revelation was something miraculous imposed upon the individual from without, and as maintaining that certain religious truths were dependent upon particular historical events. In contrast to hard-line Lutheranism of this kind, Kant refused to think of God as an agent who intervenes in states of affairs, or as an object of experience. Like many other Enlightenment thinkers, Kant denied that religious truth could depend on particular historical events, and had no respect for the notion of salvation through this or that particular belief. In particular, Kant objected to the view that divine revelation is beyond, and may even stand in contradiction to, human reason. Luther had repudiated reason as a way of knowing God, in opposition to faith for which God is both known and unknown. It followed from this that God's revelation must be apprehended by faith, not by reason.[41] As distinct from any emphasis upon revelation, Kant supports the view that:

> They who seek to become well-pleasing to Him (God)* not by praising Him...according to revealed concepts which not every man can have, but by a good course of life, regarding which everyone knows His will—these are they who offer Him the true veneration which He desires.[42]

Far from revelation being necessary, in the above it seems to be suggested that all that is required is a morally good life. And this is the conclusion which many theologians come to on reading what Kant has to say about revelation. However, such a conclusion is both misleading and one-sided. As I shall now show, Kant has a positive conception of revelation, even though it would not have been considered orthodox at the time of his writing.

The word 'alone', sometimes alternatively translated as 'mere', in the title of Kant's *Religion Within the Limits of Reason Alone,* has been taken by many to indicate that Kant is writing about religion 'without the assistance' or 'aid' of supernatural revelation. They therefore assume that the *Religion* is an attempt to rule out revelation theology. However, as Allen Wood has shown in his paper "Kant's Deism,"[43] the title by itself does not necessarily imply that Kant thinks religion can exist without revelation. Kant himself, when later speaking of the *Religion* in the preface to the *Conflict,* says that his purpose in formulating its title was:

> to prevent a misinterpretation to the effect that the treatise deals with religion *from* mere reason (without revelation). That would be claiming too much, since reason's teachings could still come from men who are supernaturally inspired. The title indicates that I intended, rather, to set forth as a coherent whole everything in the Bible—the text of the religion believed to be revealed—that can *also* be recognized *by mere reason.*[44]

And as he says in the *Religion* itself, this work is not an attempt to rule out revelation. Rather:

> Regarding the title of this work...I note: that since, after all, *revelation* can certainly embrace the pure religion of reason, while, conversely, the second cannot include what is historical in the first, I shall be able (experimentally) to regard the first as the *wider* sphere of faith, which includes within itself the second, as a *narrower* one (not like two circles external to one another, but like concentric circles).[45]

Some people might still see this claim as a cunning way of ruling out what Kant claims not to be ruling out. Yet if that had been the case, Kant would not have added the note about concentric circles, nor would he have made claims such as that ecclesiastical faith 'cannot be neglected, because no doctrine based on reason alone seems to the people qualified to serve as an unchangeable norm.'[46] It would appear difficult, given such a comment, to maintain that Kant is attempting to rule out revelation. Far from it, Kant endorses the view that revelation may facilitate the task of reason by disclosing to it various propositions which it would eventually have discovered for itself, but only at a later date.[47] Reason may accept these revealed truths as given, and devote its energies to establishing them on philosophical foundations.[48]

However, it may still be claimed that Kant is not allowing revelation a respectable role; he is allowing it only because of certain deficiencies in human nature.[49] And there is perhaps some truth in this claim, for Kant does imply that no credit can be given to revelation unless it meets the test of reason, and can be rationally interpreted in order to meet the requirements of moral faith:

> If such an empirical faith...is to be united with the basis of a moral faith... an exposition of the revelation which has come into our hands is required, that is, a thorough-going interpretation of it in a sense agreeing with the universal practical rules of a religion of pure reason.[50]

What will be conclusive for my appraisal of Kant's attitude towards revelation is whether or not the exposition suggested above is seen to be successful in Kant's eyes. It is therefore appropriate to turn now to a detailed examination of Kant's exposition of revelation, in order to see whether or not it is successful.

At the opening of Book Four, Part One of the *Religion*,[51] Kant begins to outline various attitudes towards revelation:

> A religion in which my knowledge of something as a duty depends on my knowledge of it as a divine command is a *revealed* religion, whereas a religion in which my knowledge of something as a divine command depends upon my knowledge of it as a duty is a *natural* religion. Someone who holds that natural religion alone is morally necessary, Kant calls a *rationalist.* A rationalist may either believe that there is a revealed religion, or deny that there is. A rationalist who denies the reality of all supernatural revelation is a *naturalist*, whereas one who accepts the reality of such revelation (while regarding it as unnecessary) is a *pure rationalist.* Someone who not only believes in revealed religion but also holds it to be morally necessary is a pure *supernaturalist.*

Wood has suggested that Kant's position is a rationalist one,[52] and he gives the following reasons to support this view: Kant is committed to denying pure supernaturalism which affirms that a revealed religion is morally necessary. But it is equally clear that Kant is not a naturalist: he insists that it would transcend the limits of human insight to claim that supernatural revelation has not occurred.[53] According to Wood, Kant is a rationalist because he is an agnostic about supernatural revelation. For instance, he questions whether one could ever have adequate grounds for claiming the authenticity of any putative revelation:

> If God should really speak to man, man could still never *know* that it was God speaking. It is quite impossible for man to apprehend the infinite by his senses, distinguish it from sensible beings, and *recognize* it as such.[54]

Kant's position, then, is that there may be such a thing as supernatural revelation, but if there is, no human being can ever know that there is, and no particular claim to supernatural revelation can ever be deserving of our rational assent. For that very reason, belief in supernatural revelation cannot be required of us as a duty, since it would be a duty which one could fulfil only by holding a belief which no human being could ever be justified in holding.

Although Wood is on the whole correct about Kant's attitude towards revelation, it is important to note that Kant does not quite fit into any of the positions outlined by Wood. Wood points out that a rationalist can either believe in, or deny supernatural revelation, and he goes on to say that Kant is a rationalist. But, in fact, Kant will not go so far as to say either that he believes in, or that he denies supernatural revelation. Therefore, one needs to make room for the rationalist who is an agnostic with regard to supernatural revelation. Given this further possibility, Kant's attitude towards revelation now appears as follows: he will not rule out the possibility of supernatural revelation, but he will not adopt it as an essential aspect of the religion of reason. This marks Kant's divergence from the traditional Lutheran stance, which requires a belief in revelation as one of the essential tenets of faith. However, quite remarkably in the *Conflict,* Kant maintains that Christianity adopts the same position as he does with regard to revelation:

> Only a religion that makes it a principle not to admit supernatural revelation can be called *naturalistic.** So Christianity is not a naturalistic religion-though it is a merely natural one-because it does not deny that the Bible may be a supernatural means for introducing religion and that a church may be established to teach and profess it publicly: it simply takes no notice of this source where religious doctrine is concerned.[55]

Admittedly, this is a rather unusual interpretation of Christianity, and Kant's critics would still argue that the position outlined above does not entail a positive attitude towards revelation, but rather, as has already been stated, an agnostic stance. And, in so far as the above is concerned, it would be pointless to deny this. However, there are certain statements in the *Religion* which suggest that Kant does have a positive attitude towards revelation. At one point he says that 'though each obeys the (non-statutory) law which he prescribes to himself, he must at the same time regard this law as the will of a World-Ruler, *revealed to him through reason*',[56*] and that 'the pure religion of reason is a continually occurring divine (though not empirical) *revelation for all men*.'[57*] These statements, far from suggesting a negative attitude towards revelation, seem to be making explicit appeal to divine revelation. But we are now faced with the question of whether claims such as these can be reconciled with the interpretation of Kant's agnostic position offered above. Fortunately they can, and it is in the remaining section of Wood's outline of Kant's position that one can see how this is possible.[58]

Kant provides a way of securing revealed religion, or at least parts of it. He suggests that supernatural, empirical or external revelation, revelation through scriptures or extraordinary experiences, is not the only kind, or even the most important kind:

> Revelation is either *external* or inward. An external revelation can be of two kinds: either (1) through works, or (2) through words. Inward divine revelation is God's revelation to us through our own reason. It must precede all other revelation and serve as a judge of external revelation. It has to be the touchstone by which I know whether an external revelation is really from *God*; and it must give me proper concepts of him.[59]

Kant identifies inward revelation with our pure rational concept of God as a most real being, and with our knowledge of our moral duties, since these can be represented as divine commands, and thus go to make up our concept of God.[60] We are justified in regarding all rational knowledge of God as an instance of revelation, because it hardly makes sense to suppose that we might acquire any knowledge of God whatever except through revelation. Any knowledge we might acquire about God would have to depend on a decision of self-revelation by God. Kant is convinced that 'the concept of God, and the conviction of his *existence** can be met with only in reason; they can come from reason alone, and not from inspiration or from any tidings, however great their authority.'[61] It would appear then, that the touchstone of permissible belief about God is inward revelation.

Inward revelation also serves as the judge concerning alleged external revelation;[62] and given that the concept of God revealed is a moral one, Kant goes so far as to maintain that 'even though something is represented as commanded by God, through a direct manifestation of Him, yet if it flatly contradicts morality, it cannot, despite all appearances, be of God.'[63]

Therefore, it would appear that inward revelation takes precedence over and is properly used to judge external revelation. However, even though it is epistemically dependent and secondary, external revelation has a certain value:

> An external divine revelation can be an occasion for man to come for the first time to pure concepts of God which are pure concepts of the understanding; and it can also give him the opportunity to search for these concepts.[64]

Given the above it is clear that even if Kant was unsympathetic towards, and at most agnostic about empirical revelation, he did have a positive conception of inward revelation, through reason. Thus, when Kant spoke of the inner circle of religion not being able to include the historical from the outer circle, he was not ruling out the possibility of including what amounts to revelation in the inner sense. And to those who may try to argue that Kant's belief in inward revelation pre-dates the *Religion,* and therefore may have been cast off later, I offer the following section from Kant's *Conflict,* which appeared later than the *Religion,* as a witness to Kant's belief in inward revelation.

The Bible as revelation in the Conflict of the Faculties

There is a section of the *Conflict* in which Kant refers to the Bible as divine revelation.[65] He says that 'the mark of its divinity..is its harmony with what reason pronounces worthy of God.'[66] In other words, the Bible is divine in so far as its contents are in harmony with the moral concept of God, which has been inwardly revealed to us in our reason. But in what way does the Bible correspond to inward divine revelation in human reason? According to Kant, 'we must regard the credentials of the Bible as drawn from the pure spring of universal rational religion dwelling in every ordinary man.' That is, the Bible is testimony to the predisposition to the moral religion which lays hidden in the human reason of all persons, including those who first put this disposition into words in the writing of the Bible. It is for this reason that the teaching of the Bible contains 'a faith which our reason can develop out of itself.'[67] It is the fact that the Bible has the power to nourish and nurture pure moral religion, rather than its historical status, which makes it a work of divine revelation:

> No historical account can verify the divine origin of such a writing. The proof can be derived only from its tested power to establish religion in the human heart...and we must explain it as such, so that we do not attribute the Bible's existence *sceptically* to mere accident or *superstitiously* to a *miracle*, both of which would cause reason to run aground.[68]

Kant seems to be implying that the Bible tells us what our inner conscience also tells us is required of us in order to be worthy of God. And if this is the case, then it must, as must our inward revelation, be considered as divine. Its divinity is testified to by the fact of the widespread influence it has had upon moral beings:

> The Bible contains within itself a credential of its (moral) divinity that is sufficient for practical purposes—the influence that, as the text of a systematic doctrine of faith, it has always exercised on the hearts of men...This is sufficient reason for preserving it, not only as the organ of universal inner rational religion, but also as the legacy (new testament) of a statutory doctrine of faith which will serve us indefinitely as a guiding line.[69]

Of course, the objection will be raised at this point that Kant is putting human reason before God, that it is human reason itself that is divine. I could see the force of this claim, if Kant had not himself warned against such an interpretation. He specifically says that the teaching of the Bible is in the Bible because it is from God, not from God because it is in the Bible.[70] Admittedly, Kant may be unorthodox in his view that if the teaching were from God because it is in the Bible, then that would be presupposing the divine authority of the book, before the divinity of its doctrine, and this would be a moral outrage. But his divergence from orthodoxy on this point does not alter the fact that on his view the moral content of the Bible is in the Bible because it is the revelation of the moral author, and not vice versa, as many exponents of Kant's moral theory have suggested. It is not that Kant is trying to make reason divine, but rather that in Kant's opinion it is only by reason, not by empirical, contingent fact, that we can recognise the divinity of a teaching:

> for since we cannot understand anyone unless he speaks to us through our own understanding and reason, it is only by concepts of *our*

> reason, in so far as they are pure moral concepts and hence infallible, that we can recognize the divinity of a teaching promulgated to us.[71]

There is, therefore, evidence to suggest that for Kant the moral component of the Bible is in a sense a revelation of God:

> If a people has been taught to revere a sacred Scripture, the doctrinal interpretation of that Scripture, which looks to the people's moral interest—its edification, moral improvement, and hence salvation—is also the authentic one with regard to its religion: in other words, this is how God wants this people to understand His will as revealed in the Bible.[72]

Given the above, it is easier to understand why for Kant the Bible reveals no other than the truths of reason, when he claims that the testimony of Scripture and the teachings of a sermon should be taken as examples 'in which the truth of reason's practical principles is made more perceptible through their application to facts of sacred history',[73] because reason in itself is a divine revelation. If the moral law as revealed to our reason is divine, then the moral content of the Bible, which conforms to our conception of the moral law as put into words by its writers, is also divine. Therefore, in the same way that Kant accepted internal, or general, as distinct from external, or special, revelation, so it may here be argued that he accepted the Bible as divine revelation in so far as it corresponds to internal revelation.

Nor is this interpretation of Kant pure hypothesis. Kant himself gives us the grounds for this interpretation by printing as an appendix to the section on the Bible as revelation, a letter by Carol Arnold Wilmans.[74] In the letter Wilmans claims that in a group of people called separatists, but calling themselves mystics, he found the teachings of Kant put into practice. These people lived entirely without public worship, and repudiated àll 'divine service' that did not consist in fulfilling one's duties. They considered themselves Christians, though they took as their code, not the Bible, but only the precepts of an inward Christianity dwelling in them from eternity. Wilmans found in these people a pure moral attitude of will and an almost Stoic consistency in their actions. What is most important however, is Wilmans' claim that:

> I examined their teachings and principles and recognized the essentials of your (Kant's)* entire moral and religious doctrine, though with this difference: that they consider the inner law, as they call it, an inward revelation and so regard God as definitely the author.[75]

Kant surely also takes the inner, moral law, to be an inward revelation and so, in total agreement with these people, regards God as the author. To interpret it as such is to fit entirely with what he has just said in his own section on the Bible as divine revelation.

Wilmans continues with the suggestion that these people regarded the Bible as a book which in some way or other—they did not discuss it further—was of divine origin; but they inferred the divine origin of the Bible from the consistency of the doctrine it contains with their inner law. If one asked their reason, they replied: 'The Bible is validated in my heart, as you will find it in yours if you obey the precepts of your inner law or the teachings of the Bible.'[76] For the same reason they did not regard the Bible as their code of laws but only as a historical confirmation in which they recognized what was originally grounded in themselves. This also coheres with Kant's claim that the Bible is consistent with what human reason reveals to us, and is validated by the influence it has on men's hearts.

There can be no other reason for Kant to include this letter than to point out that the position of these people, with regard to the inner law considered as an inward revelation, is no different from his own position.

Wilmans concludes that:

> If these people were philosophers they would be (pardon the term!) true Kantians...But I have never found a theologian among them—for to theologians, they are a real thorn in the eye because, while they do not support public worship, their exemplary conduct and complete submission to the civil order put them quite beyond reproach.[77]

This comment matches Kant's distrust of theologians who spend too much time concentrating upon divine worship, and belief in external revelation, and too little upon the leading of a just moral life. What Kant would advocate instead is the position of a rational theologian, that is, one versed in reason with regard to religious faith, which is based on inner laws that can be developed from every person's own reason.

By way of conclusion regarding Kant's attitude towards revelation, and the fact that it is positive in the sense outlined above, it is interesting to note Mary J. Gregor's comment in her introduction to the *Conflict*. According to Gregor Kant simply thinks that:

> As philosophical theologian...he can perform the experiment of beginning with some allegedly divine revelation and examining it, as a historical system, in the light of moral concepts, "to see whether it does not lead back to the very same pure rational system of religion"...From Kant's point of view, the experiment was successful.[78]

The experiment was successful in so far as Kant claimed to have established Christianity's credentials as divine revelation in the only way that this can be established, by demonstrating its consistency with pure moral religion.[79]

IV: KANT'S DOCTRINE OF GRACE

As with revelation, so with grace, Kant's position is determined by his divergence from the traditional Lutheran conception. The traditional view held that grace is something which invades the will from outside. God's grace is a gift and is received by humankind through faith alone, not by human merit. Lutheranism also insisted upon our complete dependence upon God's assistance in order to perform good actions. We can see this in the Lutheran claim that 'man of himself can do no good.' But if we are to take this view to its logical conclusion, it implies that if we perform good actions, no matter how objectively good our actions may be, we do not deserve any moral commendation for them, since we are impelled to do them by the grace of God. Consequently, every human deed that is not morally evil is in fact morally indifferent, since it is caused by something external to the agent.

It is important to recognize the threat that this conception of grace posed to Kant's moral theory. If the will is not independent of external forces, then in Kant's opinion it cannot be free. Since freedom is the necessary presupposition of moral responsibility, it follows that those who claim that all the good they do is the work of God are in fact denying the reality of human freedom, and with it the possibility of moral responsibility, as well as their nature as moral beings. It is no surprise, therefore, to hear Kant saying that 'to await a work of grace means,...that the good (the morally good) is not our deed but the deed of another being, and that we therefore can *achieve* it only by *doing nothing*.'[80] He simply could not accept the idea that persons can do no good of their own accord. For this would seem to relieve them of all responsibility in the moral realm. Kant wanted to give meaning not only to a more active, but also to a more responsible role for persons in the moral realm, both of which were threatened, or at least undermined, by the Lutheran conception of grace. It is for this reason that Kant speaks against those who 'intend to wait upon this moral goodness quite passively, with their hands in their laps, as though it were a heavenly gift which descends from on high.'[81] Kant's view is that 'action must be represented as issuing from man's own use of his powers, not as the effect (resulting) from the influence of an external, higher cause by whose activity man is passively healed.'

Given the above, many theologians might conclude that Kant has no sympathy whatsoever for the notion of grace. And on reading some of Kant's statements it is not difficult to understand why they should come to this conclusion. For example, he says that:

> The calling to our assistance of *works of grace* is one of those aberrations and cannot be adopted into the *maxims* of reason, if she is to remain within her limits; as indeed can nothing of the supernatural, simply because in this realm all use of reason ceases.[82]

According to Kant, it is not possible to recognise the working of grace in any human experience, nor to produce grace by activities such as prayer. He totally rejects actions normally associated with ecclesiastical faith, such as prayer, communion and church-going, as means of attaining grace. He claims that all people are doing in these actions is trying to apply themselves to God's grace 'as though thereby God were directly served.' But to think that this is possible is an illusion.[83]

Other theologians might maintain that Kant is trying to break off from the Christian tradition's belief in divine grace as the only means to morally good actions, by offering his own 'moral religion' which advocates an individualistic ethic of salvation through good works. Thus he says, 'there exists absolutely no salvation for man apart from the sincerest adoption of genuinely moral principles into his disposition.'[84]

Some theologians do admit that Kant has a use for the notion of grace, but claim that it is an entirely negative use. Keith Ward, for instance, claims that Kant's use of the notion of grace is 'a completely empty notion which merely attempts to 'explain' our moral incapacity and remove difficulties in the way of accepting the moral law.'[85] In favour of this interpretation, there is Kant's claim that:

> If man's own deeds are not sufficient to justify him before his conscience (as it judges him strictly), reason is entitled to adopt on faith a supernatural supplement to fill what is lacking to his justification (though not to specify in what that consists).[86]

However, even though Kant appears to be entirely unsympathetic towards the notion of grace when he says, for instance, that 'Reason, conscious of her inability to satisfy her moral need, extends herself to high-flown ideas capable of supplying this lack', he goes on to qualify this comment quite markedly, by adding that 'reason does not dispute the possibility or the reality of the objects of these ideas; she simply cannot adopt them into her maxims of thought and action.'[87] It is precisely because the understanding of grace is beyond us and the limits of our reason that we cannot make use of the notion in our practical and theoretical endeavours.[88] We can, however, admit the possibility of a work of grace as something incomprehensible. This suggests that when speaking of the '*parerga* to religion within the limits of pure reason',[89] Kant is not denying what is beyond the limits, but rather, acknowledging the limits of the human capacity for comprehension.

Another alternative for theologians would be to claim that Kant uses the notion of grace in a positive sense, though he does so by employing grace in a non-objective fashion. They might argue that Kant does not really believe that there is a God, who exists objectively outside of us, and who has the power to manipulate our wills. Rather, he uses the language of grace as a form of inspiration. In order to support such interpretations one might quote passages such as the following:

> That, through the moral law, man is called to a good course of life; that, through unquenchable respect for this law lying in him, he finds in himself justification for confidence in this good spirit and for hope that, however it may come about, he will be able to satisfy this spirit; finally, that, comparing the last-named expectation with the stern command of the law, he must continually test himself as though summoned to account before a judge.

And:

> To demand that more than this be revealed to us is presumptuous.[90]

The mystery of grace is thought to prevent both the sin of pride which might follow the attribution of good works to ourselves, and moral despair at the thought that our moral efforts are often of no avail. But it is not really that there is a judge of people's actions, or a divine power which can aid them, it is simply useful for people to adopt such ideas in order to test themselves, and continue to persevere in their moral efforts.

This interpretation of Kant's use of the notion of grace raises, once again, the important question of a necessary fiction.[91] Do we act 'as if' a divine power will provide what is not in our power, even though we know that there is no such divine power, or do we act 'as if' a divine power will provide what is not in our power in the true belief that there is such a divine power? The non-objective interpretation would favour the former view. However, the idea of grace as used by Kant, strongly implies a power that is, at least in some respects, beyond our own control. It is for this reason that I shall argue against the non-objective interpretation, that Kant endorses the notion of grace as a belief in the existence of a mysterious divine power which aids those who exert themselves to the uttermost in their moral endeavours. The kind of moral achievement which Kant endorses is something which is possible, but not by a person's own power or choice alone. Therefore, Kant is not using the language of grace simply metaphorically, or non-objectively. We must interpret his use of the language of grace in realist terms.

But how can one offer a realist and positive interpretation of grace without making the notion of moral responsibility incoherent, and without presuming to know too much? The answer lies in the idea of cooperation. Kant objects to the asymmetry of the Lutheran conception of grace, according to which grace is a one-way effect. He prefers instead a more symmetrical interpretation, according to which humans also have a part to play. Such an interpretation has in fact become popular amongst some theologians this century, who have placed increasing emphasis upon the ethical implications of the Christian faith. We must work towards the reception of divine grace in the moral improvement of mankind. Not only this, but it is also up to us to make ourselves receptive to the grace of God, by becoming worthy of divine grace, which we nevertheless accept as a gift that is ultimately beyond our comprehension. I shall now turn to an examination of the way in which this idea works in Kant's theology.

Kant wanted to give meaning not only to a more active, but also to a more responsible role for humans in the moral realm. Bearing this in mind, it is important to note that he felt this emphasis upon a person's responsibility to be entirely consistent with the true conception of the Christian religion as he saw it. Thus he says that:

> In the moral religion (and of all the public religions which have ever existed, the Christian alone is moral) it is a basic principle that each must do as much as lies in his power to become a better man, and that only when he has not buried his inborn talent (Luke XIX, 12-16) but has made use of his original disposition to good in order to become a better man, can he hope that what is not within his power will be supplied through cooperation from above.[92]

This gives us a hint as to Kant's position regarding the idea of grace, by implying that when we have done all that is in our power, God's grace will provide what is lacking in us. However, the most explicit outline of Kant's attitude appears in the section of the *Religion* where he deals with the question of salvation.[93] According to Kant, there are two elements in saving faith, both of which are essential. But we must be clear as to which takes precedence:

> Saving faith involves two elements, upon which hope for salvation is conditioned, the one having reference to what man himself can not accomplish, namely undoing lawfully (before a divine judge) actions which he has performed, the other to what he himself can and ought to do, that is, leading to a new life conformable to his duty. The first is the faith in an atonement (reparation for his debt, redemption, reconciliation with God); the second, the faith that we can become well-pleasing to God through a good course of life in the future. Both conditions constitute but one faith and necessarily belong together. Yet we can comprehend the necessity of their union only by assuming that one can be derived from the other.[94]

Atonement is that which persons cannot bring about, whereas moral improvement is what they can bring about. The reasonable person must:

> believe that he must first improve his way of life, so far as improvement lies in his power, if he is to have even the slightest ground for hope of such a higher gain. Wherefore, since historical knowledge of the atonement belongs to ecclesiastical faith, while the improved way of life, as a condition, belongs to pure moral faith, *the latter must take precedence over the former*.[95]

As is clear from the above, in Kant's opinion, it is inconceivable that atonement should precede moral improvement. He cannot understand how human beings can think that divine grace will be granted without the presupposition of human moral effort in order to merit such grace. At the same time, he can conceive of divine aid once humans have achieved as much morally, as is possible for them. What is important is that we must make ourselves worthy of God's grace, through actions well pleasing to God. In fact, of the two aspects mentioned, a) that of hoping that God will supply the surplus necessary, and b) making oneself worthy of this act of forgiveness, aspect b) must take precedence. However, we must not understand this as implying that b) is more important, (since both a) and b) are essential to salvation); it is rather that b) must come first in order that a person may be worthy of receiving divine grace. Kant recognizes, however, that his view is unorthodox, since ecclesiastical religion would put a) before b). But, as far as he is concerned, 'the right course is not to go from grace to virtue but rather to progress from virtue to pardoning grace.'[96] This suggests that God's grace will be available to us in order that we may attain salvation, but only after we have made ourselves worthy of such 'pardoning grace.'

In the above I have attempted a reappraisal of Kant's attitude towards grace. I have tried to show that Kant wants to emphasize the moral person's role in the process, and the need to become worthy of God's grace. However, some theologians might now argue that the above does not amount to a positive attitude towards grace, but rather a diminishing of the role of grace in a person's life. Kant's account pushes the notion of grace into the background as something not even worthy of consideration until one has improved oneself morally, whereas on the Christian understanding, without the aid of divine grace people cannot even begin to improve themselves morally. Therefore, if grace is not necessary for this, why allow it to enter in at all? This is a valid question, and I can only begin to answer it by considering Kant's position with regard to moral conversion from evil to good, to an examination of which I now turn.

Kant's Attitude Towards Evil and Moral Conversion

As a detailed account of Kant's notion of evil will be given in Chapter III,[97] I need only to point out that Kant's notion of evil appears to be very similar to the Biblical notion of original sin. Kant implies that all humans are 'under sin'[98] and therefore in need of a radical conversion in order to become good. In referring to the overcoming of evil, Kant does not speak primarily of a moral conversion, but claims that one can become good 'only by a kind of rebirth, as it were a new creation (John III, 5; compare also Genesis I, 2) and a change of heart.'[99] However, despite the explicit appeal to religious terminology here, Kant rejects all claims that the moral conversion must be dependent upon some external divine action. The change from bad to good is only possible through a free act of the agent, whereby the person transforms his or her cast of mind, and adopts a new supreme maxim as the basis of all practical behaviour. This change of heart 'must be possible because duty requires it.'[100]

There is a distinct problem here. From the above it is clear that it is a duty to overcome the evil propensity. In order to do so, one must not only adopt good maxims, but must also undergo an absolute 'change of heart.' Kant describes this change of heart as a kind of 'rebirth, as it were a new creation.' But he also says that even the best person cannot extirpate the propensity to evil in their nature, which is innate.[101] In fact, even the person whose disposition is good cannot achieve a holy will, which for Kant is necessary for moral perfection. The problem centres on how it is possible to overcome the propensity to evil, given that it happens to be the case that all human beings have adopted a morally evil supreme maxim that makes their moral characters evil.[102] This is moral rigorism. Given Kant's view then, it would seem impossible to bring about the moral conversion which he claims must be possible.

According to Philip Quinn,[103] this inconsistency in Kant's doctrine of evil reflects the tension which the Christian interpretation of the human situation presents. According to this perspective, all human characters are ineradicably stained, the moral evaluation of each is negative, but sin is self incurred. Yet, only morally perfect characters can be justified by a morally perfect God. Therefore, all humanity can hope for is some miraculous dissolution of its moral inadequacies before God. Normally of course, this tension is resolved by an appeal to the divine grace of God's mercy. Kant's problem lies in his attempt to resolve the tension in order to make room for hope without stepping beyond the limits enforced by reason. But this means that for him the conversion must precede grace. This precludes the possibility of grace to dispel the evil propensity. Quinn concludes therefore, that Kant simply does not have the resources necessary to the construction of an acceptable solution to the tension in his doctrine of radical evil.

However, in my opinion, Quinn has failed to see the significance of freedom in Kant's notion of moral conversion, which both creates the tension in his theory, and at the same time explains why the moral conversion cannot simply be attributed to divine grace in the Lutheran understanding of that concept. Once again, the thought is that if we were to rely totally upon grace from God, then we would be passive instruments in the divine network of things. And this would once again preclude the possibility of moral responsibility. One must take responsibility for one's own moral change of heart, which cannot be produced *in toto* from without. And, contrary to Quinn's thought, there is evidence in the *Religion* to suggest that Kant's understanding of evil as inextirpable is not inconsistent with the view that we can overcome the evil tendencies in our nature. Even though Kant says that evil is inextirpable, he means by this only that humans will always be open to a disposition to evil, not that we cannot overcome this disposition. First, when referring to radical evil Kant says that '*so long as** we do not eradicate it, it prevents the seed of goodness from developing as it otherwise would.'[104] Secondly, he implies that it is only if we are not capable of overcoming our disposition to evil that all people can be said to be under sin. He does not say 'they are all under sin' and no more, but rather '*if there is no virtue for which some temptation cannot be found capable of overthrowing it*'* then 'they are all under sin.'[105] Unfortunately, no clue is given in the *Religion* as to how we can overcome the evil in our nature. One needs, instead, to refer to the *Conflict* for guidance concerning Kant's thoughts on moral conversion.

Moral Conversion in the Conflict of the Faculties

In a section which deals specifically with the question of moral conversion,[106] Kant offers his own answer as follows: the call to moral conversion comes to a person 'through his own reason, in so far as it contains the *supersensible principle** of moral life.'[107] Kant does not clarify the exact nature of the supersensible principle. But he does distinguish it from alleged supersensible experiences, saying that 'a direct revelation from God embodied in the comforting statement "Your sins are forgiven you" would be a supersensible experience, and this is impossible.'[108]

However, Kant does go on to say that the Bible contains the supersensible principle necessary for the rebirth in that its teaching 'works with divine power on all men's hearts toward their fundamental improvement.'[109] What then is this supersensible principle? The closest Kant comes to telling us is in the following:

> Even the Bible...seems to refer, not to supernatural experiences and fantastic feelings which should take reason's place in bringing about

> this revolution, but to the spirit of Christ, which he manifested in teachings and examples so that we might make it our own-or rather, since it is already present in us by our moral disposition, so that we might simply make room for it.[110]

It would seem from the above that the supersensible is something akin to the power or spirit of Christ.

Given that moral conversion is not to be understood in terms of an external influence, Kant seems to be implying here that it has something to do with the 'supersensible principle' in humankind. This supersensible principle is given through a person's reason. What are we to conclude from this notion of the supersensible in humankind? It may remind one of Aquinas, and the idea that 'grace perfects nature.' Perhaps the most likely explanation of the supersensible principle is as something which is of us, and yet not of us; it is both a part of us, and beyond our natural powers. There is a similarity here with some kinds of modern theology which insist that we must understand God's grace as something which works through the natural world, and yet is not of it. The same is the case with the supersensible principle Kant attributes to humankind. Kant wants to lodge it safely in the natural world of human reason,[111] and yet it is ultimately supersensible, ie.beyond human nature. And in answer to those who might say that this line of argument is not consistent with the *Religion*, or with Kant's attitude towards grace displayed there, the following passages from the *Religion* can be offered to show that it is:

> But we cannot know anything at all about supernatural aid—whether a certain moral power, perceptible to us, really comes from above or, indeed, on what occasions and under what conditions it may be expected.[112]

This shows that Kant does already have a notion of the supersensible, and that he believes that it is beyond human comprehension. Also, in line with the interpretation of grace as working through human nature, though beyond natural means or comprehension, Kant says that:

> the persuasion that we can distinguish the effects of grace from those of nature (virtue) or can actually produce the former within ourselves, is fanaticism; for we cannot by any token, recognize a supersensible object in experience, still less can we exert an influence upon it to draw it down to us; though to be sure, at times there do arise stirrings of the heart making for morality, movements which we cannot explain

> and regarding which we must confess our ignorance: "The wind bloweth where it listeth...but thou canst not tell whence it cometh."[113]

Having given an outline of Kant's position with regard to moral conversion, I am now in a position to answer the criticism that Kant was attempting to diminish the role of grace in the life of the religious person, by ruling it out totally in the process of improving oneself morally. On Kant's view, there is something supersensible which works in us through our moral conversion, though he will not go so far as to assign to it the traditional Lutheran title of heavenly grace, because this would be something external. Yet, at the same time, it does seem to be a way for Kant to rescue something of the sense of supersensible grace working through human nature, though not as an external, but as an inward principle. In this way, by adopting a notion of the 'inward' as distinct from the 'external', Kant rescues something of the sense of grace in the same way that he rescued something of the sense of revelation. If grace is present in the moral conversion, then it is plausible to suggest that grace aids human progress in the moral realm. Kant's emphasis upon the 'inward' brings us to the very heart of his religion, namely a religion which we must seek within. Kant admits as much when he says that he is afraid that we might 'render ourselves unfit for all use of reason or allow ourselves to fall into the indolence of waiting from above, in passive leisure, what we should seek within.'[114] All of the dangers which traditional religion raises cannot in Kant's mind be avoided 'so long as we seek religion without and not within us.'[115]

In summary, it may be suggested that as with revelation, Kant seems to be ruling out grace in one sense, that is the external sense, and allowing it in an inward sense. Instead of conceiving of grace as some kind of special miraculous intervention, one ought to view it in more general terms as a supersensible principle within human nature. And once such an internal sense of grace has been established, there is no reason to rule it out as a force at work in the human conversion from evil to good, or in the supplement to human moral effort in the quest for salvation.

CONCLUSION

The first part of this chapter was concerned with the need to show that Kant continued to engage in theology in his *Religion*, a work which has, somewhat mistakenly, been accepted as a philosophical treatment of religion, and no more. I suggested that Kant's treatment of religion met with the conditions for philosophical theology rather than the philosophy of religion. I did not, however, go so far as to claim that Kant was a philosophical theologian. The reason I gave for not doing so was that there was already too much significance given to titles, when what was important was the activity pursued. I also referred to a certain confusion concerning the various disciplines within theology and philosophy. It is now appropriate to explain what I meant by these claims. The significance given to labels in philosophy and theology is somewhat misplaced, given that such labels are often arbitrarily changed for particular uses. For instance, when people trained in theology apply for positions in philosophy faculties they conveniently become 'philosophers of religion', and philosophers who have studied a little theology and want to work within a theological faculty become 'philosophical theologians.' In cases such as these the significance attached to a particular label can be advantageous. But it can also be disadvantageous, when, as I would claim is the case with Kant, the label 'philosopher of religion' carries with it negative connotations. The attribution of the title 'philosopher of religion' to Kant restricts one's impression of his engagement in theology. It is the significance given to a title carrying such negative connotations which I object to. By confusion concerning the various disciplines within philosophy and theology I mean the kind of ambiguity which results in many works in academia carrying the title 'philosophy of religion' when they are in fact examples of 'philosophical theology', and vice versa. However, confusion over philosophical theology and the philosophy of religion is not the only one. Other examples include those between theology and religious studies, or dogmatic and systematic theology. Such confusion suggests that the dividing line between these and other disciplines is rather ambiguous. But if I am not incorrect, it appears that in the history of theology and philosophy it has been the case that those advocating views which diverge from traditional interpretations of theology have been more often associated with philosophical interpretations of religion, whilst those advocating more traditional interpretations have been accepted as theologians. It is perhaps for this reason that Kant's account of religious doctrines has not been acceptable to most theologians.

Upon turning to an examination of Kant's attitude towards revelation and grace, an encounter with his anti-ecclesiasticism was unavoidable. Kant spoke out against those for whom the Christian faith had deteriorated into a matter of correct ceremonial and Orthodox belief. He describes orthodoxy as 'the view that belief in dogma is sufficient for religion.' It is the unconditional value which Orthodoxy gives to religious doctrines such as revelation, that Kant objected to, not revelation itself. In Kant's opinion it was a superstition to hold that historical belief was a duty and essential to salvation. He was also afraid of the possibility of someone professing to believe in such things while being 'the most evil and worthless person.' Add this to the fact that according to Kant, Orthodoxy regarded the natural principles of morality as of secondary importance, and it is not surprising that he tried to offer an alternative exposition of religious doctrines.

From my examination of revelation and grace, two things have become clear. First, in each case Kant wanted to rule out miraculous divine intervention in the world. Secondly, he allowed for an internal sense of both revelation and grace. With regard to revelation and the Bible, it is plausible that Kant was attempting to assimilate what had traditionally been thought of as special revelation into general revelation. Something similar applies to the concept of grace, concerning which Kant sought to replace the notion of external divine intervention with a supersensible principle, or power, within human nature. It is at this point that I think one can see the coming together of Kant's notions of revelation and grace. If the supersensible principle is given in reason, and if one bears in mind that reason is in a sense a divine revelation, then there is also a sense in which the supersensible principle is divine, whilst ever remaining quite different from miraculous supernatural interruption.

I have also emphasized the guiding theme of freedom, which is essential to the whole of Kant's thought. Kant wanted to preserve human nature's absolute autonomy. In order to do this he thought it necessary to cut humanity off from all external influences, divine, human and physical alike. However, I have argued that he did leave open the possibility of inward influence, even though we could not and must not seek to explain away the means by which this occurred. In this respect Kant is similar to the libertarian who has to confess that a person's freedom is ultimately a mystery, not to be fathomed by the human mind:

> It is as though we wished to *explain* and to *render comprehensible* to ourselves in terms of a man's freedom what happens to him; on this question God has indeed revealed His will through the moral law in us, but the *causes* due to which a free action on earth occurs or does

> not occur He has left in that obscurity in which human investigation must leave whatever (as an historical occurrence, though yet springing from freedom) ought to be conceived of according to the laws of cause and effect.[116]

The above statement suggests that freedom is a mystery which is linked to the moral law as revealed to us by God. It also suggests that the cause of our free actions is a mystery. Given that true freedom amounts to obedience to the moral law, the mystery of free actions must also therefore be the mystery of how we can become good persons. And this leads to the mystery of the supersensible principle in humankind. From this we may conclude that freedom itself amounts to a supersensible principle. To acknowledge this fact is to recognize the link between revelation, grace and freedom in Kant's theology. It is through supersensible freedom that persons are able to recognize the moral law as revealed to them, and it is through the supersensible power of grace within them that they are able to act upon it.

ENDNOTES

1 Hereafter to be referred to as the *Religion*.

2 Initially, one might think of Bernard Reardon's *Kant as Philosophical Theologian*, Macmillan, 1988, as an exception. On page 168 Reardon claims that the *Religion* is 'undoubtedly a landmark in the history of philosophical theology.' However, one wonders how significant Reardon's use of the title 'philosophical theology' instead of 'philosophy of religion' really is. For, in the preface Reardon says that Kant's 'philosophical treatment of religious problems was, however, of such scope and importance that he may fairly be described as the founder of the study now known as the Philosophy of Religion', and he calls his last main chapter on Kant, "Last thoughts on the Philosophy of Religion." Moreover, in his analysis of the *Religion* on page 91, he claims that 'In approaching this work...Kant is deliberately taking up a position of independence.' Thus, it would seem that, far from trying to show that Kant was a philosophical theologian, Reardon is advocating the idea that Kant is a philosopher of religion.

3 A more detailed examination of the title occurs later in this chapter. See p.68.

4 It is worth noting that the kind of reason usually associated with the philosophy of religion is more like the theoretical, speculative, or in other words, deductive reasoning which Kant rules out in relation to theology proper.

5 KW V, 482; Third *Critique*, II, General Remark on Teleology, p.159.

6 KW XXVIII 2.2, 997; *Philosophical Theology*, p.26

7 In the *Lectures on Ethics* Kant says that religion is morality applied to God (p.81), or the combination of ethics and theology (p.79). He even goes so far as to say that religion without morality and theology is an absurdity and impossible. Cf. KW XXVIII 2.2, 1983; *Lectures on Philosophical Theology*, p.122.

8 Kant's account of the kingdom of God will be dealt with again in Chapter III. See pp.113f and 123.

9 This title hints at an extremely significant element which is to be considered in connection with the kingdom of God, namely, the battle between good and evil, which will be considered in Chapter III. See pp.96ff, 116ff.

10 KW VI, 97-8; *Religion*, Book III, Division I, ii., p.89.

11 Ibid., 98; Ibid.

12 Ibid., 152; Ibid., Book IV, p.140.

13 Ibid., 100; Ibid., Book III, Division I, iv., p.92.

14 Ibid., 99; Ibid., iii.,p.91.

15 Ibid., 100; Ibid., iv., p.92.

16 Ibid., 101; Ibid.

17 Ibid., 152; Ibid., Book IV, p.140.

18 Cf. KW III, 522ff; First *Critique*, A804-807 / B833ff, where Kant considers the three questions: What can I know?, What ought I to do?, and What may I hope? The third question concerns the hope which we are justified in having, if we fulfil our moral obligations. In a letter to Carl Friedrich Stäudlin, dated May 4th, 1793 (KW XI, 414, transl. in *Immanuel Kant: Philosophical Correspondence*, p.205-6), Kant implies that the *Religion* is concerned with the question 'What may I hope?'

19 Such hope is also expressed in later works by Kant, as in his essay " An Old Question Raised Again: Is the Human Race Constantly Progressing" (KW VII, 80-174, transl. in the *Conflict of the Faculties*, pp.141-171).

20 See Hebblethwaite, "The Philosophy of Religion," in *The Threshold of Theology*, ed., P. Avis, Marshall Pickering, 1988.

21 KW VI, 13; *Religion,* Preface to the Second Edition, p.12.

22 Ibid., 9-11; Ibid., pp.8-10.

23 See p.9f.

24 See Hebblethwaite, "The Philosophy of Religion."

25 *Philosophical Theology,* translator's introduction, p.10.

26 KW VI, 9; *Religion,* Preface to the First edition, pp.8-9.

27 For references to the biblical theologian in the *Religion* see: Ibid., 7-10, 13, 85, note; Ibid., Preface to the First Edition, pp.7-10, Preface to the Second Edition, p.12, Book II, General Observation, p.80, note.

28 Hereafter to be referred to as the *Conflict.*

29 KW VII, 36; *Conflict,* p.61.

30 Ibid., 66; Ibid., p.121.

31 Ibid., 38; Ibid., p.65.

32 Ibid., 45; Ibid., p.79.

33 Jean-Louis Bruch, Aubier 1969, p.145.

34 KW VII, 38; *Conflict*, p.65.

35 I am therefore led to a different conclusion concerning Kant's *Religion* than that of Hebblethwaite in *The Threshold of Theology*.

36 Kant dedicated the *Conflict* to Stäudlin.

37 C.F. Stäudlin, *Beitrage zur Philosophie und Geschichte der Religion und Sittenlehre*, Lübeck, 1797, Vol. V, xi., pp.344-350. Stäudlin refers continuously to Kant's 'moral theology' in this and other works.

38 *Religion*, Preface to the Second Edition, p.11.

39 See Ch. 1, endnote 171.

40 The significant contribution which the *Conflict* will be shown to make to our understanding of Kant's doctrines of revelation and grace, hopefully disproves Reardon's claim that the *Conflict*, 'adds nothing of significance to what had been more fully said before.' See *Kant as Philosophical Theologian*, p.157.

41 This contrasts with the Enlightenment view that claims to revelation are acceptable only when they are rationally justified and their contents subject to reason's judgement.

42 KW VI, 104-5; *Religion,* Book III, v., pp.95-6. *My brackets.

43 A.W. Wood, "Kant's Deism" in *Kant's Philosophy of Religion Reconsidered*, ed., P. Rossi and M. Green, Indiana U.P., 1991, pp.1-21.

44 KW VII, 6, note; *Conflict*, pp.9-11, note.

45 KW VI, 12; *Religion*, Preface to the Second Edition, p.11.

46 Ibid., 112. Cf. 103; Ibid., Book III, vi., p.103. Cf. Book III, v., p.94.

47 Ibid., 155-6; Ibid., Book IV, i., pp.143-4.

48 Here we have yet another allusion to philosophical theology.

49 KW VII, 9; *Conflict*, p.17: Kant says that 'revelation is useful in making up the theoretical deficiency which our pure rational belief admits it has.'

50 KW VI, 110; *Religion,* Book III, vi., p.100.

51 Ibid., 153-4; Ibid., Book IV, i., p.143.

52 See Wood, "Kant's Deism."

53 KW VI, 154; *Religion*, Book IV, i., p.143.

54 KW VII, 63; *Conflict*, p.115.

55 Ibid., 44-5; Ibid., pp.77-79. * My italics.

56 KW VI, 122; *Religion*, Book III, vii., p.112. * My italics.

57 Ibid.; Ibid., p.113. * My italics.

58 See Wood, "Kant's Deism."

59 KW XXVIII 2.2, 1117; *Philosophical Theology*, p.160.

60 Ibid, 1117-8; Ibid., pp.160-1.

61 KW VIII, 142; "What is Orientation in Thinking?" p.301. * My italics.

62 KW XXVIII 2.2, 1117; *Philosophical Theology*, p.160.

63 KW VI, 87; *Religion*, Book II, General Observation, pp. 81-2.

64 KW XXVIII 2.2, 1118-9; *Philosophical Theology*, p.161.

65 KW VII, 46ff; *Conflict*, p.81ff.

66 Ibid.

67 Ibid., 63; Ibid., p.115.

68 Ibid., 59; Ibid., p.107

69 Ibid., 64; Ibid., p.117.

70 Ibid.

71 Ibid., 65; Ibid., p.119.

72 Ibid., 48; Ibid., p.85.

73 Ibid; 67; Ibid., p.123. See also, same page: 'The God Who speaks through our own (morally practical) reason is an infallible interpreter of His words in the Scriptures, Whom everyone can understand.'

74 Ibid., 69; Ibid., p.127.

75 Ibid.

76 Ibid., 74; Ibid., p.137. * My brackets.

77 Ibid.

78 Ibid., 74-75; Ibid., pp.137-9.

79 *Conflict,* translator's introduction, p.xiii.

80 Ibid.

81 KW VI, 53; *Religion,* Book I, General Observation, pp.48-9.

82 Ibid., 161; Ibid., Book IV, Section I, p.149.

83 KW VII, 42; *Conflict,* p.73.

84 KW VI, 53; *Religion,* Book I, General Observation, p.48.

85 Ibid., 199. Cf. 194; Ibid., Book IV, General Observation, p.187. Cf. p.182.

86 Ibid., 83; Ibid., Book II, Section II, p.78.

87 K.Ward, *The Development of Kant's View of Ethics,* Basil Blackwell, Oxford, 1972, p.150.

88 KW VII, 43; *Conflict,* p.75.

89 KW VI, 52; *Religion,* Book I, General Observation, p.47.

90 Ibid., 52; Ibid., p.48.

91 Ibid., 53; Ibid., p.49.

92 Ibid., 52; Ibid., P.47.

93 Ibid., 144-145; Ibid., Book III, vii., p.135.

94 I have already argued against the interpretation of the Kantian 'as if' as a necessary fiction in Chapter I. See p.19.

95 KW VI, 52; *Religion,* Book I, General Observation, p.47.

96 Ibid., 116ff; Ibid., Book III, vii., p.106ff.

97 Ibid.

98 Ibid., 117; Ibid., pp.107-8.

99 Ibid., 118-9; Ibid., p.109.

100 Ibid., 202; Ibid., Book IV, General Observation, p.190.

101 See pp.96ff and 116ff.

102 Ibid., 39; Ibid., Book I, iii, p.34.

103 Ibid., 47; Ibid., Book I, General Observation, p.43.

104 Ibid., 66-7; Ibid., Book II, Section I, C, p.60.

105 Ibid., 22; Ibid., Book I, p.17.

106 Ibid.

107 P. Quinn, "Original Sin, Radical Evil and Moral Identity," *Faith and Philosophy* 1, 1984; pp.197-201.

108 KW VI, 38; *Religion*, Book I, iii., p.34. * My italics.

109 Ibid., 39; Ibid. * My italics.

110 KW VII, 54ff; *Conflict*, p.97ff.

111 Ibid., 47; Ibid., p.83. * My italics.

112 Ibid.

113 Ibid., 59; Ibid., p.107.

114 Ibid.

115 Ibid., 46; Ibid., p.81.

116 KW VI, 191; *Religion,* Book IV, General Observation, p.179.

117 Ibid., 174; Ibid., Book IV, Part Two, 2, p.162.

118 Ibid., 191; Ibid., Book IV, General Observation, p.180.

119 Ibid., 167; Ibid., Book IV, Part I, Section II, p.155.

120 KW VII, 60; *Conflict*, p.109.

121 KW VI, 144; *Religion,* Book III, General Observation, p.135.

III: KANT AND HIS RELIGIOUS PREDECESSORS

INTRODUCTION

The main part of the last chapter dealt with Kant's positive appraisal of the religious doctrines of revelation and grace. Integral to my analysis was the suggestion that Kant's interpretation was at odds with the Orthodox Lutheran interpretations of these doctrines prevalent in his day. The fact that I argued to this effect may come as a surprise to those familiar with Kant's treatment of religion. Even today, many people are still under the impression that if Kant had any religious tendencies whatever, they went in the direction of Lutheranism. Moreover, despite the fact that Kant lived more than two hundred years later than Luther, links between his philosophy and the theology of Luther are still being advocated, and the claim continues to be made today that Kant was the philosopher of Protestantism. It was for this reason that I found it necessary to point out Kant's divergence from hard-line Lutheranism in the previous chapter, and it is for the same reason that I now find it essential to dispel the—if I may refer to it as such—'myth' that Kant is the philosopher of Protestantism, or the Enlightenment fulfiller of what Luther had initiated with the Reformation. I shall do this by examining the two main religious themes, radical evil and freewill, with regard to which Kant's treatment of religion cannot be reconciled with the theology of Luther.

However, showing that the thought of Kant, far from being as close to the thought of Luther as it has often been made out to be, amounts in fact to a contrast to the Lutheran position, does not in itself avoid the detrimental effect which such comparisons have had upon conceptions of Kant's theology. After all, the idea that Kant's position is in opposition to that of Luther might result in the assumption that Kant is even more far removed from any valid version of religiosity than has been supposed by those attempting to link him with Luther. Therefore, in an effort to vindicate Kant's theology by showing that it is a valid alternative to the Lutheran account, I will examine in detail the most fascinating similarities between Kant and the well-known adversary of Luther, namely, Erasmus of Rotterdam. Even though two centuries separate the thought of Erasmus and Kant, Kant's account of evil and freewill as well as his personal outlook and ethical religion will be shown to bear striking resemblance to the theology of Erasmus. Thus, in this chapter I will do three things:

I) Contrast Kant's conception of radical evil and freewill with that of Luther, in an effort to show that Luther is not the religious fore runner of Kant.

II) Compare Kant's conception of evil and freewill with that of Erasmus.

III) Show that Kant's religious ethic, which lies at the heart of his theology and personal outlook, is also similar to that of Erasmus, and that therefore Erasmus is the appropriate religious forerunner with whom Kant can be compared.

I: KANT AND LUTHER

Introductions to Kant's analysis of religion usually refer to the influence upon him of Pietism.[1] Given that Pietism was a major force in Königsberg, where Kant lived, and that Kant's parents were Pietists, this is not so surprising. Kant attended a Pietist school and later University, where one of the main influences upon him was a Wolffian pietist named Knutzen. Also, bearing in mind that the orientation of Pietism is Protestant, it is not so strange that Kant should be associated with the Protestant tradition. After all, Kant was most probably baptised a Protestant, and he used the Lutheran Bible. What is interesting, however, and what will concern us in the first part of this chapter, is the fact that attempts have often been made to draw a comparison between Kant's appraisal of religion, and the theology of Luther.

At the beginning of this century an expanse of literature concerned with the effort to examine the links between Kant and Luther appeared in Germany. Undoubtedly, the same literature has been the influence behind the more recent appraisals of Kant and Luther.[2] Although I do not intend to spend a great deal of time on the attempts which have been made to reconcile the thoughts of Kant with those of Luther,[3] it is worth mentioning briefly some of the links that have been found to exist between them. One such link has been the fact that both Kant and Luther favour personal autonomy in their fight against ecclesiastical orthodoxy. Kant, like Luther before him, rejects the authority and hierarchy of the church, emphasizing instead the personal, individual responsibility of persons towards God. Both Kant and Luther foster self-reliance in religious matters. Such self-reliance has been viewed as a great campaign for personal liberty and individualism, which in Luther's time had been destroyed by the Catholic church.

Another link which has been made between Luther and Kant concerns the emphasis both place upon personal conscience. Luther is seen as an advocate of the religious freedom of conscience; that is, as advocating the right of individuals to possess and to practice those convictions of religious faith that their conscience compels them to accept as true. Likewise, Kant's belief in God comes from an undeniable moral certainty. This moral certainty is thought to reflect the idea that God speaks to people through their moral conscience. Therefore, Kant's moral religion seems to be further developing the freedom of conscience begun with Luther.

There are many more similarities with regard to the concepts used by Kant and Luther, which, for those concerned, point to the fact that Kant is continuing the line begun with Luther. Although it is undeniable that comparisons can be made in this way, since Kant and Luther did both work with concepts of individual responsibility, autonomy and conscience, the extent to which the concepts used by Kant reflect those used by Luther has been over-estimated. There are, in fact, significant differences in the presuppositions underlying the concepts as used by Kant in distinction from Luther. To give an example, the essential fact that for Luther the authority of the institutional church is replaced by the authority of Holy Scripture severely affects his conception of the freedom of conscience. In Luther's opinion, Scripture, which is divine revelation, possesses divine authority, so that obedience to the written word is substituted for obedience to the institutional church. Luther's obedience to the will of God as expressed in the written word is total, therefore his conception of conscience cannot be equated with freedom of thought in regard to religious matters. It is not just personal conviction that counts, since faith is directed in all respects by the written word. Rather, far from Scripture being subject to conscience, conscience is dependent upon scriptural revelation. Thus, as Kohls has remarked in *Luther oder Erasmus*, 'the Godsent independence of the Bible is the key to Luther's self-understanding and to the true understanding of the Evangelical movement in general.'[4]

Bearing this in mind, as well as the fact that it was the historical criticisms of the Enlightenment which undermined confidence in Scripture as an objectively clear and simple revelation of Divine authority,[5] one must not over-exaggerate the degree to which Kant's concept of conscience can be compared with that of Luther. In fact, Kant wanted to redirect the emphasis of faith away from obedience to the written word, to the domain of ethics, and one cannot simply ignore his divergence from Luther in this respect.

Differences like this one mean that there is a sharp dividing line between the correct suggestion that Luther and Kant both work with concepts such as that of freedom of conscience, autonomy and so on, and the very different claim that the thought of Kant is in fact very similar to that of Luther. It will be the aim of the following analysis of Kant and Luther on evil and freewill to further clarify this difference.

Original Sin

Anyone who is acquainted with Kant's interpretation of evil as given in the *Religion* will undoubtedly also have come across the suggestion that it bears striking resemblance to the Lutheran notion of human depravity. Luther accepted the traditional Biblical notion of original sin, as well as the belief in deliverance from this evil through renewal in Jesus Christ. Kant's doctrine of evil astounded other philosophers of the Enlightenment. This was not only because of his conception of what he referred to as the 'radical evil in human nature,' but also because of his emphasis upon the need for a conversion from evil to good, which sounds very similar to the religious need of God's grace in order to overcome evil. My present task is to show that however similar Kant's account of evil appears to be to that of Luther, this is not in fact the case. I shall do this by listing the apparent likeness, and then identifying the dissimilarity between the underlying presuppositions in the views of Luther and Kant.

To begin with, the apparent similarities between the views of Kant and Luther with regard to original sin are as follows:

I) Original Sin—Far from denying the biblical notion of original sin, Kant, like Luther, seems to affirm it.[6]

II) All are under sin—Kant, like Luther, entertains the Biblical idea that after the fall, all men are sinners. Both Kant and Luther even use the same quote from St. Paul: Luther—'None is righteous, no not one; ...all have turned aside, together they have gone wrong';[7] Kant—'They are all under sin, -there is none righteous (in the spirit of the law), no, not one.'[8]

III) Evil is irradicable—Luther advocates the idea that we have inherited from our first parents, a tendency to sin which cannot be overcome. Similarly, Kant favours the view that evil is innate,[9] and inextirpable by human powers. Both Kant and Luther use the example of the bad tree which cannot bring forth good fruit: Luther—'A good tree cannot bear evil fruit, nor can a bad tree bear good fruit';[10] Kant—'How it is possible for a naturally evil man to make himself a good man wholly surpasses our comprehension; for how can a bad tree bring forth good fruit?'[11]

IV) Rigorism—Both Kant and Luther appear to be rigorists. According to Luther, 'with God there is no intermediary between righteousness and sin,'[12] and with Kant, 'it is, however, of great consequence to ethics in general to avoid admitting...of anything morally intermediate...for with such ambiguity all maxims are in danger of forfeiting their precision and stability.'[13]

V) Conversion—In referring to the overcoming of evil, Kant uses the Biblical notion of a change of heart, and rebirth, drawing specifically on John 3:5 when he says that 'a person can become a new man only by a kind of rebirth, as it were a new creation...and a change of heart.'[14] This notion of the change of heart, or rebirth, which amounts to a complete change of character rather than simply the decision to change the maxims upon which one acts, sounds very close to the Lutheran notion of deliverance through God-given grace.

These are the main lines of similarity between the Kantian notion of radical evil and the Lutheran conception of original sin. However, as I shall now show, the likenesses are not as close as they at first appear. Kant actually has an entirely different conception of the problem of evil to that of Luther, with regard to which the following observations can be made:

1A) Original Sin?—Luther believes in the historical fall of humankind from grace, whereas the belief in a lost Eden is implausible for Kant. Even though Kant uses the notion of sin, he does not, as Luther does, believe in or imply the historical fall of humankind in the biblical sense. According to Kant, 'of all the explanations of the spread and propagation of this evil…the most inept is that which describes it as descending to us as an *inheritance* from our first parents.'[15] Rather, with Kant, the ideas of the historical fall and of inherited sin give place to the conception of a fundamental propensity to act out of mere self-love and without regard to universal moral laws. This propensity is simply an empirical fact, concerning which we can give no ultimate explanation, though the Bible does so in picture language.

IIA) All are under sin?—It is important to realise that Luther's doctrine of original sin entertains an absolute moral pessimism. Human nature is impotent, and has absolutely no remaining ability for good. When he says that 'all are in sin' Luther means that humankind is entirely wicked:

> The righteousness of God is revealed in the gospel as being of faith, so it follows that all men are ungodly and wicked. For it would be foolish of God to reveal righteousness to men if they either knew it already or possessed the seeds of it.[16]

Kant appears to be maintaing something similar when he claims that in saying that a person is by nature either good or evil we mean 'there is in him an ultimate ground…of the adoption of good maxims or of evil maxims.'[17] The distinction here between a good person and one who is evil is the distinction between the person who acts upon a good maxim, and the person who acts upon an evil maxim. However, Kant adds that a person is evil 'only in that he reverses the moral order of the incentives when he adopts them into his maxim.'[18] Therefore, the proposition, 'Man is evil' means simply that 'He is conscious of the moral law but has nevertheless adopted into his maxim the (occasional) deviation therefrom.'[19] This is a much less radical claim than the Lutheran notion of total wickedness. Yet Kant continues by stating that depending upon whether people adopt or do not adopt the moral law into their maxims, they are said to have '*a good or an evil heart.*'[20] Now, it might be claimed that this notion of the evil heart is just the same as the Lutheran notion of total wickedness. But, according to Kant, the mildest form of evil actions result from the frailty, or weakness of human nature.[21] In other words, as St. Paul tells us: 'What I would, that I do not!'[22] Moreover, even evil at its worst does not amount to absolute wickedness, since such a heart may in fact co-exist with a will which in general is good. Thus, when Kant says that 'all are under sin' this does not mean that he believes in the absolute wickedness of human nature.

IIIA) Evil is innate and inextirpable?—In Luther's opinion, since the fall, each person has evil in their nature. When Luther refers to Genesis 6: 5 he says that 'every imagination of the thoughts of his heart was only evil continually.'[23] Here he is stressing that it is not that people are intent on or prone to evil, but that they are altogether evil, and that nothing but evil is imagined and thought by people all their lives. Evil is as much a part of human nature as living and breathing. Indeed, not only are the motives of fallen humankind thoroughly bad, they also have no ability to change this. Kant appears to be saying something similar when he suggests that the evil in human nature is innate and inextirpable. To say that something is innate to human nature usually means that it is inherent. But Luther adds to this the idea that we have inherited evil, and as I pointed out above, Kant rules out the suggestion that one might inherit evil. In his opinion evil is innate in the sense that it lies at the 'root' of a person's character as a free being, and is woven into human nature. Admittedly, this sounds no different from the Lutheran view. However, Kant also suggests that to say that the good or evil in human nature is innate means 'only… that it is posited as the ground antecedent to every use of freedom in experience.'[24] The 'only' here is of great significance, as is the reference to freedom, for this claim amounts to the idea that evil results from the freely chosen actions of human beings.[25] Thus:

> Man *himself* must make or have made himself into whatever, in a moral sense, whether good or evil, he is or is to become. Either condition must be an effect of his free choice; for otherwise he could not be held responsible for it and could therefore be *morally* neither good nor evil.[26]

The significance of the emphasis Kant gives to absolute freedom has already been referred to in Chapter II,[27] but it is again worth pointing out that if evil is the result of free choice, then it is also, according to Kant, possible to overcome it:

> This evil is *radical*, because it corrupts the ground of all maxims; it is, moreover, as a natural propensity, *inextirpable* by human powers…yet at the same time it must be possible to *overcome* it, since it is found in man, a being whose actions are free.[28]

Kant also changes the normal meaning of a word when he suggests that 'man is evil *by nature* ' implies that 'evil can be predicated of man as a species,'[29] since he adds that this does not mean that 'such a quality can be inferred from the concept of his species (that is of man in general),' but rather that 'from what we know of man through experience we cannot judge otherwise of him.'[30]

In saying that evil, which he refers to as a disposition, is not involved in the concept of a person, Kant is contrasting it with the good, which he calls a predisposition, and which does belong to human nature as a necessary feature of its make-up. Therefore, evil is not a natural predisposition of humankind in the way that the good is. Evil consists in maxims of the will which are contrary to the law, and these maxims are both contingent and the result of a free choice. Evil is both a propensity which can be overcome, and something for which people themselves are responsible because they choose it.

This interpretation of 'evil by nature' also affects one's understanding of what Kant means when he says that evil is *radical*. He claims that there is a *radical* innate evil in human nature and yet this is brought upon humankind by itself.[31] Evil is *radical* because it corrupts the ground of all maxims.[32] But when Kant refers to the *radical* evil in human nature, he is not referring to something that is a necessary part of human nature, because if a person were by nature necessarily evil, then that person would have a predisposition to evil, and perhaps only a disposition to good. The evil that we do is so *radical* because we choose to do it through freewill, not because it belongs to humankind by nature.

Also, whereas Luther took the Pauline phrase that 'all are sinners' to mean that we are totally corrupt, Kant agrees with this only in the sense that a propensity to evil lies in us all. For, as I have already shown in Chapter II,[33] even though Kant says that evil is inextirpable and cannot be eradicated, he means by this only that human nature will always be open to a disposition to evil, not that it cannot overcome this disposition. Therefore, Kant's understanding of evil as innate and inextirpable, contrary to how it at first appears, is far from the Lutheran view of evil as inherent. The stress Luther places upon each person's paralysing sin and impotence is a much harsher judgement than that of Kant. I have already pointed to Kant's optimism in Chapter I.[34] Here it is also essential to deny the idea that Kant is an absolute pessimist about human nature. For Luther, human nature is almost devilish, whereas with Kant, after humankind's fall from innocence 'a seed of goodness still remains in its entire purity, incapable of being extirpated or corrupted.'[35] Moreover, this is a capacity which a person could never lose, otherwise it would be impossible to regain it:

> The restoration of the original predisposition to good in us is therefore

> not the acquiring of a *lost* incentive for good, for the incentive which consists in respect for the moral law we have never been able to lose, and were such a thing possible, we could never get it again.[36]

Thus, even though we commit evil acts, there are seeds of good left in us. If this is the case, then Kant must in fact be denying the Lutheran notion of absolute depravity. If anything, Kant's emphasis upon evil is an attempt to encourage a change in human action towards the good end of human nature, whereas with Luther it amounts to resignation to a lost beginning.

IVA) Rigorism?—It was suggested earlier that Kant and Luther are rigorists. According to Luther, without God humankind is entirely wicked, but when humankind has been saved by God it is entirely righteous. In Kant's opinion, people cannot be morally good and morally evil at the same time, simply because they can only make one moral maxim the rule by which they act. The choice between moral good and evil is a radical one precisely because we can only have one supreme maxim, which determines the choice of all other secondary maxims, and thus all our actions. Therefore, as far as morality is concerned, Kant is as strict in his rigorism as Luther. However, this moral rigorism does not apply to human nature in general, because Kant does not rule out the possibility of an evil propensity existing together with a good predisposition. His view is actually in agreement with the claim in Romans 7, namely, that 'although we want to do the good, we do not.'[37]

VA) Conversion?—In Luther's opinion, human nature is bound to sin to the extent that it can do no good whatsoever. Thus:

> The entire Scripture of God is divided into two parts: commandments and promises. Although the commandments teach things that are good, the things taught are not done as soon as they are taught, for the commandments show us what we ought to do but do not give us the power to do it. They are intended to teach man to know himself, that through them he may recognize his inability to do the good and may despair of his ability.[38]

From this we can gather that the Commandments of God cannot be fulfilled by the human will. The Law exists only to tell us what we cannot do, and thereby, to convince us of our sin. Thus, 'through the law, says Paul, comes knowledge of sin.'[39] It follows from this that a moral command to become good would be a command that human nature in itself could not fulfil. The conversion from evil to good is not therefore brought about by human nature, or any moral acts which it may perform. According to Luther, the conversion is made possible through Jesus Christ. Moral acts play no part whatsoever in the person's conversion. By contrast, Kant simply cannot accept the idea that the conversion from evil to good is established through the act of another. According to him, the rebirth is an immanent, ethical occurrence, for which the individual is responsible, whereas for Luther the triumph of the good over the evil principle lies totally in the hands of God. So between Kant and Luther we have the difference between human activity and the activity of God. Kant's view becomes clear in what follows:

> But if a man is corrupt in the very ground of his maxims, how can he possibly bring about this revolution by his own powers and of himself become a good man? Yet, duty bids us do this, and duty demands nothing of us which we cannot do.[40]

Moreover, 'the injunction that we *ought* to become better men resounds unabatedly in our souls; hence this must be within our power.'[41] This suggests that it is possible for people to improve through their own efforts. Kant could not allow the idea that the conversion from evil to good is achieved through Christ, since 'this debt can never be discharged by another person.'[42] Rather, if the moral law commands that we should become good, it must be possible that we ourselves can fulfil that command. In fact, the idea that 'ought implies can' is one of the most well-known notions of Kant's entire moral theory. The moral law tells us what we must, and can, do. We have a duty to make ourselves good, as well as the capacity to realize this.[43]

From the above it should be clear that although Kant is making use of traditional religious concepts in his theory of radical evil, the presuppositions underlying the concepts made use of by him are completely at odds with the Lutheran interpretation prevalent in his day. Despite the apparent similarities, there is also a total dichotomy between Luther and Kant on what amounts for both to be the central and most significant concern of religion. This is the question of freewill, with regard to which the thought of Kant simply cannot be reconciled with that of Luther, as I shall now demonstrate.

Freewill

In my examination of the attitudes of Kant and Luther towards freewill, I shall employ the same method as used in relation to evil, namely, an outline of the apparent similarities, followed by discussion of the differences. With regard to the similarities the following can be noted:

VI) Dualism—Luther's theology entertains a spirit / flesh dualism. This dualism is represented by the idea that humanity belongs to two worlds, the kingdom of God, and the kingdom of the devil. The world of the devil is the world of the flesh, moreover it is also a world of natural determinism and sin. Thus, what is flesh is under the kingdom of Satan. By contrast, the world of God is the world of the spirit, which is at the same time a world of grace and freedom. According to Luther's dualism, one can deduce the following: As beings of the flesh, we are bound to the world of natural determinism, and are in bondage to sin. As beings of the spiritual world, we are members of the kingdom of grace, in which we are free and righteous.

Consequently, there are two levels of truth about us, according to our spiritual or carnal nature. Concerning a person's place in the two kingdoms Luther adds that:

> In one ......he is directed by his own choice and counsel, apart from any precepts and commandments of God, namely in his dealings with the lower creatures...In the other Kingdom, man is not left in the hand of his own counsel, but is directed and led by the choice and counsel of God, so that just as in his own kingdom he is directed by his own counsel, without regard to the precepts of another, so in the Kingdom of God he is directed by the precepts of another without regard to his own choice.[44]

Therefore, what freedom we have is only in terms of our power over the animals in the natural world. In the kingdom of God we are under God's direction. Yet at the same time there is no actual freedom of self determination since 'Christians know that there are two kingdoms in the world which are bitterly opposed to each other, in one Satan reigns, in the other Christ.'[45] This implies that a person is ruled by either Christ or Satan. We have no actual freedom in the natural world because we are ruled by Satan. Nor have we any actual freedom in the spiritual world, for there we are ruled by Christ. It is not the freedom of self determination, but rather, the freedom of God, who acts through human nature. This is hinted at in Luther's definition of Christian liberty, which he claims is:

> A spiritual and true freedom and makes our hearts free from all sins, laws and commandments, as Paul says, I Timothy 1:9, "the law is not

> laid down for the just:" It is more excellent than all other liberty, which is external, as heaven is more excellent than earth. May Christ give us this liberty both to understand and to persevere. Amen.[46]

Hence, when Luther refers to spiritual freedom he is actually referring to the power of God. It is for this reason that the doctrine of predeterminism can be attributed to Luther. We can compare this to the idea of the potter fashioning the clay, an example Luther actually uses.[47] On Luther's account, religious freedom is actually a kind of determinism by God.

Kant also appears to entertain a dualism of human nature. He refers to the intelligible and sensible worlds, and suggests that as far as the sensible, or empirical, world is concerned, determinism reigns. But, whereas the sensible world is determined, the intelligible world is that of free causality. By 'free causality,' Kant means that the freedom which belongs to the intelligible world is law-governed:

> freedom of will, although it is not the property of conforming to laws of nature, is not for this reason lawless: it must rather be a causality conforming to immutable laws, though of a special kind; for otherwise a free will would be self-contradictory.[48]

In Kant's view law is not the antithesis of freedom, but its foundation, despite the independence of freedom from the mechanisms of nature. Freedom and law are not only consistent, they are identical, given that we distinguish the law in question from a law of nature. Thus, Kant's account sounds just like that of Luther, in the sense that both sensible and intelligible realms seem to be determined, the former by desires, the latter by the moral law, which might as easily be referred to as the will of God.

VII) The Corruption of Human Freedom—The severity of Luther's attitude towards human freedom is best illustrated in his well known debate with Erasmus over the freedom of the will.[49] Luther provides a brief summary of his opinion in saying that 'free choice is nothing but a slave of sin, death and Satan, it does nothing and is not capable of doing or attempting to do anything but Evil.'[50] Thus: 'And of the things without the spirit is that very power of free choice...Free choice by itself is so blind that it is not even aware of sin, but has need of the law to teach it.'[51] It is obvious that the freedom referred to here is human, not of God. Such freedom belongs to the world of flesh and sin: 'When Isaiah in 40: 6 says that all flesh is grass, he means all that belongs to the person, reason, judgement, and what is most excellent in man.'[52] Therefore, if we 'take free choice then, or take whatever may be regarded as the highest or the lowest in a people: Isaiah calls it all flesh and grass.'[53] Freedom of this kind is of the flesh in distinction to the spirit. On Luther's view his opinion is supported by St. John's claim that 'what is born of the flesh is flesh, and what is born of the spirit is spirit.'[54] Freedom of choice has very little worth, it is scarcely distinct from sin itself. One could even say that the two kinds of freedom, human and Godly, are in conflict. Hence, 'free choice is nothing else but the supreme enemy of righteousness.'[55] This is because it is a slave to sin. Luther even goes so far as to say:

> I was wrong in saying that free choice before grace is a reality only in name. I should have said simply: "free choice is in reality a fiction, or a name without reality..."..everything(as Wycliff's article condemned at Constance rightly teaches) happens by absolute necessity.[56]

This statement makes it unquestionable that Luther believes in predeterminism. Freedom in the full and proper sense of the word belongs only to God. It is for this reason that Luther also claims that 'we must therefore go all out and completely deny free choice, referring everything to God.'[57] This confirms Luther's view that all good is determined through the will of God. His appraisal suggests that human freedom is really of no significance or value whatsoever.

If one applies a similar distinction to Kant's account of the sensible and intelligible realms it appears that sensible desires would be responsible for our evil choices, and intelligible freedom would enable us to follow the moral law.[58] Therefore, Luther's dualism, as well as the predeterminism between the kingdom of God and that of the devil that goes with it, appears to be entirely reflected in Kant's account of the sensible and intelligible worlds.

However, despite all appearances to the contrary, Kant's view of freedom is in fact far removed from the view of Luther, as will now be shown.

VIA) Predeterminism?—Most significantly, Kant's notion of intelligible freedom is a part of us in a way that it is not for Luther. When Kant refers to our intelligible nature, he means the supersensible within us. And if one bears in mind Kant's distinction between the supersensible and supernaturalism as outlined in Chapter II,[59] it becomes clear that Kant will not accept the view that an external will controls our actions by means of some supernatural fiat. The supersensible is wedded to human nature and moral actions performed thereby: 'For unless the supersensible (the thought of which is essential to anything called religion) is anchored to determinate concepts of reason, such as those of morality, fantasy inevitably gets lost in the transcendent.'[60] Such fantasizing would lead to the kind of claims made by Luther concerning God's action through human nature. The fact that Luther attributes spiritual freedom to God as distinct from human nature makes his theory supernaturalist, in the sense that the spirit belongs to God, whereas for Kant the supersensible is as much a part of human nature as the sensible. It is for this reason that Kant claims there can be no real contradiction between freedom and natural necessity,[61] since the determinism of the natural world and the freedom of the intelligible world must, in human nature itself, be reconciled.

VIIA) Human Freedom And Sin?—Luther's negative conception of human freedom, as linked to sin, cannot ultimately be reconciled with the view of Kant, simply because Kant believes in freedom. Freedom is 'the one sole and original right that belongs to every human being by virtue of his humanity.'[62] Freedom is also a fact: 'Man acts according to the idea of freedom, he acts *as if* he were free, and *eo ipso* he is free.'[63] Admittedly so far, this conception of freedom could, like Luther's, be a freedom to sin. However, bearing in mind that sin for Luther is tied to the empirical world, Kant makes it quite clear that our freedom is not only a part of our empirical nature, though it is this as well. Also, where Luther refers to free choice, Kant refers to freewill. Thus: 'as a rational being, and consequently as belonging to the intelligible world, man can never conceive the causality of his own will except under the Idea of freedom.'[64] This means that the freedom of the will is an attribute of our intelligible nature. All rational beings possess freewill: 'to every rational being possessed of a will we must also lend the Idea of freedom as the only one under which he can act.'[65] There is an important distinction at work here between the thoughts of Kant and Luther. Ultimately, the kind of free choice Luther refers to dissolves into determinism, as was made clear above. Kant advocates freewill, which is not compatible with determinism, since it involves the capacity to overcome the determinism of our desires. Thus:

> As a free will, and thus not only without co-operating with sensuous impulses but even rejecting all of them and checking all inclinations so far as they could be antagonistic to the law, it is determined merely by the law.[66]

Of course, this again sounds like Luther's spiritual freedom which is determined by the will of God, but in fact, for Kant, freedom amounts to self determination. As distinct from being determined by either Satan or by God: 'we must attribute to every being endowed with reason and a will this property of determining himself to action under the idea of his own freedom.'[67] And when I ask myself what my duty is, 'I ask only, what I now have to do, and in that, freedom is a necessary practical presupposition and an idea, under which alone I can regard the command of reason as valid.'[68] The claim here that freewill amounts to self determination might appear to contradict Kant's claim that freewill is determined by the moral law. However, according to Kant, there is an integral relationship between the moral law and freedom. Human freedom is bound to the moral law in the sense that 'if the freedom of the will is presupposed, morality, together with its principle, follows by mere analysis of the concept of freedom.'[69] Moreover 'morality must be derived solely from the property of freedom.'[70] And so, 'we have at last traced the determinate concept of morality back to freedom.'[71] In other words, without freedom there could be no morality. Not only is this so, but freedom is also tied to autonomy, for 'what else then can the freedom of the will be but autonomy, that is, the property which the will has of being a law to itself.'[72] Thus, self determination, morality and autonomy are all integral to Kant's notion of human freedom, whereas they are ruled out by Luther's notion of human freedom. And when autonomy, morality and self determination are added to the notion of the intelligible, one has the result that 'when we think of ourselves as free, we transfer ourselves into the intelligible world as members and recognize the autonomy of the will together with its consequence—morality.'[73] It should be clear from this outline that Kant's account of human freedom actually turns the Lutheran account on its head. For Kant, human freedom amounts to no less than the freedom that Luther attributes only to God.

Kant makes it clear that freewill, far from being the result of an external will, is actually independence from a foreign will. He speaks of 'independence from the constraint of another's will,'[74] and stresses that 'reason must look upon itself as the author of its own principles independently of alien influences. Therefore as practical reason, or as the will of a rational being, it must be regarded by itself as free.'[75] There is no better example of the distinction which lies between the views of Luther and Kant than in Kant's appraisal of what he refers to as *fatalism:*

> Fatalism in general...transforms all human actions into a mere puppet

> show, and totally annuls the conception of obligation. That which is against the ought or the imperative, which differentiates between the practical law and the natural law, also sets us totally outside of the chain of nature, whilst it, without regarding our will as free, is impossible and inconsistent, and much more leaves us with nothing to do, than to wait and to observe what kind of decisions God, by intervening in and through the natural way of things, will effect in us, not however, what we from ourselves as authors can and should do, out of which then must spring coarse superstition, which annuls all influence of healthy reason...Even the resolute fatalist himself must act every time as if he were free, and this idea therefore also truly produces the unanimous action and only this idea can produce it.[76]

The kind of attitude which Kant describes as *fatalist* is precisely that which Luther maintains with regard to freedom through faith, when he claims that God works through us, and free choice is nothing.[77] According to Kant, without freedom of the will we are marionettes. The Lutheran view makes us little more than marionettes. In Luther's opinion, we do not have the liberty necessary to lead the moral life without God. From Kant's viewpoint, predeterminism presupposes 'an immoral order of nature.'[78] In other words, we must have liberty if the moral life is to make sense. Consequently, there is no way in which Kant can submit to the concept of predeterminism.[79]

All that Kant and Luther really have in common with regard to the notion of freedom is the idea of independence from ecclesiastical religion. In this respect there is an affinity between Luther and the Enlightenment of which Kant was a part, because both emphasise freedom from an external ecclesiastical authority. But it is only in this sense that one can see the Protestant heritage at work in Kant. Moreover, this conception of freedom has little to do with freewill. Kant's understanding of freewill is in terms of the unity of human nature with the moral consciousness. It amounts to the autonomy of the moral person and has implications concerning moral responsibility. Freewill is a human capacity. For Luther, freewill in this sense of the word could only rest with God. Luther's understanding of freedom comes from his christology. It means nothing in distinction from faith. It is a spiritual freedom which is grounded outside a person, in God. As such, it is a pseudo-freedom. Such a suggestion for Kant would mean the greatest insult to human autonomy. Therefore, there is no real connection between Kant's moral freedom and Luther's spiritual freedom. Luther conceptualises freedom through the power of God. Accordingly, before each individual is saved they are ruled by the devil, and afterwards by God. Therefore, actions in the moral sphere are never really our own. On the other hand, for Kant, without freedom of the will, the moral law is unthinkable.

It should now be clear that there is a totally different orientation in the thought of Kant to that of Luther on freedom. Kant affirms freewill, Luther denies it. Of course, one might deduce from this that the difference between Kant's perspective and that of Luther is so great because Luther is dealing with the question of human freedom from a position of religious commitment, whereas Kant is not. Such a conclusion would go some way towards meeting the views of those scholars who maintain, not only that Kant's account of radical evil is an attempt to demythologise the Lutheran account, but also, that Kant offers a secular interpretation of religious themes, and attempts to reduce religion to morality. From the two previous chapters of this study it should already be clear that the charge of reductionism is misplaced.[80] Unfortunately, it is not difficult to find grounds for such reductionist interpretations when scholars such as Takuji Kadowaki in *Das Radikal Böse bei Kant* argue that Kant allows no other possibility of overcoming evil than through obedience to the moral law.[81] Likewise, when Kadowaki suggests that for Kant, 'the good is the real principle of human existence,'[82] one is strongly tempted to interpret the 'good' in moral, non-religious terms. Such reductionist interpretations, which completely ignore facts such as that for Kant the supersensible within human nature is a prerequisite to the overcoming of evil, have meant that valuable aspects of Kant's theology have been neglected. But even if it is correct to say that Kant attempts to demythologise the Lutheran tradition of religious interpretation, in the sense that he makes use of the same concepts whilst giving them a non-supernaturalist interpretation, it does not follow that he is offering a secularised, non-religious, or reductionist version of Lutheran doctrines. Rather, as I will presently attempt to show, Kant offers an alternative religious interpretation of traditionally Lutheran doctrines.

The divergence in the understanding of Kant and Luther on the notion of freedom has even more far reaching implications than those outlined above. In order to consider these implications, which offer great insight into the religious perspectives of Kant and Luther, I need to return to Luther's debate with Erasmus over the freedom of the will.[83] Upon closer reading of this work, it becomes obvious that the debate is not just about freedom, but about grace in relation to human freedom. According to Luther 'grace is preached therefore free choice is abolished; the help of grace is commended, therefore free choice is destroyed.'[84] Thus for Luther divine grace and human freedom are contradictory concepts in the sense that when grace is given, human freedom is ruled out. B.A. Gerrish has suggested that Luther's theology operates with an opposition between grace and reason. I would argue that the opposition is really between grace and freedom. In contrast to Luther, Kant could never submit freedom to grace;[85] to do so would entail supernaturalism, which he cannot endorse. Hence any notion of grace which is to be acceptable to Kant has to make a place for freewill. It is for this reason that although Kant allows some sense of grace in the conversion from evil to good, as referred to by his notion of the supersensible in human nature, he will not allow the supersensible to be divorced from the free actions of human nature in itself.

One might ask why it is that for Luther grace rules out freedom. In his opinion, the answer is quite clear, since 'what need is there of the spirit of Christ or of God if free choice can overcome the motions of the mind towards evil.'[86] Such a claim sounds strikingly similar to Kant's pronouncement of the need for something akin to the spirit of Christ in order to overcome evil, as outlined in Chapter II.[87] In fact, the meaning of Kant's claim is far removed from that of Luther. In Kant's opinion, the spirit manifested in Christ is a potential to overcome evil which all human beings have within them. According to Luther, the spirit of Christ refers to the unique act of pardoning grace brought about by Christ's sacrifice for the sake of the sins of others. Therefore, to suggest that human effort is necessary to overcome evil means a cheapening of grace in neglect of the significance of the life and death of Jesus. Furthermore, 'the righteousness of faith comes from grace apart from the law. This apart from excludes works, moral righteousness, and preparation for grace.'[88] Consequently, in Luther's opinion, grace not only rules out freedom, but also works, (by which one can assume that Luther means human actions), which can play no part in a person's attainment of righteousness. This attitude is reinforced by claims Luther makes elsewhere, such as that:

> The believer, through his faith, has been restored to Paradise and created anew, he has no need of works that he may become or be righteous; but that he may not be idle and may provide for and keep his body, he must do such works freely only to please God.[89]

This suggests three things: Firstly, that before people do any good work, they have all the righteousness that they require through faith. Secondly, the works themselves have nothing to do with Christian righteousness. Thirdly, that one becomes righteous simply by believing. Here we have a renewal of the Pauline 'justification by faith' doctrine. For Luther however, this also entails that all good works happen through belief, and all bad works through unbelief, so that it is unbelief that makes a person wicked. Thus, in the "The Freedom of a Christian" Luther says 'let him who wishes to do good works begin not with the doing of works, but with believing, which makes the person good, for nothing makes a man good except faith, or evil except unbelief.'[90] He also claims that he has 'no quarrel with any man concerning his morals, but only concerning the word of truth,'[91] and that he is attacking ungodly doctrines, and his opponents, not because of their bad morals, but because of their ungodliness. He gives the perfect summary of his view with regard to works and righteousness when he says that 'works follow after righteousness and are free and are done only to serve others and to give them an example of good works.'[92] Although he does not reject good works, he objects to the idea that they are essential to Christian righteousness, since 'our faith in Christ does not free us from works but from false opinions concerning works, that is, from the presumption that justification is acquired by works.'[93] Thus, in an attempt to prevent the confusion of faith and morals, Luther has separated the two quite clearly. He has done this by claiming that faith is all that is required for righteousness, works have absolutely no part to play. Thus:

> If works are sought after as a means of righteousness...and are done under the false impression that through them one is justified, they are made necessary and freedom and faith are destroyed; and this addition to them makes them no longer good but truly damnable works. They are not free and they blaspheme the grace of God since to justify and to save by faith belongs to the grace of God alone.[94]

According to the above, righteousness is not the result of moral worthiness, but a free gift given before any true moral obedience to God is possible. According to Luther, a person's cooperation with God is not a precondition of righteousness, it is rather a consequence of it. Moral goodness is the result of a passive submission to the divine act of grace. Therefore, although Luther is not opposed to good works he distinguishes good works as produced by faith. No merit goes to the individual. It is only after people have been made righteous through faith in

Christ that they can fulfil the moral life. In fact, it is only when our ultimate destiny does not depend upon moral rectitude that we can be free to pursue and achieve justice. Righteousness therefore occurs before good works.

This distinction between faith and works makes Luther's whole conception of human effort and the moral life quite different from that of Kant. Henri d'Aviau de Ternay has argued convincingly[95] that Kant lives by Deuteronomy 30:12-14: the notion of the moral law in a person's heart, and the idea that we must obey in order to obtain blessedness, for we will perish if we disobey. If d'Aviau de Ternay is correct, then Kant's moral religion, even though not a form of legalism in religion, is at least closer to the Torah of Judaism, (in that we have a duty to fulfil the moral law and thus perfect ourselves), than to the 'justification by faith alone' of Luther's religion. As a result, the biblical claim "You shall know them by their fruits" would have an entirely different meaning for Luther than for Kant. According to Luther:

> It is indeed true that in the sight of men a man is made good or evil by his works; but this being made good or evil only means that the man who is good or evil is pointed out and known as such, as Christ says in Matthew 7:20 :"Thus they will know them by their fruits." All this remains on the surface, however, and very many have been deceived by this outward appearance and have presumed to write and teach concerning good works by which we may be justified without even mentioning faith.[96]

One must bear in mind that Luther was reacting against hypocrisy in religion. He had personally witnessed those who appeared to be living a good, moral life, but who were in fact making a mockery of religious sincerity through their wicked ways. It is for this reason that he objects to actions as a sign of sincerity in religion. Kant was also reacting against hypocrisy in religion, and from what has already been said it is clear that Kant also denies that actions in themselves are proof of the goodness of a person. However, it is interesting that the hypocrisy against which Kant found the need to object was a kind brought about by an overemphasis upon faith alone, in complete neglect of moral responsibility. He believes that moral effort, inseparable from the supersensible principle of grace, is a presupposition of the attainment of righteousness. We can improve ourselves morally, and the best way in which to do this is to strive, through our actions. The outer action is not then the result of inner goodness, but part and parcel of it.

Given this inseparability of inner and outer sincerity for Kant, to 'know them by their fruits' cannot be something which merely 'remains on the surface.' Rather, given that belief and moral action are in a sense one and the same, it is of great consequence that we are 'known by our fruits.'

Furthermore, the divergence between Kant and Luther goes even further. According to Luther, because we are made righteous not by our own merits, but by the merits of another, namely Christ, it follows that 'true faith in Christ is a measure beyond all comparison which brings with it complete salvation.'[97] Whereas Luther claims in this way that those who have been saved by the spirit of Christ already possess salvation, and can be certain of this, Kant suggests that we should never rest in the false confidence that we possess the perfect spirit and could never fall back into moral wickedness. Rather, he advocates that we should 'work out our salvation with fear and trembling.'[98] Kant objects to the idea that God can make someone into a better person without some effort on the part of the person. Accordingly, each must do 'as much as in his power lies to become a better man.'[99] That is, we cannot think that God will simply make us good without our striving to improve ourselves morally. There is absolutely no certainty of salvation here. Kant uses the example of the parable of the talents in order to suggest that we must make use of our capacity for the good,[100] and advocates that we should strive for moral perfection to the extent that, as in Matthew 5: 48, we should be 'holy as our Father in Heaven is holy.'[101] His moral religion is in every respect an imperative to action. What is pleasing to God is the moral intention of the heart, as in Matthew 5: 20-48: 'The true (moral) service of God...is itself, indeed...a *service of the heart*...It can consist solely in the disposition of obedience to all true duties as divine commands.'[102] He stresses the necessity of inner goodness before an outer action can be performed, but he argues that good works must precede salvation.[103] Salvation without good works is not possible. Salvation can only be something we acquire after our moral striving, not before. It is the sincerity of our inner motives together with a morally good life which makes us worthy of salvation. Salvation is in proportion to moral worthiness.

In Chapter II I briefly outlined Kant's notion of the kingdom of God,[104] according to which three elements were found to be of central significance: the moral, that is, human moral actions, the theological, namely God, and the religious, which was found to involve both the moral and the theological, whilst also entertaining the notion of hope. It does not take long to see that in the debate over freewill and salvation one is also dealing with the question of the kingdom of God, only re-phrased in terms of 'What do human works have to do with the realisation of the kingdom?' And it is not difficult, given the Lutheran understanding of righteousness and salvation, to work out the Lutheran interpretation of the kingdom of God. The natural conclusion of justification by faith alone is that the coming of the kingdom lies with Jesus and God-given grace, which is prior to any human effort. It is through Jesus that our new life in the Kingdom becomes possible. The kingdom of God, which must be foreign to the sinful world, is guaranteed in Christ, through whom we have deliverance from our sins.

It follows from Kant's denial that the overcoming of sin is made possible through Jesus Christ alone, that he also rules out the idea that we gain access to the kingdom through Jesus alone. Rather, each moral individual must anticipate and work towards the realisation of the kingdom. Given such emphasis upon the need for human effort, there can be no guarantee that the kingdom will be realised. However, this is not to suggest that individual moral achievement alone will be responsible for the realisation of the kingdom. Kant's point is that there are two sides to the Kingdom: the side of humanity and the side of God. We can understand this in terms of the idea that the kingdom is both gift, and a task for human nature. The gift is also a responsibility; that which is given is also something that is earned. Kant cannot accept that our moral actions have no consequence in the establishment of the kingdom, whereas Luther would completely deny any idea of the kingdom as something that human actions can have a part in achieving. For Luther, the kingdom is Christ's, and it will be only by Christ's almighty power that it will come to fruition as a glorious fact. Kant, whilst not maintaining that the kingdom is achievable solely by human effort, would argue that humanity has an active role and duty even to help bring in the kingdom. Thus, as strongly as Kant would object to the view that human efforts alone can realize the kingdom of God, so would he deny that the realization of the kingdom of God has nothing to do with human effort. The kingdom must be brought about by human effort in cooperation with God.

Kant also brings to the forefront the significance of hope to the religious perspective with regard to the kingdom of God. As was emphasised in Chapter II,[105] his account of the kingdom involves an attitude of religious hope, both that human effort will work towards perfection, and that God will supply that which is lacking in order to achieve salvation. Kant's hope and optimism is grounded in the moral nature of humanity. But it is also grounded in God. The moral end is a God-given scheme, and as such, it can only be hoped for, not assumed. The Lutheran notion of assured salvation makes such hope almost redundant. This reflects yet another significant divergence in the outlooks of Kant and Luther, which, in addition to the differences already highlighted above, enables us to conclude that Kant and Luther have two different kinds of religiousness, because they entertain quite different theologies of salvation. For Luther, if human works are a prerequisite to salvation and the realisation of the kingdom of God, then Christ has died in vain. For Kant, without human moral effort, salvation and the realisation of the kingdom of God is not possible.

The contrast offered above between Kant and Luther has been useful for two reasons. Firstly, and most significantly, it illustrates the way in which the same concepts can be used by two people with an entirely different meaning and orientation. Secondly, it emphasizes the radical difference in opinion between Luther and Kant. The divergences in the theological presuppositions of Luther and Kant are simply too great to maintain that Kant is a follower of Luther or the Philosopher of Protestantism.[106] Luther's theology of grace separates him radically from Kant. Given that moral freedom is central to Kant's theology, it is very hard to justify Kant as bringing to fulfilment what Luther had begun, because he has a totally different conception of what the religious life entails: Kant's religion of moral worthiness is incompatible with Luther's theology of the Cross. However, to argue to this effect is not to suggest that Kant's position is not the result of a religious commitment. Rather, Kant's religious perspective involves the presupposition that freewill, and human effort in general, must work in cooperation with grace in order to attain salvation. And grace must be conceived in terms other than salvation solely through Jesus Christ. As will become clear in what follows, Kant's religious perspective offers the potential for an equally valid, although alternative theology of salvation to that of Luther.

II: KANT AND ERASMUS

So far in this chapter, I have argued against the assumption made by much German literature at the beginning of the twentieth century, that Luther is the religious forerunner of Kant. Even though it is the Lutheran mythology that Kant is demythologising, Luther still cannot be considered as the religious forerunner of Kant. There are two main reasons for this. Firstly, Kant's view of evil and human nature in general is far removed from the Lutheran conception of human depravity. Luther claims that human beings are totally corrupt, and in need of God's grace in order to become good. Kant argues that although human beings have a disposition towards evil, their underlying nature is good. Secondly, Kant has an entirely different conception of the religious life in terms of freewill and salvation. Kant affirms freewill, Luther denies it. Kant considers good works as a prerequisite to salvation, Luther rules out works as playing any part in the quest for salvation, since justification is by faith alone.

The main source used to contrast Luther's perspective with that of Kant has been Luther's famous debate with his contemporary, Erasmus of Rotterdam. During my examination of that debate it became evident that despite two hundred years difference, the stance taken by Erasmus has striking affinities with Kant's position. In fact, from a re-reading of this text it seems reasonable to suppose that as far as evil and freewill are concerned, the main religious forerunner of Kant is in fact Erasmus.[107] My aim is now to show that on the two most essential features of his religious outlook where Kant cannot agree with Luther, that is concerning evil and freewill, his thought is similar to that of Erasmus. I shall begin with a comparison of the views of Erasmus and Kant concerning evil. I shall then turn to a comparison of their views on freewill. In each case, Erasmus' view is presented in his debate with Luther, which, as has already been demonstrated, is also a debate about grace and salvation.

Evil And Human Nature

1) Evil is a free choice—In Erasmus' opinion, humans were upright and free before the fall. The act of evil was a free choice.[108] Similarly, as Wolfgang Ritzel correctly interprets Kant, 'man stands at the deciding way, he has the choice, the law to obey or to override, the choice between good and evil.'[109]

2) Evil results from the corruption of the will—On Erasmus' view, through the fall, the wills of human beings were corrupted, as shown by their disobedience to the commandment of God. The will was then so far depraved that by its natural powers it could not amend its ways, but once its liberty had been lost, it was

'compelled to serve that sin to which it had once for all consented.'[110] Likewise with Kant's notion of radical evil, all are under sin, none can do the good.[111]

3) The co-operation of divine grace and human effort in overcoming evil—Erasmus' view of human nature after the fall is as follows:

> This proneness to evil which is in most men does not take away free choice altogether, even though evil is not fully to be overcome without the aid of divine grace. For if no part of repentance depends on the will, but all things are done through God by a sheer necessity, why is man there given room for repentance?[112]

Likewise, Kant emphasises that people themselves, through their own powers, must be able to overcome evil, yet at the same time they need the supersensible principle to bring about the change of heart, or repentance.[113]

4) Human effort as a means to gaining salvation—According to Erasmus, 'at the same time, by the grace of God, when sin has been forgiven, the will is made free to the extent that...even apart from the help of new grace it could attain eternal life.'[114] As Allen Wood maintains,[115] Kant also uses the notion of the forgiveness of sins, and then suggests that it is possible for people, through their moral efforts, to achieve the good.

5) The distinction between overcoming the evil propensity and the continuing disposition to evil—On Erasmus' view, even though a person can continue in the right, that person is 'not without a tendency to sin, owing to the vestiges of original sin in him.'[116] Grace mitigates sin so that it can be overcome, but not rooted out. Likewise with Kant, we cannot extirpate our *disposition** to evil.[117]

6) Optimism concerning human nature and moral improvement—Erasmus is not pessimistic about this evil disposition, for he asserts that 'the will after the fall is impelled to better things.'[118] This makes it clear that people have not lost their good predisposition and suggests that Erasmus believes in the goodness of human nature, but acknowledges at the same time the human propensity to evil. Likewise with Kant, we never lose our predisposition towards the good, which makes moral improvement a possibility, despite the fact that we also never lose the propensity to evil either.[119]

From the above, it is clear that with regard to the question of evil, Kant and Erasmus are closer in thought than Kant and Luther. However, the real test of whether one can reconcile the thought of Kant with that of Erasmus will involve a comparison of Kant's notion of freewill in relation to grace and salvation with Erasmus' view. It is to this comparison that I now turn.

Freedom And Salvation

1) Definition of Free Choice—According to Erasmus free choice is 'a power of the human will by which a man can apply himself to the things which lead to eternal salvation, or turn away from them.'[120] Kant is entirely in agreement with Erasmus on this point of the relationship between freedom and salvation. Free choice is for Kant the moral ability to choose between evil and good, the moral good being that which leads to salvation, the moral evil that which detracts from it.[121]

2) Why Freewill is Essential—Erasmus also suggests that 'if the will had not been free, sin could not have been imputed, for sin would cease to be sin if it were not voluntary.'[122] The thought here is that if there were no freedom of the will, then there would be no sin either, because evil actions would never be chosen, they would simply be the result of our natural impulses. And if there were no freedom of choice, then there would be no moral responsibility either; there would be no attribution of either good or evil. Sin is, and must be, the result of a free choice. Erasmus' aim in his debate with Luther is not only to defend freewill, but more significantly to stress the fact of moral responsibility. Such a conception of freedom also appears to be the essential component of moral responsibility in Kant's view. As Kadowaki puts it, the leading question for Kant is, 'if man didn't have a free will, how could he be evil?'[123] And as Erasmus argues, it also follows from this that 'if man is not the author of good works then he is not the author of bad works either.'[124] Consequently, if there is no freedom of the will and all good is attributable to God as Luther had maintained, then on Erasmus' view we would have to attribute all evil to God also.

3) The Conflict of Good and Evil in Human Nature—Erasmus recognises the conflict of good and evil in the individual. He holds to the idea in Romans 7:18: 'I can will what is right, but I cannot do it.'[125] Erasmus claims that in this passage St. Paul is affirming our power to will what is good even in circumstances where we eventually succumb to evil. This idea is reflected in Kant's claim that an evil disposition can exist together with a good will.[126]

4) Work Out Your Salvation in Fear and Trembling—Most significantly, Erasmus advocates the Biblical command 'work out your own salvation in fear and trembling,'[127] which is a major imperative in Kant's *Religion.*[128]

5) Grace and Salvation—Luther accused Erasmus of defining freedom with regard to salvation, without mention of grace. This accusation is false. Erasmus is not trying to rule out Godly grace, for he admits that 'the will is not powerless, though it cannot attain its end without grace.'[129] From this it is clear that Erasmus does not intend to disparage grace, but rather, to establish freedom and human responsibility. What he cannot allow is grace to the exclusion of human effort. The same is exactly the case with Kant, who in the *Religion* specifies that we have every right to hope for God's assistance in order that we may achieve moral perfection, but 'only by qualifying for it through our own efforts to fulfil every human duty.'[130]

6) Grace and Repentance—One might argue that Erasmus is finally separated from Kant in his admittance that 'those who support free choice nonetheless admit that a soul which is obstinate in evil cannot be softened into true repentance without the help of heavenly grace.'[131] However, Wood has argued convincingly in *Kant's Moral Religion* that divine forgiveness and human repentance are both notions at work in Kant's treatment of religion.[132] In addition, as has already been shown in Chapter II, Kant's notion of the change of heart, which appeals to the idea of the supersensible in human nature, bears close resemblance to the concept of grace.[133] In this respect it is interesting to note the distinction used in Catholic theology between prevenient and peculiar grace, a distinction which Erasmus makes use of in the debate on freewill. He claims that peculiar grace is present in those who strive,[134] whereas prevenient grace is the extra help that God gives to human beings.[135] The former is that which enables people to move from the evil to the good, the latter that which complements their moral efforts in order that they may achieve salvation. In this distinction between prevenient and peculiar grace one can also identify a direct parallel with Kant. It is possible to compare the conversion from evil to good in human nature with peculiar grace, and the help which God gives after a person has striven for moral perfection to prevenient grace. Kant does not rule out the possibility of additional grace, he simply stresses the need for human effort first.[136] Thus, there is a place in Kant's theology for what has traditionally been referred to as prevenient and peculiar grace.

7) Moral Optimism and Pessimism—According to Luther, after the fall of humankind freewill is nothing but the freedom to sin. In contrast, Erasmus holds to the belief that through freewill a person can choose the good. Erasmus is therefore an optimist concerning the possibility of moral improvement. Just as for Kant ought implies can, similarly for Erasmus, 'there is nothing that man cannot do with the help of the grace of God, and that therefore the works of all men can be good.'[137] Moreover, if people do as much as lies within them, God's assistance will be given, for divine grace always accompanies human effort.[138] We can see this claim reflected in the *Religion* where Kant says that if people do as much as they can to become better people, they can hope for the help of God in those areas where they are lacking.[139]

There are two general points to be gained from the above comparison of Kant and Erasmus on freewill and salvation, both of which occur in contrast to the view of Luther:

Firstly, Luther demanded the certainty of salvation. In contrast, Kant and Erasmus emphasize that people have a duty to improve themselves morally, thus making themselves worthy of salvation, hence 'work out your salvation in fear and trembling.' Some of the responsibility for salvation lies with people themselves, because whether or not they improve themselves morally will affect whether they achieve salvation. It is for this reason that people must do as much as lies within them in order that God will then supply what is lacking to achieve salvation. Inevitably however, if people have to cooperate in the realization of their salvation, then there can be no certainty of it. Erasmus recognises that in Luther's theology of the certainty of salvation a person's cooperation vanishes, and he realized that this idea was extremely dangerous for religious ethics. It is one thing to say that a prerequisite for sincerity in action is a good heart, but quite another to imply that actions have no bearing, which could mean the ruin of all moral effort. It is for this reason that, as Bainton insists, 'Erasmus would rather give up God's absolute power than to make Him no longer amenable to the questions of human reason and the moral sense.'[140] It has been said that 'to find in Erasmus... anything like a doctrine of justification along Lutheran lines, or a theology of the cross results in a very un-Erasmus like Erasmus.'[141] The same must be said when one compares Kant with Luther.

Secondly, neither Erasmus nor Kant could accept the Lutheran idea that God would save some and damn others, without regard to moral effort. If that were the case, then God would be a tyrant.[142] It follows from this that both Erasmus and Kant believe not only in the concept of divine justice, but also in divine judgement. The suggestion made by Phillips in *Luther, Erasmus and the Reformation*, that 'if Luther founded himself on Romans 5, Erasmus certainly founded himself on Romans 14,'[143] is most telling. If given the choice between Romans 5 and Romans 14, Kant would also found himself upon Romans 14. The distinction is between grace through the sacrifice of Jesus alone, and human accountability to divine judgement. It reflects the conflict between the idea that moral works do not count, and the conviction that they must make a difference.

So far as freewill, grace and salvation are concerned, Kant and Erasmus are in agreement: salvation without freedom of choice and moral responsibility is not possible. On Erasmus' view the question of freewill exposed Luther's fatalism.[144] Kant argued strongly against fatalism: heavenly grace can be assumed, but only in connection with moral effort. Thus, the plan of salvation is under the sign of the moral law. For both Kant and Erasmus, salvation and moral attainment go together. Tracy suggests that Erasmus' human-centred philosophy of humanity was not compatible with the God-centred theology of the Reformation.[145] I do not find this comment to be fair to Erasmus because it suggests that human beings have more significance than God, and that Erasmus lacks a theology. I would prefer the idea that one can attribute a philosophical theology to Erasmus, which is not the case with Luther's theology. Nevertheless, the comparison does hit the point that for Erasmus a strong emphasis is placed upon what we must do in order to achieve salvation, and exactly the same can be said for Kant.

In light of the above appraisal of the similarities between Kant and Erasmus concerning freewill and salvation, an important consideration must be acknowledged. Often, where the thought of Kant is close to that of Erasmus, Erasmus' view is in line with Catholic thought. Concerning grace, freewill and salvation, Erasmus appears to be adhering to mainline Catholic doctrine in his argument. Does this mean therefore, that one should also place Kant within the tradition of Catholicism? There are problems with such an alignment. For instance, Catholic salvation theology has often been criticised for being a merit theology, the idea being that a person can gain salvation through earning merits. And if one is inclined to align Kant to Catholic salvation theology, then he appears to be open to the same objection. However, given that Kant advocates duty for the sake of duty alone, to the extent that if people were to act morally in order to gain salvation, then their motive would be corrupt and their morality would be a means to an end, it appears inconsistent to align Kant with a salvation theology based upon gaining merits. In fact, Kant fought against such an idea in his moral theory as much as he fought against the idea that moral action has no bearing upon salvation. Yet this apparent inconsistency is in fact no inconsistency, though not because Kant's thought is not close to Catholic salvation theology, but rather, because the interpretation of Catholic salvation theology as a merit theology is entirely mistaken.[146] As Robert E. McNally argues in *Luther, Erasmus and the Reformation*, Catholic salvation theology, when taken in its true sense, is not concerned with buying, earning or meriting eternal salvation by human work. Rather:

> The Catholic doctrine of good works has profound humanistic implications. First of all it is based on the belief that man, even though fallen, is still capable of doing natural good; his fallen human nature is not totally and intrinsically vitiated and corrupt... Second, the Catholic doctrine of good works, properly understood, exalts human life as such, and the totality of all the good that man accomplishes here and now, in the order of faith and history. Every good work, performed by man as a faithful friend of God, is of eternal value and merit. Human accomplishment here below is not of passing significance; it is more than ripe fruit falling in its fullness from a good tree. It merits God's consideration for all eternity.[147]

Thus, in Catholic theology there is both a basic optimism that human life in itself has value, and an ultimate confidence in the goodness of people and their accomplishments. There is no discrepancy between this view and that of Kant; in fact, the similarities are obvious. I have also pointed to the similarity between Kant's view and the Catholic doctrines of peculiar and prevenient grace. In particular, Kant's notion of the supersensible in human nature comes close to the implication in Catholicism that grace and nature are so related causally as to produce Christian goodness. Therefore, it is appropriate to suggest that with regard to evil, freewill and salvation, Kant's position, like that of Erasmus, falls within the perspective of Catholic theology.

I can also support my suggestion that Kant has closer links with Erasmus than with Luther, by appeal to two recent German works. The first is Kohls *Luther oder Erasmus*.[148] This work is concerned with the differences between Luther and Erasmus. Kohls sets out a number of contrasts between the views of Luther and Erasmus, such as the divergence in their attitudes towards revelation, scepticism, and theology in general, as well as the themes I have already dealt with specifically, namely, active and passive justification, grace and salvation in relation to works, and freewill and determinism. Without going into great detail it is fascinating to remark that if one were to substitute Kant for Erasmus in Kohls' contrast with Luther, the results would be exactly the same. Had Kant been in dialogue with Luther concerning evil and salvation, Luther would have differed from Kant on all of the points upon which he differs from Erasmus.

Even more fascinating than the insight to be gained from Kohls work, are the conclusions which can be drawn from Richard Schaeffler's *Was Dürfen Wir Hoffen?*[149] Schaeffler thinks that Kant's understanding of the kingdom of God provides the foundation upon which a Catholic theology of hope can be developed. That is, a theology of hope which takes a middle way between justification through faith alone and utopian thinking. The details of justification by faith alone have already been dealt with and therefore do not need to be repeated here. As an example of utopian thinking Schaeffler uses Ernst Bloch's *The Principle of Hope*.[150] Bloch maintains that one can entertain the notion of hope in relation to the idea of the perfect kingdom, which can be realised on earth, but without the religious presupposition of the existence of God. In contrast to both the Lutheran justification by faith alone, which places all hope for the kingdom in God, and the Blochian utopia, which places all hope for the kingdom in humankind, Kant stresses the need for both God and humankind. He does this by acknowledging the need for a joint effort between God and humanity in the hope and practice necessary for the kingdom of God. The emphasis of a Catholic theology of hope to be developed from the Kantian account would be upon human practice together with the acceptance of the limitations of the human capacity to bring in the kingdom. Where human limits lie, there begins the work of God.

Schaeffler's suggestion fits entirely with Kant's account of the kingdom of God as outlined in Chapter II.[151] It also agrees with the analysis carried out in this chapter, which aims to show that Kant offers an alternative, but equally valid, theological perspective with regard to salvation from that of Luther. To Schaeffler's profound insight I would also add the suggestion that Erasmus might be seen as an early initiator of an alternative theology of hope to the Lutheran justification by faith alone. Also, in light of Schaeffler's suggestion, it is worth noting that in the New Testament Jesus places a very high value on human action. If one can accept such action as decisive for the coming of the kingdom of God, then it is possible to conceive of the role of the church in the world as being that of maintaining the correlation between absolute hope and practical world duty. One might even go so far as to say that this is the position of the Catholic church since Vatican II, which emphasises the role of the church in society. Finally, we can conclude from this that there are strong grounds for advocating Kant's theology of salvation as a valid alternative to that of Luther.

III: KANT AND ERASMUS: PERSONAL THEOLOGIES

Ethical Religion

So far I have linked Kant and Erasmus on the two main doctrinal concerns where Kant's attitude differs from that of Luther. In addition, a consideration of Erasmus' attitude towards religion and ethics in general reveals that the personal theologies of Kant and Erasmus have much in common.

1) The emphasis upon the ethical in religion—a) Erasmus wrote many works concerned with religion and ethics, with regard to which he claimed that , 'what I have aimed at in publishing all of my books was to serve some useful purpose.'[152] That purpose was to 'reform the morals of man.'[153] Moral instruction is also at the heart of Erasmus' *Adages*.[154] He criticises those who give too much attention to dogma without giving enough attention to the ethical teaching of the Gospel. In the same way in the *Religion* Kant tries to redirect attention from dogma to ethics by emphasising the moral aspects of Christianity to the exclusion of dogma. He objects to a religion of mere rites and observances.[155] b) DeMolen argues that through his philosophy of Christ Erasmus envisioned a new world committed to the exercise of Christian virtue and individual responsibility.[156] If this is correct, then it sounds similar to Kant's ethical kingdom of God in the *Religion*. c) Erasmus, just as Kant, is sceptical about speculative theology or philosophy: the real test of the truth of a dogma is not in its logical coherence, but in its practical effects in the lives of people.[157] d) Erasmus' theology is very moralistic. In his theological works he placed great emphasis upon moral respon-

sibility. We can compare this to Kant's stress in the *Religion* upon an ethical faith.

2) Jesus as Moral Teacher—a) As O'Donnel points out, Erasmus gives scant attention to the historical Jesus.[158] For Kant also, the historical question is not significant; what matters is the practical result of the example of Jesus upon the moral lives of people in general. b)Erasmus' interpretation of the life and teaching of Jesus is often in line within Kant's view. He speaks of Jesus the moral teacher rather than Christ the redeemer: 'the end and aim of the faith of the Gospel is conduct worthy of Christ. Why do we insist on those things which have nothing to do with morality, and neglect the things which are like pillars of the structure?'[159]

3) A philosophy of Christ which amounts to human betterment—a) Erasmus makes it clear that he is attempting to find a Christian philosophy in the Gospel.[160] This, according to some, is exactly what Kant does in the *Religion*.[161] b) In defining his *philosophia Christi* in the *Paraclesis* Erasmus asks, 'what else is the philosophy of Christ, which He himself calls a rebirth, than the restoration of human nature originally well formed?...if we seek a model for life, why does another example take precedence for us over that of Christ himself?'[162] His philosophy of Christ is thus in many respects a practical guide, similar to Kant's moral theology. c)Erasmus suggests that the betterment of human nature is the true philosophy of Christ when he says that 'to overcome evil with good is to emulate the perfect character of Christ Jesus.'[163] Likewise with Kant, the main concern of religion is the overcoming of evil and moral improvement.[164]

4) A Religion of the Heart—Erasmus' theology does not lack a personal quality:

> But on the other hand, do not think that Christ is found in ceremonies, in doctrines kept after a fashion, and in constitutions of the church. Who is truly Christian? Not he who is baptised and anointed, or who attends the church. It is rather the man who has embraced Christ in the innermost feelings of his heart, and who emulates him by his pious deeds.[165]

Kant also recognizes the personal quality of faith when, in the *Religion,* he states that true service to God amounts to service of the heart.[166]

5) The Inseparability of Inner and Outer Religion—Erasmus insists that external steps are not useful unless they are disposed in our hearts. This suggests that Christianity is lived interiorly and reflected externally through good deeds.

Kant also stresses the importance of seeking religion 'within' rather than 'without.'[167] It is the moral disposition of the heart, not the outward moral act that makes a person good or bad. Thus for both religion is within. But at the same time this recognition of the necessity of inner sincerity does not lead to neglect of the significance of morality to religion. Erasmus and Kant attempt to get the balance right, so that both inner and outer sincerity are necessary, thus avoiding the danger of an either / or situation which arises with Luther.

6) The Limits of Human Reason—Erasmus recognizes the limits of human reason in attempting to decipher religion. In "The Freedom of the Will," he suggests that the human mind is unable to freely understand all the mysteries of Scripture:

> For there are some secret places in the Holy Scripture into which God has not wished us to penetrate more deeply and, if we try to do so, then the deeper we go, the darker and the darker it becomes, by which means we are led to acknowledge the unsearchable majesty of the divine wisdom, and the weakness of the human mind.[168]

One can compare this to Kant's reference in the *Religion* to the mysteries of religion.[169]

7) Conflict with Theologians—Erasmus often had conflicts with theologians, and in particular he labels scholastic theologians as "fools" in the *Praise of Folly*. One can compare this to Kant's lack of understanding with the theologians as referred to in the *Conflict*.[170]

8) Reason / Passion -Spirit / Flesh distinction—In the *Enchiridion* Erasmus claims that the Pauline distinction of flesh and spirit is equivalent to the philosophical distinction between reason and the passions.[171] This philosophical distinction between reason and the passions is central to Kant's philosophy. Erasmus also recommends that one should live according to reason, and not according to affections,[172] something advocated by Kant's moral outlook in works such as the *Groundwork* and the second *Critique*.

9) A Moral Interpretation of the Bible—Erasmus suggests that certain things in the Bible must be understood as allegory.[173] He interprets the Bible in terms of its literal and spiritual meanings. The spiritual meaning of Scripture refers to its allegorical (ie. moral) sense. And, as DeMolen suggests, in those places where Erasmus thought that Scripture should be interpreted allegorically,

he was actually concerned with identifying the meaning of Scripture so that it could be made applicable to human conduct. Moral action lay at the heart of his exegesis.[174] Therefore, Erasmus' purpose is very similar to that of Kant in the *Religion*, who wants to give a moral interpretation of the Gospel.

10) Inner / Outer Revelation—DeMolen notes that the divine revelation by which the apostles were guided, had, in Erasmus' opinion, long ago ceased to be operative.[175] It is possible to identify a similar attitude in Kant's lack of enthusiasm for the idea of external revelation. Yet, at the same time, Erasmus refers to the eternal law of God and reason in humankind.[176] This bears resemblance to Kant's notion of inner revelation[177] and suggests that Erasmus may be working with a distinction between inner and outer revelation similar to that used by Kant. For instance, within the sphere of moral teaching, Erasmus sometimes maintains that the New Testament ethic is already present in the human spirit.[178] The similarity between this view and that of Kant, as expressed in the *Conflict*, is striking.[179] According to Erasmus, the inner promptings of human nature itself are in sympathy with the message of the New Testament, and the words of the New Testament have a power to change the lives of men.[180] This idea is also present in the *Conflict*.[181]

11) Human Dignity—Erasmus speaks of human dignity,[182] a notion which also plays a primary role in Kant's ethics.[183] For Erasmus human dignity is confirmed by Christ's emphasis upon the worth of even the poorest soul, for Kant it is due to each person's nature as a rational, moral being.

The concerns of Erasmus and Kant with regard to religion and ethics are shown in the above eleven points to be remarkably similar. However, it is important to note that although it has been suggested that Erasmus adhered to Catholic doctrine with regard to freewill and evil, the same cannot be said for his ethics, with regard to which his adherence to Catholic teaching has often been questioned. One might for instance query how Erasmus could promote such a morality based religion and yet at the same time, support Catholic doctrine. Tracy has suggested that although Erasmus held an outward loyalty to the Catholic church, inwardly he looked forward to the emergence of a new ethical form of Christianity in which there would be no fixed or unchanging dogmas.[184] In fact it may be that on many of the points regarding ethics in religion where Kant and Erasmus are in agreement, this results from a divergence on Erasmus' part from mainline

Catholicism. But, as I shall now illustrate, it is not only on the points of specific theology that Kant and Erasmus are similar.

Character And Outlook

Character studies of Erasmus are also informative. Erasmus dislikes the idea of war, and suggests that we 'Be bolde therefore in the conflict to hope for perpetual peace.'[185] According to James Froude, Erasmus hated lies;[186] but he also loved humanity.[187] Margaret Mann Phillips sees Erasmus as 'a rationalist and precursor of enlightened agnosticism,'[188] and Preserved Smith insists that Erasmus was a champion of rational Christianity, who saw religion as an ethical concern and who sought to reduce its emphasis upon dogma.[189]

Each of these points of character mentions something which places Erasmus' character close to that of Kant. It is not hard to find a parallel to Erasmus' hope for perpetual peace in Kant's work of that name.[190] The works on ethics display both Kant's opposition to lies and his love and concern for humanity. It is taken for granted that Kant is a rationalist, and it is often argued that he is an agnostic.[191] Kant continually insists that the main concern of religion is ethics rather than dogma.

In terms of personal outlook, Erasmus and Kant share a common view of the human situation. Both are concerned with opposites such as freedom and determinism, evil and good, abasement and dignity, reason and passions, spirit and flesh. Both recognised that these opposites, which compose the human paradox, must be reconciled. Kant's attempt at such a reconciliation is given in his appraisal of the intelligible and the sensible worlds. Some may question whether such a reconciliation is possible. For Erasmus and Kant it is essential. And, as Phillips suggests, to have one's cake and eat it is not only possible, it is absolutely necessary if one is to be really human.[192] Both Erasmus and Kant saw this. Thus, there are not only similarities in the thoughts of Erasmus and Kant on religion and ethics in general, but also in their personal characters and outlooks.

CONCLUSION

Given the above appraisal, I would suggest that there are good grounds for considering Erasmus to be the most appropriate religious forerunner with whom Kant can be compared. The issue is less clear cut with regard to the positions of Kant and Erasmus in relation to Catholicism. As was shown above, there are grounds for placing Kant's thought with regard to evil and salvation closer to Catholic doctrine than to the Lutheran. Yet there are also grounds for questioning Kant's allegiance to Catholic theology on points of his ethical religion. Erasmus' views on ethics, which compare with those of Kant, are in many respects too radical to meet with traditional Catholic theology. Therefore Kant, like Erasmus, is both close to Catholic doctrine in his appraisal of evil and salvation, and removed from it in many of his ethical claims. This does not, however, reflect a contradiction in the views of either Erasmus or Kant. Rather, it illustrates clearly that the personal theology of an individual does not always meet with the boundaries demarcated by ecclesiastical faith. It is worth bearing in mind here that as well as on evil and salvation, another reason for distinguishing Kant from Luther was that Kant could not entertain the idea of obedience to the written word. Catholicism advocates not only obedience to sacred Scripture, but also to sacred tradition. Thus, with regard to what has Divine authority, Kant's stance is even less in line with "orthodox" Catholicism, than with "orthodox" Lutheranism. This, and many more objections, could be raised to reject the idea that Kant may be considered an adherent of Catholicism.

However, if Kant is, strictly speaking, neither an adherent of Protestantism, nor of Catholicism, what in fact can we conclude with regard to his theological perspective in light of his religious forerunners? In my opinion we can only begin to give a conclusion which is true to the thought of Kant when we acknowledge that the very question as to whether Kant is an adherent of either Protestantism or of Catholicism is misplaced, given that Kant is critical of both:

> If a church which claims that its ecclesiastical faith is universally binding is called a catholic church, and if that which protests against such claims on the part of others...is called a protestant church, an alert observer will come upon many laudable examples of protestant Catholics and on the other hand, still more examples, and offensive ones, of arch-catholic Protestants.[193]

Kant does not seek to be identified with either Protestantism or Catholicism. Whereas the Reformation substituted Protestantism for Catholicism, Kant wanted to substitute his moral faith for Protestantism, that is, a pure moral religion no longer tied to institution. However, there is no contradiction in pointing out Kant's lack of allegiance to either Protestantism or Catholicism, and at the same time suggesting that Erasmus, rather than Luther, is the religious forerunner with whom Kant has most in common.

ENDNOTES

1 In *Kant as Philosophical Theologian*, Reardon attempts to show that throughout his life Kant never lets go of the influence of Pietism, and that this influence can be identified in his treatment of religion.

2 See for instance B. Wand, "Religious Concepts and Moral Theory: Luther and Kant," *Journal of the History of Philosophy* 9, 1971, and a paper given at the 7th International Kant Congress, Mainz, Germany, 1990, by R. Saarinen, "Kant's Kritik der praktischen Vernunft als 'Philosophie des Protestantismus' bei H. Cohen und W. Hermann."

3 Examples of such attempts are: B. Bauch, *Luther und Kant*, Berlin, 1904; F. Paulsen, "Kant der Philosoph des Protestantismus," *Kant-Studien* 4, 1900.

4 E.W. Kohls, *Luther oder Erasmus*, Basel, 1978,Vol.II, p.183. My translation: Die gottesgechenkte Selbsttändigkeit der Bibel ist der Schlüssel zu Luther's Selbstverständnis und zum wahren Verstehen der evangelischen Bewegung uberhaupt.

5 As Michael G. Baylor has pointed out in *Action and Person: Conscience in Late Scholasticism and The Young Luther*, E.J. Brill, 1977.

6 See p.81ff.

7 "The Freedom of a Christian," transl. W.A. Lambert, revised by Harold J. Grimm, in *Selected Writings of Martin Luther*, 1520-1523, ed., T.G.Tappert, Fortress U.P., 1967, p.23. Cf. Romans 3:10-12.

8 KW VI, 39; *Religion*, Book I, iii., p.34.

9 Ibid., 21; Ibid., Book I, p.17.

10 "The Freedom of a Christian," p.37.

11 KW VI, 44-45; *Religion*, Book I, General Observation, p.40.

12 Luther, "The Bondage of The Will" (taken from "De Servo Arbitrio"), in E.G. Rupp et al., transl. and ed., *Luther and Erasmus: Free Will and Salvation,* Westminster Press, 1986, p.308.

13 KW VI, 22; *Religion*, Book I, Observation, p.18.

14 Ibid., 47; Ibid., Book I, General Observation, p.43.

15 Ibid., 40; Ibid., Book I, iv., p.35.

16 "The Bondage of The Will," p.294.

17 KW VI, 21; *Religion*, Book I, p.17.

18 Ibid., 36; Ibid., Book I, iii, p.31.

19 Ibid., 32; Ibid., p.27.

20 Ibid., 29; Ibid., Book I, ii., p.24.

21 Ibid., 37; Ibid., Book I, iii, p.32.

22 Ibid; Ibid., Book I, ii., p.25. Cf. Romans 7:15.

23 "The Bondage of The Will," p.266.

24 KW VI, 22; *Religion*, Book I, p.17.

25 Ibid., 22; Ibid.

26 Ibid., 44; Ibid., Book I, General Observation, p.40.

27 See pp.76, 82, 87-88.

28 KW VI, 37; *Religion*, Book I, iii., p.32.

29 Ibid., 32; Ibid., p.27.

30 Ibid.

31 Ibid; Ibid., p.28.

32 Ibid., 37; Ibid., p.32.

33 See p.83.

34 See pp.2, 34, 50-51.

35 Ibid., 45; Ibid., Book I, General Observation, p.41.

36 Ibid., 46; Ibid., p.42.

37 Ibid., 29; Ibid., Book I, ii., p.25.

38 "The Freedom of a Christian," p.24.

39 "The Bondage of The Will," p.190.

40 KW VI, 47; *Religion*, Book One, General Observation, p.43.

41 Ibid., 45; Ibid., p.40.

42 Ibid., 72; Ibid., Book II, Section 1, C, p.66.

43 In "Ought Implies Can: Kant and Luther, a contrast," *Kant and His Influence,* Thoemmes, 1990, pp.1-72, Roger White is strongly critical of the Kantian stance, and openly admits that his sympathies lie with the position of Luther. I will have reason to take issue with White's criticism of the Kantian stance later in this chapter.

44 "The Bondage of The Will," p.183.

45 Ibid., p.327.

46 "The Freedom of a Christian," p.47.

47 "The Bondage of The Will," pp.255-258.

48 KW IV, 446; *Groundwork of the Metaphysic of Morals*, III, p.114. Hereafter to be referred to as *Groundwork.*

49 See *Luther and Erasmus: Free Will and Salvation.*

50 "The Bondage of The Will," p.317.

51 Ibid, p.305.

52 Ibid, p.271.

53 Ibid.

54 Ibid, p.270. Cf.John 3: 6.

55 Ibid, p.296.

56 Ibid, p.13, and Luther's reference to this on p.219.

57 Ibid, p.291.

58 In the second *Critique* Kant does seem to endorse such a view, but it is important to note a development in his conception of the relationship between freedom and evil which occurs between the writing of the second *Critique* and the *Religion*. In the second *Critique* Kant tends to the opinion that a freewill will always choose the good and that it is only when free choice is obstructed by sensible desires that evil is performed. By the time of the *Religion* he has realized that our choice of evil is itself a free act, otherwise there would be no moral accountability. The interpretation of evil and freedom presented in the *Religion* is both later, and more consistent with Kant's moral theory as a whole, and will therefore be considered as representative of Kant's perspective for the purposes of this study.

59 See p.83ff.

60 KW VII, 46; *Conflict*, p.81.

61 KW IV,456; *Groundwork*, III, pp.123-4.

62 KW VI, 237, *The Metaphysical Elements of Justice*, pp.43-4.

63 KW XXVIII 2.2, 1068; *Philosophical Theology*, p.105.

64 KW IV, 452; *Groundwork*, III, p.120.

65 Ibid., 448; Ibid., p.116.

66 KW V, 72; Second *Critique*, I, I, III, p.75.

67 KW IV, 449; *Groundwork*, p.116.

68 KW VIII, 13; My translation from "Rezension von Schulz's Versuch einer Anleitung zur Sittenlehre,"1783: Ich frage nur, was ich nun zu tun habe, und da ist die Freiheit eine notwendige praktische Voraussetzung und eine Idee, unter der ich allein Gebote der Vernunft als gültig ansehen kann.

69 KW IV, 447; *Groundwork*, p.115

70 Ibid.

71 Ibid., 448; Ibid., p.116.

72 Ibid., 447; Ibid., p.114.

73 Ibid., 453; Ibid., p.121.

74 KW VI, 237; *The Metaphysical Elements of Justice*, pp.43-44.

75 KW IV, 448; *Groundwork*, p.116.

76 KW VIII, 13 My translation from "Rezension von Schulz's Versuch einer Anleitung zur Sittenlehre": Der allgemeine Fatalism...alles menschliche Tun und lassen in bloßes Marionettenspiel verwandelt, den Begriff von Verbindlichkeit gänzlich aufhebe, das dagegen das Sollen oder der Imperativ, der das praktische Gesetz vom Naturgesetz unterscheidet, uns auch in der Idee gänzlich außerhalb der Naturkette setze, indem er, ohne unseren Willen als frei zu denken, unmöglich und ungereimt ist, vielmehr uns alsdann nichts übrigbleibt, als abzuwarten und zu beobachten, was Gott vermittelst der Natursachen in uns für Entschließungen wirken werde, nicht aber was wir von selbst als Urheber tun können und sollen; woraus dann die gröbste Schwärmerei entspringen muß, die allen Einfluß der gesunden Vernunft aufhebt...Eben so muß der entschlossenste Fatalist jederzeit so handeln, als ob er Frei wäre, und diese Idee bringt auch wirklich die damit einstimmige That hervor und kann sie auch allein hervorbringen.

77 See "The Bondage of The Will," p.289.

78 KW XXVIII 2.2, 1116; *Philosophical Theology*, p.159.

79 It is interesting to note that in the *Conflict* Kant refers to what he calls St. Paul's 'teaching on predestination,' and says that this teaching cannot be reconciled with the Apostle's teaching on freedom of action. See KW VII, 41 and 66; *Conflict*, pp.71 and 121.

80 See pp.21f. and 61f.

81 See *Das Radikal Böse bei Kant*, Dissertation, Bonn 1960, p.85. My translation: Im menschlichen Dasein gibt es aber...keine andere Möglichkeit der Überwindung des Bosen als den Kategorischen Imperativ des Moralgesetzes.

82 Ibid., p.70. My translation: Das Gute das eigentliche Prinzip menschlichen xDaseins ist.

83 See *Luther and Erasmus: Free Will and Salvation.*

84 "The Bondage of The Will," p.290.

85 See pp.76f, 82f, 87-88.

86 "The Bondage of the Will," p.188.

87 See p.83f.

88 "The Bondage of the Will," p.307.

89 "The Freedom of a Christian," p.36.

90 Ibid.,p.38.

91 Ibid., p.11.

92 Ibid. p.45.

93 Ibid. pp.48-49.

94 Ibid. p.39.

95 See Traces *Bibliques Dans La Loi Morale Chez Kant*, Beauchesne, 1986.

96 "The Freedom of a Christian," p.38.

97 Ibid. p.23.

98 KW VI, 68; *Religion,* Book II, Section 1, C, p.62. Cf. Philippians 2: 12.

99 Ibid., 52; Ibid., Book I, General Observation, p.47.

100 Ibid. Cf. Luke 19: 12-16.

101 Ibid., 66; Ibid., Book II, Section 1, C, p.60.

102 Ibid., 192; Ibid., Book IV, General Observation, p.180.

103 See pp.81.

104 See pp.61-62.

105 Ibid.

106 MacKinnon rightly observes in "Aspects of Kant's Influence On British Theology," *Kant and His Influence*, p.350, that the idea that Kant is the philosopher of Protestantism is somewhat paradoxical.

107 I must therefore disagree with White, who, in "Ought Implies Can: Kant and Luther, a contrast" rules out the possibility of linking Kant to Erasmus. Not only does White fail to account for Kant's version of religious doctrines such as revelation and grace, but he also suggests that the factor ruling out a specific link between Kant's position and that of Erasmus is that Erasmus has a theodicy, whereas this is not possible for Kant. As should be clear from Chapter I, I do not agree with this claim. See p.34ff.

108 Erasmus, "The Freedom of the Will" (taken from Erasmus' De Libero Arbitrio), in: *Luther and Erasmus: Free Will and Salvation*, p.48.

109 *Immanuel Kant—Eine Biographie*, Berlin, 1985. My translation: Der Mensch steht am "Scheideweg"; er hat nur die Wahl, dem "Gesetz Gehör zu geben" oder es zu übertreten, die Wahl zwischen Gut und Böse.

110 "The Freedom of the Will," p.49.

111 KW VI, 39; *Religion*, Book I, iii., p.34.

112 "The Freedom of the Will," p.75.

113 See p.83ff.

114 "The Freedom of the Will," p.49.

115 *Kant's Moral Religion*, pp.240-244.

116 "The Freedom of the Will," p.49.

117 KW VI, 37; *Religion*, Book I, iii., p.32. * My italics.

118 "The Freedom of the Will," p.79.

119 KW VI, 44-46; *Religion*, Book I, General Observation, pp.40-42.

120 "The Freedom of the Will," p.47.

121 See KW VI, 51-52. Cf. 83; *Religion,* Book I, General Observation, p.47. Cf. Book II, Section Two, p.78.

122 "The Freedom of the Will," p.50.

123 *Das Radikal Böse bei Kant,* p.26. My translation: Wenn der Mensch in der Willkür nicht frei wäre, wie könnte er böse sein?

124 "The Freedom of the Will," p.92.

125 Ibid., p.63. Cf. Romans 7:18, See also KW VI, 29; *Religion*, Book I, ii., p.25.

126 KW VI, 37; *Religion,* Book I, iii., p.32.

127 "The Freedom of the Will," pp. 73, 81. Cf. Philippians 2:12.

128 KW VI, 68; *Religion,* Book II, Section 1, C, p.62. Cf. Philippians 2:12.

129 "The Freedom of the Will," p.79.

130 KW VI, 118; *Religion,* Book III, Division One,vii., p.108.

131 "The Freedom of the Will," p.73.

132 *Kant's Moral Religion,* pp.240-248. Cf. p. 106.

133 KW VII, 46-47; *Conflict,* pp.81-83. See p.77ff.

134 "The Freedom of the Will," pp. 49, 52.

135 Ibid. pp. 52, 66, 84.

136 See pp.81.

137 "The Freedom of the Will," p.85.

138 *Luther and Erasmus: Freewill and Salvation*, introduction, p.15.

139 KW VI, 51-52; *Religion,* Book 1, General Observation, p.47.

140 R. H. Bainton, *Erasmus of Christendom*, Charles Scribners Sons, 1969, p.187. Cf. pp.188, 190.

141 *Luther and Erasmus: Freewill and Salvation*, introduction, p.8.

142 See KW XXVIII 2.2, 1115; *Philosophical Theology*, p.158.

143 *Luther, Erasmus and the Reformation -A Catholic Protestant Reappraisal*, ed., J.C. Olin et. al., Fordham U.P., 1969, p.108.

144 *Luther and Erasmus: Freewill and Salvation*, introduction, p.9.

145 J.D. Tracy, "Erasmus the Humanist," in *Erasmus Symposium of 1971*, ed., R.L. DeMolen, Twayne, p.29.

146 In "Ought Implies Can: Kant and Luther, a contrast," White accuses both Kant and Erasmus of advocating versions of merit theology. The fact that he does so is due to his failure to recognise the significance of freedom in relation to salvation for both Erasmus and Kant, but also due to a misconception of Catholic salvation theology.

147 *Luther, Erasmus and the Reformation: A Catholic Protestant Reappraisal*, p.40.

148 See footnote 4, this chapter.

149 Darmstadt, 1979.

150 Transl., N. Plaice et. al., Basil Blackwell, 1986.

151 See pp.61-62.

152 Letter to Maarten van Dorp, May 1515, transl. J.C. Olin in *Desiderius Erasmus: Christian Humanism and The Reformation*, Fordham U.P., 1975, pp. 57, and 78.

153 Ibid., p.60.

154 M. Mann Phillips: *The Adages of Erasmus: A Study with Translations*, Cambridge U.P., 1964.

155 See KW VI, Viertes Stück; *Religion*, Book IV.

156 "Erasmus of Rotterdam in Profile," in *Erasmus Symposium of 1971*, p.23.

157 Ibid., p.40.

158 See Erasmus, *Enchiridion*, transl. and ed., R Himelick, Indiana U.P. 1963, p.xvi.

159 *The Adages of Erasmus,* p.346.

160 *Enchiridion*, p.11.

161 Cf. Stephen Palmquist " Faith as the Key to the Justification of Transcendental Reflection," *The Heythrop Journal* 25, 1984.

162 *Desiderius Erasmus: Christian Humanism and The Reformation*, p.90.

163 *Enchiridion*, p.197. Cf. R.L. DeMolen, *Spirituality of Erasmus of Rotterdam*, De Graaf, 1987, p.176.

164 See KW VII, 121. Cf. 49; *Conflict,* p.121. Cf. p.87.

165 Erasmus, *The Education of a Christian Prince*, 1516, transl. and ed., L.K. Born, Columbia U.P., 1963, p.153.

166 KW VI, 192; *Religion,* Book IV, General Observation, p.180.

167 Ibid., 167; Ibid., Book IV, Part 1, Section Two, p.155.

168 *Luther and Erasmus: Free Will and Salvation*, p.38.

169 KW VI, 52. Cf. 142-147; *Religion*, Book I, General Observation, p.47. Cf. Book III, General Observation, pp.133-138.

170 KW VII, 36-75; *Conflict,* pp.61-139. See also Chapter II, p.58ff.

171 *Enchiridion*, p.xvi.

172 Ibid., p.66.

173 Ibid., p.47.

174 *The Spirituality of Erasmus of Rotterdam*, p.123.

175 Ibid., p.81.

176 *Enchiridion*, p.65.

177 KW XXVIII 2.2, 1117; *Philosophical Theology*, p.160. See p.65-66.

178 *Erasmus Symposium of 1971*, p.40.

179 KW VII, 63; *Conflict,* p.115. See p.66ff.

180 *Erasmus Symposium of 1971*, p.41.

181 KW VII, 63-65; *Conflict*, pp.115-119.

182 *Enchiridion*, p.180.

183 See KW IV, 434ff. Cf. 438-440; *Groundwork,* p.102ff. Cf. pp.105-108.

184 *Erasmus Symposium of 1971*, p.41.

185 *The Spirituality of Erasmus*, pp.174-175.

186 *Life and Letters of Erasmus*, Longmans and Green & Co., 1899, p.6.

187 *Erasmus Symposium of 1971*, p.24.

188 M.M. Phillips, *Erasmus and The Northern Renaissance*, Collier Books, 1965, p.11.

189 *Erasmus: A Study of his Life, Ideals and Place in History*, Harper and Brothers, 1923, p.325.

190 KW VIII, 341-386, *Perpetual Peace*.

191 See p.70f.

192 *Luther, Erasmus and the Reformation*, p.111.

193 KW VI, 109; *Religion* Book III, v., p.100.

IV: KANT AND CHRISTIAN THEOLOGY

INTRODUCTION

This chapter deals specifically with the relationship between Kant's theology and Christian theology. Some insight into this relationship has already been given. For instance, in previous chapters I have shown the extent to which Kant's treatment of typically Christian themes such as revelation, grace, the kingdom of God and salvation, has diverged from Christian interpretations in some respects, and yet also retained distinctly Christian features in others respects. I have pointed to Kant's dislike for ecclesiastical religion. At the same time, I have shown that Kant's interpretation of religion includes the view that Christianity is *the* moral religion. However, the specific details of the relationship between Kant's perspective and that of the Christian tradition have yet to be examined. It is important to get to the heart of that relationship for two main reasons. First, Kant's analysis of religion has been seen to have posed a great threat to Christian theology, and the reluctance to associate Kant with theology often comes from those eager to defend the Christian faith against such a threat. Clarifying Kant's stance will alleviate such concern. Secondly, it will enable us to distinguish between those elements of Kant's theology which are the result of his historical and cultural context, and those which truly reflect his theological initiative.

My appraisal of the relationship between Kant's theology and Christian theology will neither claim, nor attempt, to be exhaustive. First, I shall examine an aspect of Kant's theology which has been misunderstood by most Christian theologians. That is, his interpretation of incarnational theology. In order to counter the widespread opinion that Kant devalues the human Jesus I will then consider the significance of the humanity of Jesus for Kant's theology. Next, I shall examine Kant's attitude towards the historical Jesus. In response to the criticism that Kant neglects the historical Jesus, I will show that Kant is constantly seeking to offer an alternative version of theology to that based upon historical faith. The question then follows, as to whether Kant's alternative version of theology remains, or even ought to remain, within the boundaries of Christian theology. Therefore, in this final chapter I shall do four things:

I) Outline standard interpretations of Kant's attitude towards the incarnation, and then specify, by detailed examination of Kant's appraisal of incarnation, the respects in which they are mistaken.

II) Examine the significance of Jesus' role as human exemplar in Kant's theology.

III) Consider the criticism that Kant, in contrast to Christian theologians, neglects the historical Jesus.

IV) Defend the absence of historical faith in Kant's theology as a presupposition of the establishment of a universal religion, and consider whether that universal religion can be retained as a version of Christian theology.

I: INCARNATIONAL THEOLOGY

Before I can begin to examine Kant's stance with regard to incarnational theology it is necessary to specify the form of such theology against which Kant's interpretation is set. This can be done by stating the main portion of the official teaching of the Christian Church as laid down in the Nicene (A.D.325) and Chalcedonian (A.D.451) creeds, to the effect that Jesus Christ is:

> the only-begotten Son of God, Begotten of the Father before all the ages, Light of Light, true God of true God, begotten not made, of one substance with the Father, through whom all things are made; who for us men and for our salvation came down from the heavens, and was made flesh of the Holy Spirit and the Virgin Mary, and became man, and was crucified for us under Pontius Pilate, and suffered and was buried, and rose again on the third day according to the Scriptures, and ascended into the heavens.[1]

According to this statement of Christian belief, Jesus Christ was both fully human and fully divine, more specifically, he was God incarnate. It is this belief that 'God the Son was made man for our salvation,' a belief which still represents the official teaching of the Christian Church today, which forms the basis of the incarnational theology against which Kant sets his own interpretation.

I shall begin my exposition with what most Christian theologians and philosophers have taken Kant's interpretation to be.[2] Inevitably, such accounts always commence with Kant's treatment of the Son of God in the *Religion.* The passage most often referred to is the one which makes frequent appeal to the fourth gospel, and begins with references to 'Mankind...in its complete moral perfection,' and goes on to say that 'Man so conceived, alone pleasing to God, "is in Him through eternity..."hence he is no created thing but His only begotten Son...and only in him and through the adoption of his disposition can we hope "to become the sons of God."[3] Kant says that 'this archetype has *come down* to us from heaven and has assumed our humanity,' and that 'Such union with us may therefore be regarded as a state of humiliation of the Son of God if we represent to ourselves this godly-minded person, regarded as our archetype, as assuming sorrows in fullest measure in order to fulfil the world's good, though he himself is holy and therefore is bound to endure no suffering whatsoever.'[4] He continues that 'Man may then hope to become acceptable to God (and so be saved) through *a practical faith in this Son of God* (so far as He is represented as having taken upon Himself man's nature).'[5]

The account given above seems to involve recognition of the divinity of the Son of God. Consider, for instance, the similarity between Kant's notion of the archetype as having come down from heaven, and the statement of the Nicene creed: he 'came down from the heavens.' But Kant goes on to say that 'We need therefore no empirical example to make the idea of a person morally well-pleasing to God our archetype; this idea as an archetype is already present in our reason.'[6] Most theologians have taken this claim to suggest that, as long as we have the divine Son of God present in our reason, we have no need of a human Son of God. As a consequence of this, Kant has been accused of denying the need for the human Jesus. His interpretation is considered to be docetic, favouring the divine Son of God over the human Jesus.

However, if this is the case, what is to be said for the allusions I made to Kant's interpretation of Jesus as moral teacher and exemplar in Chapter III? According to most theologians, the answer is given in a telling passage from Kant's *Groundwork,* where he states that: 'Even the Holy One of the gospel must first be compared with our ideal of moral perfection before we can recognize him to be such.'[7] This means that the human moral teacher and exemplar must be judged according to the divine Son of God who exists in our reason. The divine Son of God, the archetype lying in human reason, is more important for Kant than the living reality of the Gospel teacher. Kant is therefore accused of having placed his 'practical' faith in a Christ of reason, rather than in the human example of Jesus, who must be examined in light of the archetype before we can attribute any moral worth to him. Kant's so-called preference for the ideal Son of God of human reason over the human figure has horrified theologians and philosophers alike. Iris Murdoch tells us, with considerable disdain, that according to Kant, 'when confronted with the person of Christ we must turn back to the pattern of rationality in our own bosoms and decide whether or not we approve of the man we see.'[8]

There is an even greater problem with Kant's claim in the *Groundwork*, for it implies that the human figure, Jesus of Nazareth, is not the Son of God. The very suggestion that we judge him according to the ideal Son of God in our reason implies that the ideal Son of God is independent of the human figure. Kant either makes the very existence of Jesus of Nazareth unnecessary, or trivialises his significance in relation to the ideal Son of God existing in our reason. Therefore, the conclusion drawn by most theologians who give an account of Kant's attitude towards the incarnation can be summed up in the words of Reardon:

> The 'Son of God' illustrates an ideal which primarily has to be sought not elsewhere than within ourselves, in human hearts and consciences. The living embodiment of the ideal, that is, is not itself the ideal; he simply exemplifies it in his teaching and good works. Hence Kant's account of Christ leans either to docetism—that the divine ideal was not really made flesh—or to Arianism, that its human embodiment was not really the ideal in its divine fulness.[9]

Needless to say, if Reardon is correct, then Kant's interpretation of the incarnation is at the very least heretical, and as Macquarrie suggests, 'simply fails to do justice to the substance of the Christian tradition.'[10]

Christian theologians might also point out that even Erasmus, with whom I compared Kant's theology in Chapter III, held to the official teaching of the Church concerning divine incarnation. As John Payne has maintained, Erasmus seemed 'fully to accept the Nicene and Chalcedonian declarations concerning Christ's deity and humanity.'[11] In fact, on the question of divine incarnation Erasmus would stand with Luther against Kant. Unlike Erasmus, but like most

Enlightenment philosophers, Kant was enchanted by and gave primary place to human reason. In fact, the ultimate explanation for his interpretation of the divine Son of God present in our reason to the exclusion of the human Christ, lies in the Enlightenment preoccupation with reason. On the other hand, if one accepts the official teaching of the Church, as both Erasmus and Luther did, and as most Christian theologians today also do, then the confession of God's incarnation in Jesus Christ forms the centre of Christian theology and it is that which distinguishes Christian theology from any other kind of theology. Such an attitude is expressed in the words of Donald MacKinnon: 'At the foundation of the faith there lies a deed done, an incarnating of the eternal in the stuff of human history.'[12] On such an evaluation, despite the similarities between the emphasis upon morality in Kant's and Erasmus' theologies, it is the attitude towards Jesus, seen as both God and man, which truly matters for Christian theology.

Many crucial issues are raised by this account of Kant's interpretation of incarnational theology. And in certain respects I would not wish to query the results. For instance, I think that Kant's attitude towards incarnational theology is undoubtedly not only at odds with the official teaching of the Church, but also with the view of Erasmus. To a certain extent, Kant's attitude can be explained in terms of Enlightenment rationalism.[13] It can also be explained in terms of the radical change which takes place between the time of Erasmus and that of Kant, when much of the official teaching of the Church concerning Jesus Christ was beginning to be severely challenged. In fact, between the sixteenth and eighteenth centuries a watershed in attitudes towards incarnational theology occurred. The official teaching of the church in the form of the Nicene and Chalcedonian creeds was increasingly subject to criticism at the time of the Enlightenment. Kant, like most eighteenth century philosophical sceptics, was willing to challenge the official teaching of the Church in a way that Erasmus was not.

Thus far, I am entirely in agreement with the standard account of Kant's interpretation of incarnational theology. However, as I shall presently demonstrate, Kant's account is neither docetic nor Arian, and it is not wholly explicable in terms of the Enlightenment preoccupation with reason. But before this can be demonstrated, I need to turn to Kant's first *Critique*, and to an analysis of terminology which proves essential to a correct account of Kant's interpretation of the Son of God.

The terminology to be referred to includes the following: idea, ideal, pattern, example, archetype and personification. According to Kant:

> if anyone is held up as a pattern of virtue, the true original with which we compare the alleged pattern and by which alone we judge of its value is to be found only in our minds. This original is the idea of virtue, in respect of which the possible objects of experience may serve as examples (proofs that what the concept of reason commands is in a certain degree practicable), but not as archetype.[14]

That is, individual persons, or even objects of experience, may serve as examples of virtue, but not as the archetype of virtue which consists in the original idea.

Kant goes on to say that every human being carries in their soul the idea of humanity as the archetype of their actions.[15] Therefore 'humanity' is an archetype, or idea of reason. At a later point Kant adds that 'human reason contains not only ideas, but ideals also, which have practical power and form the basis of the possible perfections of certain actions.'[16] Virtue, and human wisdom are ideas. The 'wise man' is an ideal, that is, a man existing in thought only, but in complete conformity with the idea of wisdom. According to Kant, 'we cannot concede to these ideals objective reality (existence).'[17] Rather, they are personifications of ideas. For instance, the 'wise man' is the personification of wisdom. Most significantly, Kant says that to attempt to realise the ideal in an example, that is in the (field of) appearance, ...is impracticable.[18] To understand why this is so one might consider the idea 'philosophy' as an archetype for the estimation of all attempts at philosophising.[19] Thus regarded, philosophy is a mere idea of a possible science which nowhere exists *in concreto* in the world, but to which, by many different paths, one endeavours to approximate. This idea of 'philosophy' can be 'personified' and its archetype represented in the 'ideal *philosopher*.' When the idea or archetype of philosophy is thus represented in the 'ideal *philosopher* ' we have the personification of the idea. However, it is one thing to think such an 'ideal *philosopher*,' and another to entitle oneself a philosopher, and to pretend to have equalled the pattern which exists in the idea alone.

To give a brief summary of the above terminology, ideas such as those of virtue, human perfection and philosophy, are the standards by which we judge approximations in nature. Ideals, such as the 'wise man' and the 'ideal *philosopher'* are personifications of the ideas in the form of individual persons in our thought. To suggest that such ideals exist in reality in human form is entirely unfounded from a practical point of view. It is with this summary of Kantian terminology in mind that I now return to Kant's treatment of the Son of God passage in the *Religion*, and to an alternative interpretation of it.

It is important to note that the passage concerned has as its sub-title: "The Personified Idea of the Good Principle."[20] Kant equates the idea of humanity in its perfection with the notion of the Son of God. Thus: 'Mankind...in its complete moral perfection...''Man so conceived, alone pleasing to God, "is in Him through eternity..."hence he is no created thing but His only begotten Son.'[21] The reason for this equation is that the Son of God is the ideal personification of the idea of human perfection. The Son of God motif is an ideal of reason.

From the first *Critique* it is clear that there is a difference between an idea of moral perfection, or even the ideal of such perfection, and the actual instantiation of such an ideal in a real, existing human person. In fact, Kant maintains that archetypes do not manifest themselves in empirical instances. Rather they serve as standards by which we judge empirical instances.[22] It therefore seems odd that Kant refers to the archetype as 'coming down from heaven,' and also says that:

> This ideal of a humanity pleasing to God (hence of such moral perfection as is possible to an earthly being who is subject to wants and inclinations) we can represent to ourselves only as a person who would be willing not merely to discharge all human duties to himself and to spread about him goodness as widely as possible by precept and example, but even...to take upon himself every affliction, up to the most ignominious death, for the good of the world and even for his enemies.[23]

In the above Kant appears to be referring to an actual living person. In fact, he is giving an account of the Gospel record of Jesus' life and death. However, the clue to his interpretation lies in the words 'represent to ourselves.' According to Kant, one limitation of human reason is that it can only represent the idea of humanity in its perfection as an ideal person living a human life. From the first *Critique* it is clear that ideals of reason do not exist in human form. Therefore, although Kant does not advocate the notion of a literal 'Son of God' existing in human form, he acknowledges that 'we must always resort to some analogy to natural existences to render supersensible qualities intelligible to ourselves... Such is the *schematism of analogy*, with which (as a means of explanation) we cannot dispense.'[24] Kant is willing to accept that as a result of the limitations of human reason, it represents the ideal of human reason in a human figure. He is also willing to allow the application of the Son of God terminology to Jesus Christ. However, what he will not allow is the attempt to claim that such a human person is the ideal in human form. That is, he will not allow the claim that Jesus is the ideal of human reason, or that Jesus is the Son of God, to be taken literally. To make such a claim is to transform a '*schematism of analogy*' into a '*schematism of objective determination* (for the extension of our knowledge)' and this amounts to '*anthropomorphism,*' which has, from the moral point of view, 'most injurious consequences.'[25] One should be reminded here of Kant's criticism of anthropomorphism in the *Prolegomena* and of his notion of symbolic anthropomorphism.[26] Kant wants to allow the use of symbolic language to make the ideal of the Son of God, the personification of humanity in its moral perfection, comprehensible to finite human understanding, without allowing anthropomorphic claims such as that a person exists, or has existed, who is the instantiation of the ideal.[27]

If one considers further the Son of God terminology as used in the *Religion* it becomes clear that all such terminology is steeped in symbolic language. It is for this reason that Kant uses the word **personified** in the sub-title to the passage. He also continually uses the word 'represent.' For instance, before referring to the archetype as having descended from heaven, Kant states quite clearly that **we represent it** as having done so because 'we are not the authors of this idea, which has established itself in man without our comprehending how human nature could have been capable of receiving it.'[28] We are not ourselves the creators of our idea of moral perfection, and we therefore seek an empirical means of describing it. But we should not then assume that the empirical elements such as existence in human form which we attribute to the ideal of a most perfect person, the Son of God, apply to the ideal itself.[29] Even the most surprising claim on Kant's part, that 'Man may hope to become acceptable to God (and so to be saved) through *a practical faith in this Son of God'* adds by way of clarification 'so far as he is **represented** as having taken upon Himself man's nature.'[30] It is simply as a result of the limits of human reason that we must represent the ideal of moral perfection to ourselves in human form.

Yet Kant fully accepts the reality of the idea of moral perfection. He says that 'From the practical point of view this idea is completely real in its own right, for it resides in our morally-legislative reason.'[31] The notion of a Son of God is a representation of the idea of moral perfection which rests in human reason and has complete reality. However, the ideal itself cannot apply literally to a divine being living among human beings. According to Kant, we ought to conform to the idea of moral perfection, and 'must *be able* to do so,'[32] whereas we could not possibly conform to anything achieved by a divine being.

Kant seems, therefore, to be denying a literal account of a Son of God coming to earth and living as a human being amongst others. Yet he will not entirely rule out such a possibility:

> Now if it were indeed a fact that such a truly godly-minded man at some particular time had descended, as it were, from heaven to earth and had given men in his own person, through his teachings, his conduct, and his sufferings, as perfect an *example* of a man well-pleasing to God as one can expect to find in external experience(for be it remembered that the *archetype* of such a person is to be sought nowhere but in our own reason), and if he had, through all this, produced immeasurably great moral good upon earth by effecting a revolution in the human race-even then we should have no cause for supposing him other than a man naturally begotten...This is not, to be sure, absolutely to deny that he might be a man supernaturally begotten. But to suppose the latter can in no way benefit us practically, inasmuch as the archetype which we find embodied in this manifestation, must, after all, be sought in ourselves.[33]

As is suggested in the above, Kant will not deny the possibility of a divine person taking on human form, but he does not think that belief in such a divine being could have any practical, or, in other words, moral value. In fact, the opposite would be true, since 'his distance from the natural man would then be so infinitely great that such a divine person could no longer be held up as an *example* to him.'[34] Similarly, in a passage from the *Conflict*, Kant says that:

> if we think of this God-man, not as the Idea of humanity in its full moral perfection, present in God from eternity and beloved by Him...but as the Divinity "dwelling incarnate" in a real man and working as a second nature in him, then we can draw nothing practical from this mystery: since we cannot require ourselves to rival a God, we cannot take him as an example.[35]

Here Kant is more explicit about the fact that he is speaking of divine incarnation. He also makes it clear that by 'God-man' he means the idea of humanity in its perfection. In the footnote to this passage he states that if we are to think in terms of a God-man at all, we must understand by such an idea 'humanity in the abstract' rather than 'a real human being.'[36] But, just as in the *Religion*, Kant is not ruling out the possibility of divine incarnation. He is only claiming that there is no practical use for such an idea since the fact of its reality or otherwise is indifferent to moral faith. However, he does raise the difficulty posed to incarnational theology of multiple incarnations: 'And I shall not insist on the further difficulty-why, if such a union is possible in one case, God has not let all men participate in it, so that everyone would necessarily be pleasing to Him.'[37] As a result, even though he will not commit himself to a denial of the possibility of divine incarnation, Kant finds the idea of a literal 'God-man' unacceptable, particularly because of the danger of anthropomorphism. However, we are entirely justified in thinking of humanity in its complete perfection. And as a result of this idea, just as with the ideal of the 'wise man,' so we have within us the ideal of a most perfect person. However, it is one thing to have the ideal of such a perfect person, and quite another to suggest that such a person exists or has existed in human form.

As far as Kant is concerned, ecclesiastical religion has committed the error of making belief in a literal divine incarnation a necessary tenet of faith. In so doing, it applies concepts to Jesus which only belong to the rational ideal of reason. In attempting to identify rational ideas of moral perfection with the human figure, Jesus Christ, it seeks to unite two principles, one empirical, the other rational.[38] In this manner, it turns a schematism of analogy into a schematism of objective determination, and falls into anthropomorphism.

This distinction between a schematism of analogy and a schematism of objective determination lies at the centre of Kant's attitude towards incarnational language. Yet it might be claimed that my exposition does not suggest anything essentially different from the standard account of Kant's interpretation of the Son of God. If after all, Kant is willing to entertain the ideal in human reason of a Son of God, but not a human person who is literally such a Son of God incarnate, then Kant's account is entirely docetic, as Reardon has maintained. As I will now attempt to show, the conclusion drawn here is actually very different.

It should be clear from the above that in the Son of God passages from the *Religion*, Kant's primary concern is with the idea of humanity in its perfection.

The tendency to view Kant's account as docetic may be associated with Kant's suggestion that the Son of God, is 'in God from all eternity.'[39] However, as one begins to realise that the Son of God is no more than a way of representing the idea of humanity in its perfection, it becomes obvious that Kant's account is not in fact docetic. At the very least we have a much weaker notion of the Son of God than the divine being of the Nicene creed who takes on human form. If the idea of humanity in its perfection exists in God, it does so in the same way that the idea of virtue, or the idea of philosophy also exists in God. If, therefore, Kant's ideal of the Son of God is docetic, his account of the wise man, or the ideal philosopher is also docetic. A clue to the fact that Kant's account is not docetic lies in his suggestion that the only way in which human reason can render supersensible qualities to itself is by representing such qualities in human guise. The clue lies in the word 'supersensible,' which has already been a subject of detailed examination in Chapters II and III.[40] There it was argued that Kant was willing to make use of the notion of the 'supersensible' in the sense of that which is beyond the limits of the sensible, but he sought always to lodge the notion of the supersensible to determinate concepts of human moral reason. As such, the supersensible is as much a part of human nature as it is that which in some way transcends the sensible in our nature. The same interpretation applies to the idea of humanity in its perfection, which is an idea existing in the reason of every human person, although it is not an idea which they have created for themselves, and must therefore be in some sense supersensible. The idea of humanity in its perfection is a supersensible principle in human reason. And, as will be shown later, this supersensible principle of humanity in its perfection is directly related to a supersensible disposition, also common to every human being.

This interpretation makes it much easier to understand why Kant says that 'We need therefore no empirical example to make the idea of a person morally well-pleasing to God our archetype; this idea as an archetype is already present in our reason.'[41] He can say this because the ideal is a personification of an idea or principle, not a divine being existing in human form. Kant's Son of God terminology is a mythological expression of the supersensible principle of humanity in its moral perfection. Therefore, what Kant calls the Son of God, and what others call his docetic christology, does not really amount to christology in the normal sense at all. Kant's Son of God is very far removed from the official teaching of the

Church concerning the incarnation. The representation of the ideal Son of God as having taken on human nature can be no more than a mythological way of representing a supersensible principle of reason. Anyone who attempts to understand such mythology in literal terms is toying with anthropomorphism.

It is worth mentioning Kant's use of references to the fourth Gospel throughout his exposition. Today it is generally accepted that the Gospel of John portrays a Jesus who was conscious of being God incarnate.[42] The fourth Gospel has also been referred to as the most docetic Gospel.[43] Contrary to the assumption that Kant uses the fourth Gospel because his own account is docetic, he actually uses the fourth Gospel in order to display just how far fetched the idea of a literal 'God-man' is. His use of the fourth Gospel is as a source of the kind of literal interpretation which he is attempting to re-describe using mythological language.

Kant's account of the Son of God coming to earth and living among human beings is a story, it is not literally true. It's truth is a practical rather than literal truth. This practical truth rests in the reality of the idea of humanity in its perfection. Kant realises that this myth is applied to Jesus Christ. In fact, all of the allusions he makes to the Son of God as represented in human form coincide with the Biblical narrative concerning Jesus. He acknowledges that Jesus, the moral teacher of the Gospels, who in his opinion is an example conforming to the archetype of a humanity alone pleasing to God, is **represented** as the ideal of humanity well-pleasing to God, and as returning to heaven, whence he came.[44] He is also aware that the official teaching of the Church views Jesus literally as this Son of God in human form, and thus as a divine incarnation. However, for Kant himself, the Son of God exemplifies the use of mythological language as applied to Jesus. And, granted that this is the case, it is inappropriate to take Kant's treatment of the Son of God as an instance of docetism.

But if this is the case, what is to be said for the charge of Arianism? After all, my exposition seems if anything to have strengthened Kant's claim that nothing in existence can match the archetype of humanity in its perfection, which is beyond empirical manifestation. To begin to answer this charge, it is useful to explain why Kant maintains that even Jesus must be compared with our notion of goodness before we can decide that he is good. First, and most significantly for Kant, morality is *a priori*, not *a posteriori*. By this he means that we obtain our moral (and religious) conceptions independent of experience. Secondly, the *a priori* idea of moral perfection is of primary significance in morality and hence also in religion. It cannot therefore be based upon empirical evidence, such as the example of moral individuals. Hence:

> morality and religion cannot be judged by examples; the examples themselves can only be judged good or bad by reference to universal principles... If, then, saintly people are presented to me as models of religion, I must not imitate them, be they ever so holy; I must judge them rather by universal rules of morality. There are, indeed, examples of righteousness, of virtue, and even of holiness, such as the Example set before us in the Gospels, but this Example of the earthly life does not serve as our ground of judgement; rather we judge it by the holy law. If it conforms to the holy law, then only do we recognize that it is an example of holiness. Examples serve for our encouragement and emulation. They should not be used as patterns.[45]

This outline explains why, in the *Groundwork*, Kant tells us that 'Even the Holy One of the gospel must first be compared with our ideal of moral perfection before we can recognize him to be such.'[46] And Kant's claim is not as horrifying as people like Murdoch take it to be. His point is simply that each person could not recognise Jesus as an example of perfect goodness if they did not already have within them an idea of what perfect goodness ought to consist of. As John Macquarrie rightly asserts, there must be some sense in which Kant is correct, for 'we could not recognize Jesus as a person well pleasing to God unless we already had some idea of what is meant by a person well pleasing to God, and we do have that idea because of our own constitution as human persons.'[47]

Kant's account is not Arian because he is not advocating a divine Christ who is superior to the human figure. His Son of God is not a divine Son existing eternally within our reason. Rather, the Son of God is a mythological way of referring to an abstract principle of humanity in its moral perfection. But, and it is at this point that many Christian theologians take great exception to Kant, Jesus does not, in his opinion, give us our conception of perfect goodness. Rather, we recognise him as the most perfect example of such goodness, the idea of which we already have within us. He is not therefore the archetype for our religious and moral life. By contrast, Christianity has always taken Jesus Christ as its pattern or ideal of the perfect moral and religious life. So, there is a sense in which Kant favours eternal ideas of reason over human figures. And it is here that Kant's Enlightenment rationalism shows. But only in so far as the foundation of morality and religion is not given by Jesus Christ, since it must be grounded *a priori* in human reason.

Is Jesus therefore redundant according to Kant? Before answering this question, it is worth noting that Kant is fully aware of the divergence of his view from standard Christian teaching about Jesus, who is seen as the ideal pattern which all Christians ought to imitate.[48] However, he also says that 'If, however, others have demonstrated the practical possibility of a moral act, we should follow their example and endeavour to do the same and not let others forestall us. On the whole, examples are desirable.'[49] As was suggested in Chapter III,[50] for Kant Jesus is a moral exemplar whose example we ought to emulate. Kant is not attempting to devalue the human Jesus, he is simply holding to the foundation of his moral theory, namely that our conceptions of morality and religion are formed independently of experience; they are not empirical sciences. Kant's point then, in relation to Jesus, the moral teacher and exemplar, is that the example of the moral teacher is highly valuable, but we do not obtain our original moral concepts, nor for the same reason our religious precepts, from the example. Rather, the example serves for our encouragement and emulation. It is not a pattern upon which we should image our religious or moral precepts, but rather an example of those precepts at work in practice, and therefore a worthy source of inspiration. Jesus himself is not a moral or religious ideal or pattern, he is an example of such an ideal in practice.

All of this may in fact sound heretical from a standpoint which seeks to establish in the human figure, Jesus of Nazareth, the foundation of the moral and religious life. However, from a perspective which values Jesus because of his human excellence, it is not so outrageous to reconcile this with a morality already revealed to us by God through our human reason, by which we recognise the quality of Jesus' example. Therefore, in an effort to counter the claim that Kant devalues the human Jesus, I shall now give Kant's interpretation of Jesus' significance for morality and religion.

II: THE SIGNIFICANCE OF JESUS' HUMANITY

According to Kant, Jesus shows us what each of us can become. Moreover, his example is in a sense more than an example, since it can awaken in us our own disposition to become well-pleasing to God. Kant refers to Jesus as 'a humanitarian who brings to the heart of his fellowmen their own well-understood wills, according to which they would act spontaneously of themselves if they proved themselves fitting.'[51] Jesus wins his way into the hearts of those 'whose understanding is already illuminated by the conception of the law of their duty.'[52] The example of Jesus has the capacity, as it were, to awaken something within us, even though we are already in possession of our moral concepts. That which he awakens is the capacity to respond to our ideal of moral perfection. He awakens the moral disposition within us. Yet this moral disposition, and particularly the ideal to which it relates, is, and always has been, common to human nature in general:

> Yet the good principle has descended in mysterious fashion from heaven into humanity not at one time but from the first beginnings of the human race...And since it made its appearance in a human being, as an example to others,...by example (in and through the moral idea) he opens the portals of freedom to all who, like him, choose to become dead to everything that holds them fettered to life on earth to the detriment of morality.[53]

It is important to note in the above that Kant now speaks of the 'good principle' descending from heaven into humanity rather than the 'Son of God.' The good principle does not begin with Jesus, it has been a part of human nature since the very beginning. Jesus does not therefore have something different from other human beings, although he may be better at putting the moral disposition into practice than others, and hence a source of inspiration to them. Jesus does, however, bring with him a new source of release from bondage to life on earth for those who will make his example their own.

In spite of the evident respect for Jesus in statements such as these, Christian theologians are nonetheless perplexed by the idea that Jesus only makes us aware of something we already have within us. As Macquarrie notes with regard to Kant's understanding of Jesus, 'at most he serves to awaken our awareness of the archetypal humanity already discoverable in our reason.'[54] Therefore, even if Jesus is, to begin with, necessary to awaken such a principle within us, he is like a midwife who is necessary at the birth, but all the while dispensable. This dissatisfaction with Kant's interpretation of Jesus highlights the difference between Kant and those who want to hold on to some sense whereby Jesus is unique or ultimate in a way that another human person could not be. The difference can be seen by comparing the significance of Jesus to that of Martin Luther King, who fought for the rights of black people in America. King claimed that black people ought to have the same rights as white people, that they were not second rate citizens. He was in this way teaching something which every black person knew in their heart. However, he was also able to activate something within other black people, namely a sense of pride and self worth. In Kant's opinion, Jesus gave people a sense of their moral potential. And thus, in the same way as with King, Jesus awakened within others an awareness of something ultimate. But there is a sense in which, after King had set off the black civil rights movement, he was dispensable. This is not to say that the example, and memory of him, does not live on in the minds of people today as a form of inspiration. Ultimately, however, the continued realisation of rights for blacks in the future does not depend upon King, no matter how much his significance is still felt. Many Christian theologians might argue that even black Christians would want to put the example of Jesus, and his ultimate significance, beyond that of Martin Luther King in a way which is not a possibility for Kant.

This is an entirely valid criticism, but it does assume that Jesus is to be valued in a way that other human beings, such as Martin Luther King, are not to be valued. Whereas if Jesus is solely human, then the most that can be done is to value his significance in relation to other human achievements. This is not to say that there is no difference between the example of Jesus and that of Martin Luther King. There is always the possibility that one human individual might set a standard, or be valued for his achievements in a way that no other has been valued. But it is to lodge the significance of Jesus to the realm of humanity. And this is precisely what Kant does. Jesus' value as a teacher and as an example is bound to his being solely human. In the passages above Kant has referred to Jesus as a 'human being,' and as a 'humanitarian.' Elsewhere, he also refers to Jesus as 'a person whose wisdom was purer even than that of previous philosophers, as pure as though it had descended from heaven. This person proclaimed himself as indeed truly human with respect to his teachings and example.'[55] Jesus is a kind of super-philosopher, excelling in wisdom more than any other, rather than God. Yet we are also told that Jesus is 'an envoy from heaven who, through an original innocence, was not involved in the bargain with the evil principle into which. ...the rest of the human race had entered.'[56] By this Kant means that Jesus did not succumb to evil in the way that the rest of the human race did, and continues to do today. However, far from seeing this as grounds to separate Jesus from the rest of the human race, Kant sees the example of Jesus as something which every person can achieve. What is so special about Jesus is that he demonstrates the possibility to overcome evil. If he were not solely human, if he were in some sense a God, he would not be such an important person for Kant's interpretation of morality and religion. He is also a source of hope and inspiration. The difference between optimism and pessimism for Kant is the crucial difference between denying that true goodness is a possibility, and actually being shown in the example of Jesus that this goodness can be achieved. Given that Jesus was a man who rose above evil, there must reside in every human nature the potential to do the same. And if, on these terms, others speak of the divinity of Jesus, then they must also speak of the inherent divinity of humankind in general. In this sense we can all be 'Sons of God.'[57]

Admittedly not every human being will make use of his potential in the way that Christ has. In fact it is possible that very few will. But it is precisely for this reason that the example of Jesus, and the response which he can awaken in us, is all the more important. Kant's respect for this human person who has risen above evil in a way unrivalled in the whole of human history shines through his writing.

And what is most fascinating about the significance of Jesus for Kant, is that even though Jesus is solely human, Kant still speaks in terms of incarnation in connection with him:

> Now such a godly-minded teacher, even though he was completely human, might nevertheless truthfully speak of himself as though the ideal of goodness were displayed incarnate in him(in his teachings and conduct). In speaking thus he would be alluding only to the disposition which he makes the rule of his actions;...to the supremely pure moral disposition of the man himself. When a disposition such as this,...is taken as the ideal of mankind, it is,...a perfectly valid ideal for all men, at all times and in all worlds, whenever man makes his own disposition like unto it, as he ought to do.[58]

In this passage we have a summary of all that has been argued in my alternative account of Kant's attitude towards the incarnation. Jesus, although a Godly minded teacher, is completely human. The 'Son of God' has been replaced by the 'ideal of goodness.' This ideal of goodness is the supersensible principle of humanity in its perfection. To say that Jesus incarnates such an ideal, is to suggest that he has made use of the moral disposition within him, a disposition which exists in all people, if they will only let it work within them. One is reminded here of the supersensible disposition within human nature as referred to in Chapters II and III[59] in connection with the overcoming of evil. The supersensible disposition needed, in Kant's view, to be wedded to determinate concepts. Yet Kant appealed to the spirit of Christ as integral to that disposition being activated within us. The disposition may be supersensible, but it is not some supernatural phenomenon making its way miraculously into human nature. As Kant says 'This ascendency of the *supersensible* man in us over the *sensible*,...is an object of the greatest *wonder*, and our wonder at this moral predisposition in us, inseparable from our humanity, only increases the longer we contemplate this true (not fabricated) ideal.'[60] Each person has within them a supersensible principle of humanity in its moral perfection, and a supersensible disposition to act in accordance with this principle. It is this same supersensible disposition raised to its highest level that Jesus exemplifies in his capacity to overcome evil. However, the supersensible principle, and the disposition to act in accordance with it, are both so far removed from any notion of a God incarnate, that the stark divergence of Kant's perspective from the notion of a literal incarnation is obvious.

Furthermore, far from Kant devaluing the human Jesus in favour of eternal principles of reason, the interpretation given above shows remarkable theological initiative on Kant's behalf. His interpretation of Jesus actually bears striking resemblance to a twentieth century alternative to the official teaching of the Christian Church concerning the incarnation. It is to a brief consideration of this twentieth century equivalent that I now turn.

Admittedly, according to many Christian theologians the alternative referred to will be simply a restatement of past heresy. For in its most basic form, it denies that Jesus Christ is God incarnate. However, I would suggest, that contrary to positions held in the past which have been condemned for Arianism, this view differs in that it does not imply that the human Christ is in any sense subordinate to the Divine Christ, rather, it holds that a fully adequate Christian theology can be built upon a Jesus who was human only. It thus amounts to a non-incarnational Christian theology. A version of such non-incarnational theology has been offered by John Hick in the notorious Myth of God Incarnate debate which took place in the 1970's.[61]

Hick argues[62] that the idea of divine incarnation is a mythological idea. He uses the term 'myth' in the sense of a story which is told but is not literally true, or an idea or image which is applied to someone or something but which does not literally apply. The statement 'Jesus was God the Son' is not literally true since it has no literal meaning, but is an application to Jesus of a mythological concept. The divinity accounts attributed to Christ are the result of human speculative thinking rather than divinely revealed truths. He also maintains that whatever truth a myth might have is a kind of practical, rather than literal truth. Yet he does not seek to abandon incarnational language. Indeed he believes that the metaphor of incarnation is a powerful one. To take two examples: Joan of Arc incarnated the spirit of France, or Winston Churchill the defiance of the British people. When someone thus embodies some ideal in their life, we can say that this ideal is being incarnated in that life. And it is also possible that something has been more perfectly or absolutely embodied in one life than in any other. However, the Christian church attempted to turn the metaphor of incarnation into a metaphysical theory by implying that the human Jesus was also literally divine. According to Hick, Jesus was solely human, he was not also divine. Therefore, to call Jesus God, Son of God, or God incarnate, is to use mythological language which is misused when it is treated as a set of literal propositions from which to draw further literal conclusions.

Although the kind of view which Hick advocates today was not available to Kant, the same essential differences between Kant's account of Jesus Christ and the official teaching of the Church also exist between Hick's account and official teaching. Kant uses the term 'Son of God' in the way that Hick says it ought to be used when applied to Jesus, namely, as a mythological concept. And he would certainly agree with Hick, that the divinity accounts applied to Jesus are the result of human speculative thinking rather than divinely revealed truths. His account of the Son of God is in part an attempt to show this. But neither Kant nor Hick seeks to abandon incarnational language in reference to Jesus. In Kant's opinion, Jesus incarnates the ideal of goodness. According to Hick, the spirit of love was incarnated in Jesus.[63] In both cases, however, the language used is not to be understood literally. Rather, Jesus displays a quality so close to our notion of complete goodness or perfect love that we cannot but make this statement about him. Thus, both

Hick and Kant entertain the possibility of using mythological incarnational language to refer to Jesus, even though they both believe that he was solely human.

If Christian theology is defined by literal belief in the divinity of Christ, that Jesus was God on earth, then Kant cannot be associated with Christian theology. On this definition, Erasmus' theology is Christian and Kant's is not. But if, as Kant assumes, and Hick specifically maintains, we can retain the language of the incarnation whilst re-defining it in mythological terms, then the interpretation of Jesus present in the work of Kant and Hick offers exciting possibilities for an alternative approach to Christian theology. And it is fascinating that Kant was presenting such a mythological interpretation two hundred years before its popular twentieth century exposition.[64]

However, it is far from my intention to imply that Hick and Kant share precisely the same kind of theology. Hick does not, for instance, entertain the notion that morality and religion must be founded upon *a priori* principles as Kant does. I have used the example of Hick only to support Kant's interpretation of the incarnation as a viable alternative to the official teaching of the Christian Church. In fact, as I turn now to the most challenging objection to Kant's theology from a Christian perspective, it will become clear why Hick and Kant cannot share the same theology.

III: THE HISTORICAL JESUS

The greatest objection to Kant's theology comes from a perspective which can be equally shared by those who deny a literal incarnational theology as well as by those who favour it. I have shown that Kant has great respect for Jesus and for the practical implications of Jesus' life. However, from the point of view of Christian theology, it is regrettable that his theology does not give more attention to the personality of Jesus, as well as to the significance of Jesus' life, death and resurrection, all of which are just as crucial to Christian theology as the practical, or ethical implications of his life.

In contrast to Kant, Hick would stress that the person and personal story of Jesus Christ is of great importance for Christian theology.[65] In stressing only the practice of Jesus and the way in which he sets the right way of life before us, Kant loses so much of the historical person, whose significance for Christian theology goes far beyond what he taught. From the point of view of historical faith, Kant misses half of the story.

The extent to which the significance of the person, life, death and resurrection of Jesus Christ is lacking in Kant's theology can be illustrated by reflecting back over some of the central themes dealt with in earlier chapters.

In Chapter I Kant's treatment of theodicy was examined.[66] He chose the book of Job from the Old Testament as his text for an analysis and interpretation of the problem of evil, whereas an analysis and interpretation of the problem of evil from within the perspective of Christian theology always attempts to understand evil in relation to Christ's death on the Cross. Kant fails entirely to appeal to the experience of Jesus' suffering, death and reported resurrection for his treatment of this theme. Although trust in God is integral to Kant's theodicy, Jesus is not referred to at any time. Kant's opinion is that we should accept the incomprehensible fact of evil, and trust in a God of justice. In contrast, the suffering and death of Jesus Christ is crucial to the Christian understanding of evil and suffering, and therefore to any attempted theodicy. Pope John Paul II, in his play 'Job,' even suggests that without the cross of Jesus Christ, we have no ultimate explanation or justification for the immeasurable sufferings of Job.[67]

In Chapter II, it was suggested that as far as revelation was concerned, Kant denied the notion of a specific revelation of God to humankind at a special time in history.[68] It is now clear that he also denies the idea that Jesus was God incarnate. Even Hick, who also denies that Jesus is literally God incarnate, allows for the possibility that through Jesus, God was being revealed to the world.[69] Kant only allows a sense of revelation through the mediating principle of human reason. And because this revelation must come through our own reason, it automatically rules out the possibility of another person, such as Jesus Christ, revealing God to us. In contrast, Hick is fully willing to accept that Jesus reveals God, and particularly God's love, to humankind.[70] The revelation of God in Jesus Christ is entirely lacking in Kant's account. In fact, it must be if the only access we have to God is through our own reason. For Kant, Jesus is not the revealer of God, but rather one who gives us an insight into our own souls and into the way in which we can become pleasing to God.

Inevitably, with regard to grace, something similar is the case.[71] Kant objected to the idea of divine grace as a supernatural power invading the human will. He needed a notion of grace which worked in cooperation with human nature. Because of his emphasis upon individual responsibility he would not entertain the idea that through Jesus the world was being reconciled to God. But even from Hick's point of view, we need to safeguard the divine initiative at work in Christ. Jesus was a man approved by God for a special role. In fact, one might go so far as to say that Jesus was not only love incarnate, but that he was God's love incarnate, a man in whom God's inspirational grace was effectively at work. Jesus was an instrument of the divine purpose on earth. Jesus' capacity to heal the sick, and bring people into a new form of life, was evidence of God's grace working through him. He was one through whom others transformingly encountered God's grace.[72]

Chapter II also dealt with Kant's interpretation of the Kingdom of God.[73] Mention was made of Jesus, but only in so far as he taught the moral implications of the kingdom. Jürgen Moltmann has dealt with what he thinks are the deficiencies of Kant's account as seen from a Christian perspective.[74] He suggests that the Christian view of the kingdom of God has quite different priorities than those portrayed in Kant's ethical kingdom. From the point of view of Christian theology, all statements about the future are grounded in the person and history of Jesus Christ, but particularly, in the belief in Christ's resurrection.[75] According to Moltmann, hope for the kingdom of God rests in the resurrection of Jesus Christ. The death and resurrection of Christ is seen as our future, and it is through Jesus that our new life in the Kingdom becomes possible. With Jesus' resurrection, death is overcome and salvation is a reality. Therefore, Christian claims concerning the kingdom of God 'rest upon an eschatology which is at heart Christology in an eschatological perspective.'[76] The eschatology which moulds Jesus' conception of the kingdom of God is not to be found in Kant's interpretation of the kingdom. Nor does he emphasise the resurrection of Jesus as integral to belief in the kingdom of God.

Hick suggests that eschatology is also necessary to the Christian resolution of the problem of evil.[77] And as far as resurrection is concerned, he says that if it were not for:

> this mysterious event which dominated and coloured the thinking of the first generation of believers, Christianity would never have been more than a dying memory of a dead prophet. It is the resurrection which gives meaning to the claim that Jesus was more than a teacher, he was a Messiah, the man in whom God was at work redeeming his

> world. For so many Christians, the belief in the resurrection has been the foundation of their faith.[78]

It is the resurrection experience, regardless of the ambiguities it raises, which in Hick's opinion has created the Christian movement. It cannot therefore be neglected in any account which claims to do justice to the Christian tradition.

Chapter III was concerned with the significance of freewill for Kant's theology, especially in relation to the question of salvation.[79] According to Kant, each person is in some way responsible for their own salvation. I found an ideal contrast to Kant's theology in that of Luther, who had claimed that if salvation does not come from Christ alone, then Jesus has died in vain. By this Luther meant that if Jesus did not die for the sins of humankind, and in order that humankind might, in spite of its sin, attain salvation, then his death was pointless. This doctrine of atonement, which Luther had advocated in the sixteenth century, was that against which Kant still found the need to argue in the eighteenth century. He opposed the idea that Jesus died for our sins. In fact, it was the suggestion that he did which Kant was objecting to when he stressed that each individual is responsible for their own battle to overcome evil. No other person can bear our sins for us since: 'this is no transmissible liability which can be made over to another like a financial indebtedness...rather it is the most personal of all debts...which no innocent person can assume even though he be magnanimous enough to wish to take it upon himself for the sake of another.'[80]

Hick would also want to retain a strong sense of freewill, but he recognises the place that Jesus' death on the cross has had in the conversion of millions of people to the Christian faith.[81] It is unfortunate that Kant was not able to appreciate that the significance of the cross of Jesus for the Christian attitude towards evil and suffering does not have to be interpreted in the sense that Jesus literally died for our sins. Hick, for instance, suggests that in accepting the inevitability of his death, Jesus was accepting the claim of transcendent goodness upon him.[82] Jesus did not therefore die for humankind in any juridical sense. He did, however, die for humankind in the sense that he envisaged his death as an experience which God desired him to undergo for the sake of humankind, and it was his selfless acceptance of it that has made it a means to humankind's salvation.[83] Once again therefore, it was through Christ and his death that the world was being reconciled to God.

In contrast to Hick, the historical account of Jesus' life, death and resurrection have little significance for, or influence upon, Kant's formulation of his theology. In fact, when one looks very closely, it appears that most of what Christianity attributes to the Jesus of history, other than his status as teacher or exemplar, Kant dresses up in the mythological language of the Son of God. For instance, when Kant does refer to the idea of vicarious suffering in the *Religion*, his account is steeped in the symbolic language of the Son of God:

> And this moral disposition which in all its purity (like unto the purity of the Son of God) the man has made his own—or, (if we personify this idea) this Son of God, Himself—bears as *vicarious substitute* the guilt of the sin for him, and indeed for all who believe (practically) in Him; as saviour He renders satisfaction to supreme justice by His sufferings and death; and as *advocate* He makes it possible for men to hope to appear before their judge as justified. Only it must be remembered that (in this mode of representation) the suffering which the new man, in becoming dead to the old, must accept throughout life is pictured as a death endured once for all by the representative of mankind.[84]

It is quite clear that what Kant means in the above is that we personify our own moral act. The symbolic notion of a Son of God dying for our sins represents what Kant calls the death or dying of the old man within us, and the birth of the new. The notion of vicarious suffering together with the idea of Jesus as saviour is simply a symbolic story whose 'spirit and rational meaning have been valid and binding for the whole world and for all time...Its meaning is this: that there exists absolutely no salvation for man apart from the sincerest adoption of genuinely moral principles into his disposition.'[85] Once we divest this 'vivid mode of representation' of its 'mystical veil,'[86] it is easy to understand this. Nor does Kant recognise the significance of the ideas of Christ's resurrection from the dead and ascension into heaven. Although he is willing to allow that Jesus gives 'An example conforming to the archetype of a humanity alone well-pleasing to God, after which he is represented as returning to heaven, whence he came,'[87] on the whole he is sceptical about the ideas of resurrection and ascension just as he is sceptical about the notion of a 'God-man.'[88]

With this we must contrast the acceptance of the life, death, and claims concerning the resurrection of Jesus, as central to the Christian story for Hick. Regardless of the divine-human controversy, Kant is willing to attribute to Jesus much less than Hick is not only willing to allow, but sees as essential.

Kant also ignores the fact that Jesus lived and taught a direct relationship to God.[89] Seen from the perspective of incarnational theology, Jesus could do this because he was God. But even from Hick's point of view, Jesus' message was one of the immediate presence of God as unlimitedly gracious and unlimitedly demanding love.[90] Admittedly, his teaching had practical implications spreading beyond ecclesiastical channels, as Kant recognised, but these cannot, from the point of view of Christian theology, be divorced from the fact that his whole life was one lived consciously in the divine presence and in total response to divine purpose. As Hick suggests, God was so completely real to Jesus that it is impossible to think of him without this consciousness of God.[91]

It follows from this that for Christian theology, Jesus is central to all that concerns a person's relationship with, and understanding of, God. For Christians, Jesus is the unique focus of their perception, experience of, and response to God. For Kant God is an inferred reality, whereas for Jesus, and for the majority of Christians also, God was and is an experienced reality.[92] Therefore, as many Christians rightly feel their spiritual heritage which has to a great extent been activated in and by the religious experience of Jesus Christ, is impoverished by Kant.

According to Hick, it is out of an experience of God's dealings with humankind in the climactic few years of the life of Jesus of Nazareth that the Christian tradition of theology has been formed.[93] It would be pointless, in light of this, to try to claim that from such a perspective Kant's theology is not found to be lacking. Kant's Jesus is not the God who dies on the cross, nor is he Hick's insight into, and channel for, God's action in the world. Kant is not open to the idea of Jesus as saviour and redeemer in any of the Christian formulations of these terms. In Chapter III, I mentioned that Kant, like Erasmus, gave scant attention to the historical Jesus.[94] However, even Erasmus accepted redemption through Christ. As Payne once again shows, Erasmus acknowledged that 'God himself put on manhood and reconciled men to God by his death.'[95] Any Christian who believes that it is through the life and death of Jesus that humankind has been redeemed and brought into communion with God, must entertain a theology radically different from that of Kant.

Donald MacKinnon has expressed Kant's divergence from Christian theology clearly in saying that Kant is not an apologist of the Christian faith.[96] For

MacKinnon, to say this means that Kant did not confess Jesus as God's self revelation in history, as the one who died for our sins, and therefore not only as the key to our understanding of, but also as essential to the overcoming of evil. But one could equally well say that Kant was not an apologist of the Christian faith as Hick understands it. That is, in terms of Christ's revelation of the love of God to us, especially in the way that he deals with evil, suffering and death. From either perspective, the centrepiece of Christian theology and its experience of God disappears in Kant's theology.

There are numerous explanations for Kant's failure to appreciate the significance of the historical Jesus for Christian theology. Primary among them is the sceptical attitude towards historical faith at the time of the Enlightenment. Once again, Kant's preoccupation with reason and with the *a priori* foundations of morality and religion are to be held responsible. The extent to which Kant emphasises individual moral responsibility to the exclusion of faith in another also reflects Enlightenment individualism. He changes most of the historical account of Jesus' life into a moral story with practical lessons for the individual soul. These factors evidently point to the Enlightenment ideas moulding Kant's own attitude.

Thus, in the above, I have outlined what may be considered as the most powerful criticism of Kant's theology, as based upon acceptance of historical faith in Jesus Christ. However, if a balanced appraisal of the relationship between Kant's theology and Christian theology is to be given, then it is also necessary to consider Kant's attitude towards historical faith. In particular, one must consider why Kant finds it so important to ground morality, and hence religion also, in something other than the coincidental facts of history. The answer lies in his preoccupation with what he calls 'true universal religion.'[97] That is, not just with a, but with <u>the</u> true religion, valid for all people and for all time.[98] And as I will now show, it is not that Kant fails to appreciate the historical Jesus, but rather that from his own point of view, it is essential to avoid preoccupation with the historical Jesus if we are even to hope for the establishment of true universal religion.

IV: KANT'S ALTERNATIVE—UNIVERSAL RELIGION

The ultimate aim of Kant's theology is to develop what might be referred to as a universal religion. In fact, the notion of 'universal religion' is implicit to Kant's theology as outlined in earlier chapters.[99] To be authentic and valid for the whole world,[100] such a religion can only be based upon reason.[101] And it must consist in a purely moral faith, which is 'everywhere the same.'[102] That is, it must be based upon universal moral dogmas,[103] which are 'intelligible to all men.'[104] Only such a moral and rational faith amounts to '*pure religious faith*' which 'can be believed in and shared by everyone.'[105] This pure moral religion will be universally binding. It cannot be confined to a faith which is based upon historical events, since 'historical faith...has only particular validity...and, like all empirical knowledge it involves as well the consciousness of its contingency.'[106] Because it is grounded solely on facts, historical faith 'can extend its influence no further than tidings of it can reach, subject to circumstances of time and place and dependent upon the capacity (of men) to judge the credibility of such tidings.'[107] In fact, historical faith amounts to ecclesiastical faith, which is the opposite of pure religious faith.[108] Unlike ecclesiastical faith, pure religious faith will be devoid of all dogma, for 'to claim *universal validity* for a dogma involves a contradiction.'[109] Kant believes that in the end, religion will gradually be freed from all empirical determining grounds and from all statutes which rest on history, and thus, 'at last the pure religion of reason will rule over all, "so that God may be all in all".'[110]

Faith in the historical Jesus cannot, in Kant's opinion, be the basis upon which pure religious faith is grounded. He makes clear his attitude towards faith in the historical Jesus as distinct from pure moral faith in the following passage:

> The proposition: We must believe that there was once a man (of whom reason tells us nothing) who through his holiness and merit rendered satisfaction both for himself(with reference to his duty) and for all others(with their shortcomings, in the light of their duty), if we are to hope that we ourselves, though in a good course of life, will be saved by virtue of that faith alone-this proposition says something very different from the following: With all our strength we must strive after the holy disposition of a course of life well-pleasing to God......the first belief is not in the power of everyone(even of the unlearned). History testifies that in all forms of religion this conflict between two principles of faith has existed; for all religions have involved expiation, on whatever basis they put it, and the moral predisposition in each individual has not failed, on its side, to let its claims be heard.[111]

In Kant's opinion, faith in Jesus as saviour and redeemer is not something that everyone can believe, whereas faith that individual moral improvement will bring one closer to God, is. Furthermore, if Christian faith concentrates upon Jesus' status as redeemer and saviour, then it amounts to 'belief in a *messiah,*' and becomes 'merely a sect of messianic faith.'[112] Christianity in this sense would be:

> the faith of a certain people, based on dogmas and Scriptures, and we could not know whether it is directly valid for all men, the final revelation by which we must henceforth abide, or whether we can expect the future to bring other divine statutes that will approximate still more closely to the end.[113]

There is undeniably something true in what Kant is saying here. After all, Islam claims to be a more recent revelation from God than that of the Christian faith and therefore maintains that it, rather than the Christian proclamation, is the fullest and final divine revelation. In Kant's opinion, so long as Christianity amounts to the worship of Jesus Christ, or makes Jesus the object of its faith, it cannot become the universal religion, because 'a division into sects of messianic faith can never occur in matters of pure religious belief, for it involves a passing off of what is contingent for what is necessary.'[114] He thinks that the apostles took the essential requirement for salvation to be 'the veneration of this teacher himself and a sort of wooing of favour,...against which that teacher had so explicitly and repeatedly preached.'[115] Kant wants a universal religion, not a 'cult' which venerates Jesus.[116] It is worth noting that he distinguished himself as a philosophical theologian, not only from the Biblical theologian but also from Biblical religion in general, which included the historical faith in a Messiah.[117] In the case of Christianity, that Messiah was Jesus.[118]

Infatuation with the particularity of Christ, or, as Kant refers to it, with 'the derivation and the rank, ...of his person,'[119] is inappropriate from the point of view of a universal religion. This also explains why Kant was so reluctant to entertain the notion of divine revelation taking place in the person of Jesus Christ. Christianity, as Kant had experienced it, argued that Jesus was God incarnate and that therefore in Jesus Christ God's final revelation to the world had occurred. It claimed that belief in God's self-revelation in the person and fate of Jesus was necessary for salvation. In Kant's opinion this version of Christianity could never form the basis of a universal religion, for a special revelation taking place at a particular time in a particular place, to a particular people, is not open to universal assent:

> scriptural texts that seem to contain such a specific revelation... have to do with ecclesiastical faith...which requires historical evidence that not everyone can share,' whereas, 'religion (because it is based on moral concepts) must be complete in itself and free from doubt.[120]

As should be clear from the above, Kant favours a universal religion, which, on the very grounds that it is to be universal, cannot be bound to the historical contingencies of the Christian faith. The veneration of Christ as the ultimate figure through whom alone salvation is to be gained, as God incarnate, needs to be dispensed with for the sake of universal religion. Kant's reasons, therefore, for removing aspects central to Christian theology are based upon his efforts to make possible a universal religion. Given that this is the case, we can appreciate why he offers interpretations of theodicy, revelation, grace, the kingdom of God and salvation which do not concentrate upon Jesus Christ.

The desire to formulate a religion which has universal validity lies at the very heart of Kant's moral theology, and cannot therefore be left aside in any consideration of that theology in relation to Christian faith in the historical Jesus. In fact, Kant gives a specific account of the relationship between Christianity as historical faith and universal religion, the main aspects of which I shall now examine briefly.

According to Kant, the Christian Church 'contained within itself, from its first beginning, the seed and the principles of the objective unity of the true and *universal* religious faith.'[121] In other words, Christianity had the roots of the true, universal religion within it. In fact, 'Christianity's first intention was really no other than to introduce a pure religious faith, over which no conflict of opinion can prevail.'[122] And to some extent it succeeded. Placing its main emphasis upon the *moral disposition,*[123] Christianity effected a thoroughgoing revolution in doctrines of faith, thereby instituting a 'change of faith.'[124] Unfortunately, 'what was to serve for the introduction of this faith was made the foundation of a universal world religion.'[125] That is, the historical embodiment of the the pure religious faith came, wrongly, to be valued of more importance than the pure religious faith which it embodied.

Kant distinguishes between the historical embodiment and the pure religious faith which lies within it by referring to the former as the Christian faith, and the latter as the Christian religion.[126] Earlier in this chapter it was suggested that Kant is not an apologist for the Christian faith.[127] In light of the above one might now argue that although this is the case, he can be an apologist of his own interpretation of the Christian religion, which is destined to be the world religion. Moreover, it is the Christian religion rather than the Christian faith which is the moral religion.[128] Therefore, when Kant says that 'Christianity is not the culmination of religion, it is only its historical beginning,' we can assume that he is referring to the Christian faith as distinct from the Christian religion. And when he suggests that Christianity is best suited to become the world religion, or even that it is intended to be the universal world religion,[129] we can assume that he means the Christian religion, free of its historical embodiment. The Christian faith will eventually evolve towards a purer, higher, form that can dispense with the historical and become the pure religion of reason: 'historical faith...will itself cease and pass over into a pure religious faith equally obvious to the whole world.'[130] Therefore, the historical faith built up around Jesus Christ will, in Kant's opinion, eventually decline in order that true religious faith, which is alone universal, may be fully established.

However, to say this is not to deny a place to Jesus in pure religious faith. On the contrary, since Christianity was necessary to introduce the true religion of reason, it is inevitable that Jesus should be its first teacher.[131] Kant says that everything pertaining to the true religion of reason was 'first revealed when it was *publicly* taught and made the symbol of a wholly new religious epoch.'[132] It was Jesus who publicly taught, and therefore initiated the true religion:

> Let us suppose there was a teacher of whom an historical record (or, at least, a widespread belief which is not basically disputable) reports that he was the first to expound publicly a pure and searching religion, comprehensible to the whole world (and thus natural). His teachings, as preserved to us, we can in this case test for ourselves. Suppose further, we find that he made this universal religion of reason the highest and indispensable condition of every religious faith whatsoever...we cannot deny to him himself the prestige due the one who called men to union in this church.[133]

Elsewhere, Kant also implies that Jesus' task involved the overthrow of institutional religion.[134] He believes that Jesus was the teacher of the true religion, valid for all the world, but also that he had an authority and worth which requires no scholarly certification:

> Here then is a complete religion, which can be presented to all men comprehensibly and convincingly through their own reason; while the possibility and even the necessity of its being an archetype for us to imitate (so far as men are capable of that imitation) have, be it noted, been made evident by means of an example without either the truth of those teachings nor the authority and the worth of the Teacher requiring any external certification(for which scholarship or miracles, which are not matters for everyone, would be required).[135]

Appeals to other means of confirmation of the truth of Jesus' teachings are inappropriate to the religion of reason, which 'must be comprehensible and, without any expenditure of learning, convincing to all men.'[136] In particular, one does not need to appeal to Church teaching about Christ in order to verify them. And just as he distinguishes the Christian religion from the Christian faith, so Kant distinguishes 'the *teachings of Christ* from the *report* we have of those teachings.'[137] According to Kant, the essential and most excellent part of the teachings of Christ is:

> that righteousness is the sum of all religion and that we ought to seek it with all our might, having faith (that is, an unconditional trust) that God will then supplement our efforts and supply the good that is not in our power.[138]

The difference between this teaching, and a faith in a special revelation as essential to true religious belief, highlights Kant's divergence from the Christian faith. Historical tenets of faith have no bearing upon the true end of religion, which is a life well-pleasing to God, a life which has been exemplified in the teaching and practice of Jesus.

Christian Scripture also has a role to play in the foundation of universal religion. Although belief in Scripture is not essential for salvation, Kant finds it fortunate that the Bible contains 'the purest moral doctrine of religion in its completeness,'[139] and acts therefore as 'the organ of universal inner rational religion.'[140] In fact, 'all that we need concerning the objective rule of our behaviour is adequately revealed to us (through reason and Scripture), and this revelation is at the same time comprehensible to every man.'[141]

From the above distinction between Christianity as historical faith and universal religion the most important points can be summarised as follows. Firstly, Kant advocates the Christian religion, which consists in a moral faith based upon reason, and is devoid of historical and ecclesiastical contingencies. Such a religion can be valid for the whole world and for all time. He rejects ecclesiastical Christianity, which might otherwise be referred to as historical faith. In his opinion, ecclesiastical religion makes the inessentials of faith, such as historical revelation, dogmas, ceremonies and belief in miracles, into the essentials of correct belief. Secondly, he favours Jesus, who was the first teacher of true religion, and believes in the universal validity of the religion initiated by him. He has a great respect for the teaching of Jesus as found in the Bible and even favours an alternative to ecclesiastical religion based upon such teaching. However, he objects to the veneration, or worship, of Jesus as redeemer, saviour, or as God incarnate, as is advocated by historical faith. Thirdly, he believes that the New Testament can be used to instruct people in true, inner and universal religion, even though he rejects the idea of a faith based upon belief in Scripture as a means to salvation.

This portrayal of the distinction between pure religious faith and Christianity as historical faith reaches the heart of the true relationship between Kant's theology and Christian theology. The theology which Kant advocates is based neither upon a faith in Jesus as God incarnate, nor upon a faith in the historical Jesus. But in Kant's opinion, it is based upon what lies at the core of Christianity as a historical faith, namely a pure moral religion. It is inevitable from the perspective of Christian theology, which for the majority of Christians is based upon faith in the historical Jesus, that Kant's theology will be found to be unacceptable. Kant removes so much of what lies at the heart of the Christian faith that it is hard to see what remains. In fact, it is worth asking whether Kant's 'core' Christianity contains anything that is specifically Christian. He says that Christianity has true religion within it, and that Jesus is the first teacher of true religion, but does that true religion itself contain anything specifically Christian? For instance, in his reworking of the doctrine of the Trinity,[142] so that the Christ of the Christian tradition is no longer central to it, the concept of God which remains does not seem to retain anything that is explicitly Christian. In fact it may be that Kant's 'core' Christianity is so radically different from the Christian faith that the product is no longer Christian.

There certainly is a sense in which Kant seems to want the best of all worlds. He wants to be able to cast off as much of ecclesiastical Christianity as he sees fit, and retain just those features which meet with his approval. In a revealing statement Kant himself implies that from the point of view of 'ecclesiastical ortho-doxy'[143] he would be classed as an unbeliever: 'Now when, as usually happens, a church proclaims itself to be the one church universal...he who refuses to acknowledge its (peculiar) ecclesiastical faith is called by it an *unbeliever* and is hated whole-heartedly.'[144] On the other hand, from his lack of tolerance for 'ecclesiastical orthodoxy' it is clear that he would not value its opinion. Might one therefore conclude, from Kant's own perspective, that regardless of the judgement of 'ecclesiastical orthodoxy,' his interpretation of pure religious faith is a version of Christianity, and might therefore fall within the boundaries of Christian theology? Might one say that Kant's version of Christianity and of Christ is heretical, but that he is also in some sense clinging to the Christian tradition? Interestingly, many scholars have assumed that Kant did consider himself a Christian.[145] And certainly, if one thinks back to the separatists mentioned in Chapter II, who 'consider themselves religious people and indeed Christians, though they take as their code not the Bible, but only the precepts of an inward Christianity dwelling in us from eternity'[146] the similarities with Kant's own perspective are once again evident. It is also worth noting that if one were to follow Erasmus' suggestion as outlined in Chapter III, that 'the man who has embraced Christ in the innermost feelings of his heart, and who emulates him by his pious deeds'[147] is truly Christian, then despite the differences between Erasmus and Kant with regard to incarnation and redemption through Christ, it is plausible that on Erasmus' own account Kant might still be worthy of the title Christian. In fact, it is possible that even though Erasmus accepted divine incarnation and redemption through Christ, he did not consider belief in either of these tenets of faith as central to being a Christian.

However, quite separate from the question of Kant's allegiance or not to the Christian tradition, there are serious problems with his attempt to establish a universal religion whilst extrapolating it from the Christian faith.

Firstly, Kant's belief that there was an eternal essence living throughout all of the historical and doctrinal changes within Christianity, reflected as much as anything an Enlightenment belief about eternal truths of reason. Today, things look entirely different. As Hick rightly suggests, the very idea of an essence of Christianity, and a search for that essence, is not the most appropriate approach to the issue of Christian identity. For, in an important sense, Christianity does not have an unchanging essence; it is not a static entity but a living strand of history, continuously growing into the future.[148]

This in fact leads into the second question which concerns the notion that one can remove the essence of Christianity from its historical, and, as we are most aware today, from its cultural framework. We can no longer ignore the historical and cultural contingencies which mould the faiths of the world. Kant's belief that there could be a religious essence independent of its historical and cultural setting was simply mistaken. It was a false belief which he shared with most other Enlightenment thinkers.

The third and most important question relates to Kant's claim that, although there are numerous faiths, there is only one true religion. On occasion he even gestured towards a time when there would be 'only one shepherd and one flock.'[149] Regardless of how it may have appeared in Kant's time, such a claim cannot go unchallenged today. Critics agree that there are a variety of faiths in the world, but vehemently deny that there is one true religion. There is an even greater problem with Kant's claim that true religion is to be found within the Christian faith. He seems to have been prey to the conviction, which was paramount in the eighteenth and nineteenth centuries, of the superiority of Christianity over other world faiths. His allegiance to the Christian religion as valid for the world, to Christ as a teacher of people in general, and to Christian Scripture as the text for universal religion all imply this. Admittedly, such a belief was almost inevitable during his period of history, when there was either total ignorance, or very little knowledge of other world faiths. It was also inevitable as a result of his own upbringing and cultural setting. However, today, given a much wider appreciation of the variety of religious belief in the world, it is more difficult for Christians to cling to Christianity as the world religion. Theologians such as Hick want to abandon the myths of Christian uniqueness and superiority,[150] and maintain instead, that the Christian faith is one among many, and Jesus, although central to Christian theology, is nevertheless one among many in a way that perhaps even Kant would not allow.

Finally, it is also unfortunate that as a result of the hypocrisy Kant had experienced in religious institutions, he defines his true religion in exclusively moral terms. The difficulty with this is that someone else might just as easily define true religion in terms of its social function or in terms of its psychological effect.

The majority of Christian theologians and philosophers will conclude from this that Kant's attempt to establish a religion valid for the whole world, based upon pure religious faith, does not succeed. To a great extent this is due to the period of history in which his ideas were formulated. The very conviction that it is possible to advocate a religion for the world seems itself to be a product of Enlightenment rationalism which no longer holds in the twentieth century. But the failure of Kant's project is also due to his desire to found such a religion upon what he thought was best in Christianity.

However, in my opinion, despite his failure to establish a universal religion valid for the whole world, some of the things Kant has to say about pure religious faith show remarkable insight into religious life. In fact, although Kant neither sought, nor wanted to separate his version of pure religious faith from Christianity, I would suggest that if we view his statements about true religion as referring to religion in general, rather than to his own version of Christianity, then they uncover universal features of the religious life. In order to illustrate this I now return to the questions posed by Kant's attempt to establish a universal religion whilst extrapolating it from Christianity.

Firstly, it is worth noting that true religion for Kant amounts to a way of life, based upon a practical, moral faith, rather than the definable entity that his claims about the 'Christian religion' imply. Moreover, in Kant's opinion, the only true doctrine of religion is 'the doctrine of the purity of conscience in faith and of the good transformation of our lives.'[151] There is nothing in this that is exclusively Christian, but it does involve faith, which for Kant means 'unconditional trust in God.'

Secondly, if the essence of religion can be considered in such practical terms, then it does not involve the historical or ecclesiastical particularities of 'a religion' such as doctrines and tenets of belief, but rather, a practical way of life, based upon 'faith.' It is not a theoretical belief system built up around doctrine, but a life lived.

Thirdly, and most significantly, although Kant says that there is only one true religion, he nowhere implies that Christianity is the <u>only</u> faith which encompasses such a true religion. He suggests instead, that this religion can be found within the different faiths,[152] even though Christianity is the best expression of it: 'Although there are indeed different varieties of belief in divine revelation and its statutory teachings, which cannot spring from reason...there are not different religions. Of these forms Christianity, as far as we know, is the most adequate.'[153] He also says that pure rational faith really constitutes the religion in every faith,[154] and implies that every religion can contain elements of the one true religion within it.[155] In light of these claims, there is no reason to suggest that Kant's account of pure religious faith entails Christian exclusivism, even though he inevitably favours Christianity over other religions.

Kant's tendency to define true religion in purely moral terms is regrettable, but it is interesting to note that any religion which is worthy of the name is inseparable form a morally worthy life. As a prerequisite for such a life, Kant points to the 'good transformation of our lives.' This is something which is integral to most, if not all, of the world faiths, namely the stress upon transformation of the individual soul. Such transformation for Kant involves overcoming 'self-interest, the god of this world' in response to the ultimate claim of the moral law upon us.[156] This sounds similar to what Hick refers to in his latest work as the transformation from self-centredness to Reality-centredness.[157] However, as Hick has made clear, we must allow for the transformation of human existence going on in various ways and varying degrees throughout the world, not only within the borders of our own traditions.[158]

Hopefully, each of these responses to the problems posed illustrates the potential of Kant's claims when they are considered as applying to religion in general rather than to a specific religion. Moreover, some of Kant's other claims about the preconditions for universal religion also contain revealing suggestions. Kant's effort to move away from the centrality of Christ might be entirely worthwhile from the point of view of world religions. Hick has called for a 'Copernican revolution in our understanding of the religions.'[159] The traditional dogma has been that Christianity is the centre of the universe of faiths, with all the other religions revolving at various removes around the revelation in Christ and being graded according to their nearness to or distance from it. Hick suggests that it would now be more realistic to make the shift from Christianity at the centre to God at the centre, and to see both our own and the other great world religions as revolving around the same divine reality, even if they have a different name for it than God. This is precisely what Kant's statements about true religion can achieve, if they can resist the tendency to cling to Christianity. On at least one occasion Kant does resist such a tendency, and says that:

> If we take what is universal in religion and so is common to all religions, namely pleasing God through the disposition of our hearts, carrying out His holy law, and hoping that in His goodness God will supplement our weakness, then there is no reason why every individual should not follow the religion of his forefathers; so long as he does not believe that he can please God more by the *cultus* of his own than by that of any other religion, it can do him no harm. Let the observations be what they may, so long as they are not regarded as anything more than a means of awakening within us a godly disposition; but let them in themselves be regarded as a service to God and serious harm ensues. And under such conditions one religion is a harmful as another.[160]

Here Kant refers to what is 'universal in religion,' rather than speaking of 'one true religion.' He seems to be acknowledging the possibility that within each of the world religions there exists one basic religious factor, a human response to God. And it is fascinating that Kant could as easily be speaking from a personal perspective which is Hindu or other, rather than Christian, in this passage. In fact, this statement could have come from one of today's theologians who seek not to dissolve the plurality of faiths into one religion, but rather to recognise the central ultimate reality of all religion, and the human religious response to that ultimate reality, in each of the different world faiths. If Kant is being sincere, and bearing in mind his adamant defence of sincerity in all things we must assume that he is, then he is acknowledging the possibility of a unifying thread amidst the diversity of the world faiths, namely, that to which they respond in obedience and faith. This is remarkable in light of the almost total ignorance concerning religious pluralism in Kant's day.

For Kant, just as there is only **one** true religion, so there is only **one** God.[161] But, if he were to entertain the possibility of true religion as life lived in response to the demand of ultimate transcendent reality upon us, then his interpretation of true religiosity might in fact be close to what is required by Hick's Copernican revolution in our understanding of the religions. Hence, Kant's own Copernican revolution in theology might have the framework for a theology of the world religions within it.

CONCLUSION

This chapter has been concerned with the relationship between Kant's theology and Christian theology. In the first part I demonstrated that accounts which attempt to interpret Kant's stance with regard to incarnational theology as either docetic or Arian are mistaken. I outlined Kant's mythological interpretation of the incarnation whilst also revealing his profound respect for Jesus Christ, who in his view was solely human. Similarities between Kant's interpretation and that of the twentieth century Christian theologian, John Hick, were also highlighted, in an effort to point out that both Kant and Hick offer an alternative to incarnational theology which might still be classed as Christian.

In the second part I considered the objection that Kant fails to appreciate the significance of the life, death and resurrection of Jesus Christ for Christian theology. Reflection upon the central themes of Kant's own theology revealed his neglect for the historical Jesus, at the same time as highlighting Hick's allegiance to the historical Jesus. However, I then pointed out that, viewed from Kant's own perspective, it was not a matter of neglecting the historical Jesus, but rather, of removing the historical Jesus from the centre of theological reflection. His reason for doing so was influenced by a desire to formulate a universal religion. Kant wanted a world religion valid for all times, based upon reason and moral principles. Christianity, Jesus and Christian Scripture all play a central role in his efforts to formulate such a religion. However, it is doubtful whether the religion Kant advocates, even though in his opinion it is the religion of Christ, fits with most people's conception of Christian theology.

I have pointed to the problems with Kant's assumption that he can simply get to the essence, or core of Christianity, and take from it those moral elements which are the basis upon which he will formulate his own version of true religion. In fact, Kant's attempt to achieve a universal religion fails partly because of his allegiance to particulars of the Christian tradition of theology. However, I have suggested that although Kant fails to establish a universal moral religion, he succeeds in pointing to universal features of the religious life. In fact, Kant's account of pure religious faith offers great potential for a version of theology which bases itself upon the assumption that there is a uniting thread in each of the world religions. Integral to such an approach would be an emphasis upon ultimate transcendent reality rather than christocentrism, the sincere religious response to that reality, and individual transformation. Of course, a version of theology based upon these fundamental aspects of the religious life would no longer be Christian, but neither would it be a threat to Christian theology; and it would have universal appeal. In the concluding appraisal which follows, I will show that in his final years Kant's preoccupation with morality diminishes, and his tendency to cling to Christianity disappears completely, with the result that his theology finally focuses upon a unified religious theism.

ENDNOTES

1 Citation taken from *The Documents of the Christian Church*, ed., H. Bettenson, O.U.P., 1988 edition, p.26.

2 For instance, J. Macquarrie in *Jesus Christ in Modern Thought*, S.C.M. Press, 1990, V.A. McCarthy in *Quest for a Philosophical Jesus*, Mercer U.P., 1986, and B.M. Reardon in *Kant as Philosophical Theologian*, Macmillan Press, 1988.

3 KW VI, 60-61; *Religion*, Book II, Section I, p.54. Kant even refers to the idea of mankind in its complete moral perfection as 'God's Word.'

4 Ibid., 61; Ibid., pp.54-55.

5 Ibid., 62; Ibid., p.55.

6 Ibid; Ibid., p.56.

7 KW IV, 408; *Groundwork*, p.76.

8 *The Sovereignty of Good*, Routledge and Kegan Paul, 1971 edition, p.30.

9 *Kant as Philosophical Theologian*, p.200, note 4.

10 *Jesus Christ in Modern Thought*, p.191.

11 *Erasmus, His Theology of the Sacraments*, M.E. Bratcher, 1970, p.56.

12 *Explorations in Theology*, p.22.

13 There are grounds for taking issue not only with Kant's preoccupation with reason, but also with his whole conception of rationality. Recent feminist critiques have pointed to some of the problems with the dichotomy Kant raises between reason and emotion. However, there still remains great potential for a future critique of Kant's entire philosophy and rational moral theology.

14 KW III, 247; First *Critique*, A315/B372.

15 Ibid., 248; Ibid., A318/B374.

16 Ibid., 384; Ibid., A569/B 597.

17 Ibid.

18 Ibid; Ibid., A570/B598.

19 Ibid., 542; Ibid., A838/B866—A839/B867.

20 KW VI, 60; *Religion*, Book II, Section I, p.54.

21 Ibid.

22 KW III, 384; First *Critique*, A569/B597—A570/B598.

23 KW VI, 61; *Religion*, Book II, Section I, p.55.

24 Ibid., 65; Ibid., p.58, note.

25 Ibid.

26 KW IV, 357; *Prolegomena*, p.222.

27 Although space does not permit a detailed treatment of it here, the distinction between idea and ideal is also crucial to Kant's critique of the traditional arguments for the existence of God. See KW III, 383-392; First *Critique*, A568/B596-A583/B611.

28 KW VI, 61; *Religion*, Book II, Section I, p.54.

29 Ibid., 65; Ibid., p.59, note.

30 Ibid., 62; Ibid., p.55.

31 Ibid.

32 Ibid.

33 Ibid., 63; Ibid., p.57.

34 Ibid., 64; Ibid.

35 KW VII, 39; *Conflict*, p.67.

36 Ibid.

37 Ibid.

38 KW VI, 119; *Religion*, Book III, Division One, vii., pp.109-110.

39 Ibid., 60; Ibid., Book II, Section I, p.54.

40 See pp. 83ff, 105ff.

41 KW VI, 62; *Religion*, Book II, Section I, p.56.

42 See J. Hick, "Jesus and the World Religions," in *The Myth of God Incarnate*, ed., J. Hick, S.C.M., 1977, p.176, and *The Second Christianity*, S.C.M., 1983 edition, p.28.

43 See Macquarrie, *Jesus Christ in Modern Thought*, pp.97-122.

44 KW VI, 128-9; *Religion*, Book III, Division Two, p.120.

45 *Lectures on Ethics*, pp.109-110.

46 KW IV, 408; *Groundwork*, p.76.

47 *Jesus Christ in Modern Thought*, p.199.

48 See for instance, *Lectures on Ethics*, p.9.

49 Ibid., p.111.

50 See p.125.

51 KW VIII, 338; "The End of all Things," pp.82-83.

52 Ibid., Ibid., p.83.

53 KW VI, 82; *Religion*, Book II, Section Two, p.77.

54 *Jesus Christ in Modern Thought*, p.237.

55 KW VI, 80; *Religion*, Book II, Section Two, p.74.

56 Ibid.

57 Ibid., 60; Ibid., Book II, Section One, p.54.

58 Ibid., 65; Ibid., p.59.

59 See pp.83ff. and 105ff.

60 KW VII, 58-9; *Conflict*, pp.105-7.

61 See for instance *The Myth of God Incarnate*, *The Truth of God Incarnate*, ed., M.Green, Hodder and Stoughton, 1977, *Incarnation and Myth: The Debate Continued*, ed., M.Goulder, S.C.M., 1979.

62 See "Jesus and the World Religions," pp.167-185, "Is There a Doctrine of the Incarnation?" in *Incarnation and Myth: The Debate Continued*, pp.47-51, and "Jesus—The Centre of Christianity" in *The Second Christianity*, pp.15-33, and 92.

63 *The Second Christianity*, p.19.

64 It is interesting to note that Hick generally acknowledges the influence of Kant upon his own thought, although he does not specifically refer to Kant in his account of Jesus.

65 See "Jesus—The Centre of Christianity."

66 See pp.34ff.

67 K. Wojtyla, "Job" in The *Collected Plays and Writings on Theatre*, transl. B. Taborski, California U.P., 1987, pp.19-74.

68 See p.67.

69 See "Jesus and the World Religions," p.185.

70 *The Second Christianity*, p.16. Cf. pp.57-9.

71 See p.76.

72 *The Second Christianity*, p.172.

73 See pp.61-62.

74 See *Theology of Hope*, transl. J.W.Leitch, SCM, 1967.

75 Ibid., p.165.

76 Ibid., p.192.

77 *The Second Christianity*, p.101.

78 Ibid., p.24. Cf., pp.26, 30.

79 See esp. pp.102ff and 118ff.

80 KW VI, 72; *Religion*, Book II, Section One, p.66.

81 *The Second Christianity*, p..23. Cf., pp. 21, 99.

82 Ibid., p.21.

83 Ibid., p.100.

84 KW VI, 74-5; Cf. 76; *Religion*, Book II, Section One, p.69. Cf., pp. 68, 71.

85 Ibid., 83; Ibid., Book II, Section Two, p.78.

86 Ibid.

87 Ibid., 128-9; Ibid., Book III, Division Two, pp.119-120.

88 KW VII, 39; *Conflict*, p.67.

89 *The Second Christianity*, p.23.

90 "Jesus and the World Religions," p.172. See also, *The Second Christianity*, p.23.

91 Ibid., p.35.

92 *The Second Christianity*, p.43.

93 Ibid., p.39.

94 See p.125.

95 *Erasmus: His Theology of the Sacraments*, p.65.

96 *Borderlands*, p.71.

97 KW VI, 135. Cf. 102; *Religion*, Book III, Division Two, p.126. Cf., p.94.

98 Ibid., 127. Cf. 106, 131 136, 163; Ibid., p.118. Cf., pp.97, 122, 126, note, 151.

99 See esp. pp.73, 80.

100 KW VI, 114; *Religion*, Book III, Division I, vii., p.105.

101 Ibid., 112. Cf. 122; Ibid., vi., p.103. Cf. p.113.

102 Ibid., 132; Ibid., Book III, Division Two, p.123, note.

103 Ibid., 111; Ibid., Division One, vi., p.101.

104 Ibid; Ibid., p.102.

105 Ibid., 102-3; Ibid., v., p.94.

106 Ibid., 115; Ibid., vii., p.105.

107 Ibid., 103; Ibid., v., p.94.

108 Ibid., 105; Ibid., p.96.

109 KW VII, 49; *Conflict*, p.87.

110 KW VI, 121; *Religion*, vii., p.112.

111 Ibid., 120; Ibid., p.110.

112 Ibid., 48; Ibid., p.85.

113 Ibid., 49; Ibid., p.87.

114 Ibid., 50; Ibid., p.89.

115 KW X, 170; Zweig, *Kant's Correspondence*, p.82 (Letter to J.C. Lavater, April 28, 1775).

116 See KW VI, 160; *Religion*, Book IV, Part One, Section One, p.148.

117 KW VII, 62; *Conflict*, p.113.

118 KW VI, 166; *Religion*, Book IV, Part One, Section Two, p.153: 'one is obliged to believe that "every Christian must be a Jew whose Messiah has come".'

119 Ibid., 129; Ibid., Book III, Division Two, p.120.

120 KW VII, 44; *Conflict*, p.77. Cf. KW VI, 109, 145; *Religion*, Book III, Division One, vi., pp.100, 136.

121 KW VI, 125; *Religion*, Book III, Division Two, p.116

122 Ibid., 131; Ibid., Book III, Division Two, p.122

123 Ibid., 126; Ibid., p.116

124 Ibid., 130; Ibid., p.120

125 Ibid., 131. Cf. 165-6; Ibid., p.122. Cf. p.153

126 This distinction fits entirely with Kant's acceptance of the narrower, or moral sphere of religion, without the wider (historical and ecclesiastical): Ibid., 12; Ibid., Preface to the Second Edition, p.11.

127 See p.161-162.

128 See p.80.

129 KW VIII, 339; "The End of All Things," p.84.

130 KW VI, 135; *Religion*, Book III, Division Two, p.126, note.

131 Ibid., 112. Cf. 167; Ibid., Book III, Division One, vi., p.103. Cf. p.155.

132 Ibid., 145; Ibid., General Observation, p.136.

133 Ibid., 158; Ibid., Book IV, Part One, Section One, p.146.

134 Ibid., 81; Ibid., Book II, Section Two, p.76, note.

135 Ibid., 162; Ibid., Book IV, Part One, Section One, p.150.

136 Ibid., 163; Ibid., p.151.

137 KW X, 168; Zweig, *Kant's Correspondence*, p.80 (Letter to J.C. Lavater).

138 Ibid., 171; Zweig, *Kant's Correspondence*, p.83

139 KW VI, 107; *Religion*, Book III, Division One, v., p.98.

140 KW VII, 64; *Conflict*, p.117.

141 KW VI, 144; *Religion*, Book III, General Observation, p.135.

142 Ibid., 141-2. Cf. 145-7; Ibid., Book III, General Observation, pp.132-3. Cf. 136-8, and note.

143 Ibid, 109; Ibid, Book III, Division One, v., p.100.

144 Ibid., 108; Ibid., p.99.

145 To give some examples: Lucien Goldmann suggests that Kant 'frequently calls himself a Christian,' in *Immanuel Kant*, transl. R.Black, N.L.B., 1971. p.193. Don Cupitt maintains that Kant considered himself a Christian, in *The Nature of Man*, Sheldon, 1979, p. 53. Stephen Palmquist has argued that Kant was a Christian philosopher in "Immanuel Kant: A Christian Philosopher?," *Faith and Philosophy* 6, 1989.

146 KW VII, 74; *Conflict*, p.137. See p.68.

147 See p.125.

148 *The Second Christianity*, p.72.

149 KW VII, 53; *Conflict*, p.95.

150 See for instance, "The Non-Absoluteness of Christianity," in *The Myth of Christian Uniqueness*, S.C.M., 1987.

151 KW X, 168-9; Zweig, *Kant's Correspondence*, p.80 (Letter to Lavater).

152 KW VI, 108; *Religion*, Book III, Division One, v., p.98.

153 KW VII, 36; *Conflict*, p.61.

154 KW VI, 153; *Religion*, Book IV, p.140.

155 Ibid., 156. Cf. 112, 115, 123; Ibid., Book IV, Part One, p.144. Cf.pp.103, 106, 113, note.

156 Ibid., 161; Ibid., Book IV, Part One, Section One, p.149.

157 *An Interpretation of Religion*, Macmillan, 1989, pp.14, 45.

158 Ibid., p.380.

159 *The Second Christianity*, p.82.

160 *Lectures on Ethics*, p.110.

161 KW VI, 104; *Religion*, Book III, Division One, v., p.95.

CONCLUDING THEOLOGICAL REFLECTIONS: THE *OPUS POSTUMUM*

Before entering into my concluding appraisal of Kant's theology it is useful to draw together the threads of the exposition carried out in the previous four chapters.

Chapter I shows that even though Kant rules out theoretical knowledge of God's existence, his attitude is very close to that of negative theology, and he still offers a positive metaphysic resulting in the moral argument for the existence of God. Kant's conception of God is predominantly in moral terms, and God's relation to humankind is through the moral law. The works of Kant specifically referred to in this chapter are his three *Critiques*. From a closer analysis of these works it becomes clear that, as far as Kant is concerned, theology can no longer present itself as a factual science providing knowledge of God by theoretical argument; the only kind of theology he can allow is a practical or moral one, and he conceives of this theology in its most developed form as ethico-theology. As a result, Kant proposes a theology within the bounds of practical reason and morality.

Chapter II widens one's conception of Kant's theology somewhat, as his works specifically dealing with religious doctrines, namely the *Religion* and the *Conflict*, are brought into consideration. Kant is critical of church dogma, yet at the same time he is convinced of the rationality of the basic principles of Christian belief and uses his moral theology to support their rationality. This chapter also illustrates the closeness of Kant's approach to that of the philosophical theologian, when he offers extensive treatment of religious doctrines, and his own positive appraisal of them.

In Chapter III it is made clear that freedom, as much as reason and morality, is essential to Kant's theology. It becomes increasingly obvious that Kant's moralism and rationalism are tied to the significance he places upon individual responsibility before God. He thinks in terms of moral progress and personal salvation, and though strongly ethical, his moral theology is also humane in its recognition of human sinfulness. However, what is much more revealing is the personal character of Kant's theology, which is strikingly similar to that of the Christian humanist, Erasmus of Rotterdam.

Chapter IV examines the specific relationship between Kant's theology and Christian theology. Kant's divergence from the official teaching of the Christian Church with regard to belief in divine incarnation and the significance of the historical Jesus is evident. He offers his own version of Christianity as pure religious faith, and although his version is not incompatible with Christian theology, it certainly falls short of most people's conception of the Christian faith. In fact, Kant's version of pure religious faith is more appealing when considered as an appraisal of basic features of religion in general, rather than a complete exposition of a specific religion.

My concluding task is to demonstrate that in his final years Kant openly acknowledges the theology which has been implicit to the works of his entire lifetime. In order to do this I must turn to an examination of his last, but uncompleted treatise, the notes from which have been published and appropriately named the *Opus Postumum,*[1] or posthumous work.

Although I shall refer to the *Opus Postumum* as a 'work', it is important to bear in mind that this 'work' is not easy to understand or interpret, since it consists of repetitious notes (written by Kant and originally intended for publication, but pre-empted by the author's death) which often appear to be stating contradictory claims, and sometimes seem totally unintelligible. It is not really surprising that such notes should include contradicting lines of thought, given that Kant, like many other authors, formulated his own opinions by testing his ideas against alternative views.[2] It is however unfortunate that, as a result, there is much debate concerning exactly what Kant is trying to argue in these notes.

Most scholars interested in the religious implications of this work have been concerned with either defending or rejecting the idea that Kant's stance in relation to the idea of God is a realist one. Vaihinger, who rejects this idea, argues that Kant's reflections upon God in the *Opus Postumum* amount to no more than the approval of the idea of God as a necessary fiction.[3] Although I have already rejected the plausibility of a necessary fiction to explain Kant's conception of God in Chapters I and II,[4] it is necessary to deal with this idea again here because of the ambiguity of the statements made by Kant in the *Opus Postumum.* Vaihinger's main reason for attributing an *'as-if'* notion of God to Kant are based upon Kant's treatment of two main questions, namely, 'What is God?' and 'Does God exist?' Vaihinger rightly points out that in answer to the question 'What is God?' Kant suggests that God is a 'thought entity' (ens rationis).[5] However, Vaihinger uses this notion of the 'thought entity' to come to the conclusion that for Kant, '"God" is an expedient, a necessary idea, and ideas are "heuristic fictions", As-if modes of approach'.[6] In answer to the question 'Does God exist?' Vaihinger also correctly refers to Kant's statement that 'God is not a substance outside of me'.[7] For Vaihinger, this statement is enough to convince us of the fictional nature of the idea of God as used by Kant.[8]

In my opinion, a most adequate exposition and defence of Kant's stance against non-realist, as well as reductionist, interpretations, has already been given by Erich Adickes.[9] In response to Vaihinger, and in an effort to remain loyal to Kant's realist stance, Adickes points out that in answer to the question 'What is God?' Kant is eager to deny the idea that God is a substance but only in the empirical understanding of this term, because God does not belong to the world of sense. Adickes does not deny that Kant views God as a thought entity, but he does deny that it follows from this that God is a fiction. It is quite natural that Kant should deny that God does not exist as a substance outside of me,[10] for any proof to the contrary would limit God to the world of sensible intuitions, when the truth is that the reality of God transcends our world of sensible limitations.[11] With regard to the question 'Does God exist?' Adickes suggests that Kant denies *only* theoretical knowledge of God's existence, whilst postulating the reality of God as undeniable in moral terms. Kant takes it as self-evident that God exists,[12] he rules out the possibility of proving the existence of God in a theoretical sense *only*. And to do so is simply to repeat the claims he has already made in the first *Critique*. In Adickes opinion, Kant's whole philosophical system has no purpose without the reality of God.[13]

I entirely agree with Adickes' defence of Kant's realism in the *Opus Postumum*, and acknowledge the necessity for such a defence. However, the attention which has been given to this issue,[14] whilst entirely worthwhile, has detracted from, or at least over-shadowed, the main concern of the theological portions of this work. For, as I will now show, it is in the *Opus Postumum* that Kant comes closest to realising that the philosophical system which has been the preoccupation of his life, has in fact been grounded in theism.

Despite so much controversy over the answers to the two questions mentioned above, there is no difficulty or ambiguity concerning Kant's overall intention in the theological sections of this work (written in the very last months of his life), which is to develop a system of 'transcendental philosophy' based upon the relations of God, the world, and humankind.[15] By this Kant means that it is possible to achieve a system in which the speculative, which is concerned with our knowledge of the world or nature, and the moral, which is concerned with God and human moral obligation in relation to God, are reconciled.[16] To fail to realise the significance of Kant's intention in this respect, is to miss the main point of the *Opus Postumum.*

However, it is important to note that the emphasis Kant gives to morality is now somewhat diminished. In fact, Adickes would go so far as to say that in the *Opus Postumum* Kant gives up the notion of a moral argument for the existence of God in favour of a belief in direct, personal experience of God.[17] I cannot agree with Adickes on this matter, since, as Professor George Schrader has shown,[18] Kant does restate the moral argument in the *Opus Postumum,*[19] and continues to avoid all subjectivity in morality and religion.[20] Yet it certainly is the case that in the *Opus Postumum* Kant reduces significantly the priority he had previously given to morality. Moreover, his tendency to cling to Christianity is entirely absent. The absence of references to Christianity does not, however, imply a decrease in Kant's preoccupation with theology. On the contrary, he repeatedly states that the highest principle in transcendental philosophy is the relation of God and the world.[21] He also maintains that these two principles are combined in the human subject.[22] In other words, the factor which involves both of these two realms is human nature, because it belongs to the sensible and the intelligible realms.[23] The world does not have equal status with God, rather, it exists in a relation of subordination.[24] And it follows from this that although human nature belongs to the intelligible world, given its joint basis in the sensible world, it must also be subordinate to God. Therefore, God must be the supreme principle in the completed system. Kant gives grounds for such an interpretation when he states that God is the highest ground of the transcendental philosophy,[25] and the Being to which all things belong.[26] In other words, God is the ground and source of both the intelligible and the sensible.

Kant even goes so far as to suggest that the system of transcendental philosophy is that according to which we 'see all things in God'. Unfortunately his claims to this effect raise all kinds of negative connotations, particularly in light of the fact that he refers to either Spinoza or Zoroaster when making them.[27] Yet, to Kant's credit, he points out that his notion of 'seeing all things in God' is far removed from the pantheist tendencies of Spinoza, who uses the notion of God to mean 'world soul'.[28] The similarity Kant sees between his own view and that of Spinoza is simply in terms of God as the source of unity in all things. And the same meaning applies to the references Kant makes to Zoroaster.[29] The emphasis in both cases is upon God as the unifying principle of all things, and it is for this reason only that Kant speaks in terms of 'seeing all things in God'. It is unfortunate that the name 'Zoroaster' has become associated, in theological and philosophical circles at least, with Nietzsche, and the supposed atheism that he advocated, and therefore that Kant's use of the name Zoroaster should conjure up negative images. It is not the Nietzschean notion of a world beyond good and evil at work here, but rather, the idea of evil and good as part of the whole, and once again the implication that all things are reconciled in God's system.[30]

The only real difficulty with regard to Kant's notion of 'seeing all things in God' concerns his failure to specify the way in which one is to understand the idea that God is the unifying principle of all things. Apart from pointing out that his notion is not a pantheist one which tries to see the world and God as one, Kant offers little guidance. One possible line of interpretation is that given by Reiner Wimmer in *Kants kritische Religionsphilosophie*.[31] Wimmer suggests that Kant's concept of God refers to a particular way of seeing the world, namely as a unity, and as a purposeful whole. In the Wittgensteinian sense of the word, it is a way of 'seeing-as'.[32] The notion of 'seeing all things in God' amounts to the acknowledgement of the unity and wholeness of life itself.[33]

Although I agree with Wimmer's stress upon the integral nature of the relationship between God and the meaningfulness of existence itself for Kant, I must differ from him on the basis that Kant's theological outlook amounts to more than the Wittgensteinian notion of 'seeing-as'. Amongst other things, such an interpretation once again falls into the danger of a non-realist account of Kant's theology. Against such an interpretation must be placed Kant's frequent references in the *Opus Postumum* to God as a Person.[34] Although to the very last Kant rules out personal, intimate communion with God, in favour of a God who far transcends our powers of recognition, he does want to be able to see God as the most perfect of all Beings, and it is as such a Supreme Being that God exists as the unifying principle of life itself.

Wimmer has, however, rightly recognised the fact that in the eventual working out of his system, Kant's transcendental philosophy becomes transcendental theology.[35] Kant admits as much when acknowledging that the highest questions concerning transcendental philosophy are the theological ones, and that the highest standpoint of the transcendental philosophy becomes that of transcendental theology.[36] Thus, Kant recognises not just that theology is integral to his system of transcendental philosophy, but also that the very nature of his system is theological.

In conclusion, from the above it is clear that in the *Opus Postumum* Kant is preoccupied with the central concerns of theology, namely, God, world and humankind, in his effort to develop an overall system of explanation for the meaning and purpose of existence. God, who is already the ground of the unity of nature, morality and end-purpose in Kant's system of theology, now becomes the key to his entire philosophy.[37] There can be no clearer indication of Kant's final realization that the goal which he has spent his entire life working towards, has its basis in God. And together with this, the theology which has always been present in his writings, if in certain cases less apparent, finally comes to the fore.

ENDNOTES

1 KW XXI-XXII. An English translation of this work by Eckart Förster and published by C.U.P. appeared in 1993.

2 See N. Kemp Smith, *A Commentary to Kant's Critique of Pure Reason*, Macmillan and Co., 1923, p.610.

3 See *The Philosophy of 'As-If'*, transl. C.K. Ogden, Kegan Paul, 1924. For a more recent appraisal of Kant's concept of God in the *Opus Postumum*, which also develops an interpretation along the same lines, see A. Cortina, "Die Auflösung des religiösen Gottesbegriffs im Opus postumum Kants", *Kant-Studien* 75, 1984.

4 See pp.19, 78f.

5 *The Philosophy of 'As-If'*, p.314.

6 Ibid., p.318.

7 Ibid., p.316. Cf KW XXI, 149, 145, 144, 153. KW XXII, 123.

8 Ibid., p.315.

9 See *Kant's Opus Postumum dargestellt und beurteilt von Erich Adickes,* Berlin, 1920.

10 Ibid., p.819.

11 Ibid., p.701. Cf. F.C. Copleston, *A history of Philosophy, Vol.VI,* Burns and Oates, 1960, pp. 387-388.

12 Ibid., p.681. Cf. pp.711, 721, 776.

13 Ibid., pp.720, 782. Cf. p.831, where Adickes refers to Kant's Weltanschauung, or philosophy of life.

14 Important questions also include whether Kant relinquishes his earlier opinions in the *Opus Postumum*, or comes close to advocating a version of the Ontological argument, as he had done in his pre-critical days.

15 KW XXI, 27, 70, 80, 82, 85, 94, 157. Cf. Kants *Opus Postumum dargestellt und beurteilt von Erich Adickes*, pp. 721, 723, 725.

16 Ibid., 58, 108, 126, 127.

17 *Kant's Opus Postumum dargestellt und beurteilt von Erich Adickes,* pp.846-849. See J.R. Silber, "The Ethical Significance of Kant's *Religion*" in *Religion*, p.lxv-lxvii, for a summary of Adickes' argument. Cf. Kemp Smith, *A Commentary to Kant's Critique of Pure Reason*, pp.610, 638.

18 G. Schrader, "Kant's Presumed Repudiation of the 'Moral Argument' in the Opus Postumum: an Examination of Adickes' Interpretation", *Philosophy* **July**, 1951. The same opinion has been shared by more recent writers, such as Keith Ward in *The Development of Kant's View of Ethics* and Bernard Reardon in *Kant as Philosophical Theologian.*

19 Ibid., p.236.

20 Ibid., p.241. Cf. p.237: Kant continues to insist that the existence of God, like the concept of freedom, can never be presented or proven directly, but only through the mediation of the moral law. See KW XXI, 30. However, he does seem to be seeking a more immediate connection between consciousness of moral obligation and belief in God, as Copleston has pointed out. See *A history of Philosophy*, Vol.VI, p.389.

21 KW XXI, 13, 18. Cf. 20

22 Ibid., 22. Cf. Kants *Opus Postumum dargestellt und beurteilt von Erich Adickes*, p.770.

23 Ibid., 48. Cf. *A history of Philosophy*, Vol.VI, pp.386, 390.

24 KW XXII, 62.

25 KW XXI, 151.

26 Ibid., 63.

27 See KW XXII, 61, and KW XXI, 78.

28 Ibid., 58, 59, 62. Cf.KW XXI, 19.

29 See KW XXI, 96. Cf. 156.

30 See Kants *Opus Postumum dargestellt und beurteilt von Erich Adickes*, p.731. Cf. p.728. It is worth noting that the references Kant makes to both Spinoza and Zoroaster are the result of his reading and comparison of his own views with those of Lichtenberg, whom he specifically mentions in passages such as: XXI, 96, XXII, 54-55. Cf. Kants *Opus Postumum dargestellt und beurteilt von Erich Adickes*, p.844.

31 *Kants kritische Religionsphilosophie,* Berlin, 1990.

32 Ibid., p.267.

33 Ibid., p.268.

34 KW XXI, 9-10, 17, 24, 45.

35 *Kants kritische Religionsphilosophie,* p.15. Cf. p.267.

36 KW XXII, 63.

37 KW XXI, 151.

SELECT BIBLIOGRAPHY

H.B. Acton, *Kant's Moral Philosophy*, Macmillan, 1970.

E. Adickes, *German Kantian Bibliography*, Burt Franklin, 1970 edition.

E. Adickes, *Kant's Opus Postumum dargestellt und beurteilt,* Berlin, 1920.

H.E. Allison, *Kant's Theory of Freedom*, C.U.P., 1990.

H.E. Allison, *Kant's Transcendental Idealism: An Interpretation and Defence*, Yale U.P., 1983.

U. Anacker, "Hoffnung—Kants Versuch, die Idee der Gerechtigkeit zu denken," *Philosophisches Jahrbuch* **88**, 1981.

S. Anderson, *Ideal und Singularität: Über die Funktion des Gottesbegriffes in Kants theoretischer Philosophie*, Berlin, 1983.

R. Attfield, *God and the Secular, a philosophical assessment of secular reasoning from Bacon to Kant*, University College Cardiff Press, 1978.

J.E. Atwell, *Ends and Principles in Kant's Moral Thought,* Martinus Nijhoff, 1986.

B. Aune, *Kant's Theory of Morals*, Princeton U.P., 1979.

P. Avis, ed., *The Threshold of Theology*, Marshall Pickering, 1988.

R.H. Bainton, *Erasmus of Christendom*, Charles Scribners Sons, 1969.

K. Barth, *Protestant Theology in the Nineteenth Century,* transl. B. Cozens and J. Bowden, S.C.M., 1972.

B. Bauch, *Luther und Kant*, Berlin, 1904.

O. Bayer, "Vernunftautorität und Bibelkritik in der Kontroverse zwischen Johann Georg Hamann und Immanuel Kant," *Neue Zeitschrift für systematische Theologie und religionsphilosophie* **28**, 1986.

M.G. Baylor, *Action and Person: Conscience in Late Scholasticism and The Young Luther*, Brill, 1977.

H. Beck, "Kant und die Scholastik heute," *Zeitschrift für philosophische Forschung* **12**, 1958.

L.W. Beck, *A Commentary on Kant's Critique of Practical Reason*, Chicago U.P., 1960.

L.W. Beck, *Early German Philosophy: Kant and his Predecessors,* Harvard U.P., 1969.

L.W. Beck, "Kant on Faith and Reason," *Times Literary Supplement* **4342**, 1986.

L.W. Beck, ed., *Proceedings of the 3rd International Kant Congress*, D. Reidel, 1972.

L.W. Beck, *Six Secular Philosophers*, The Free Press, 1966.

L.W. Beck, "Was Haben Wir von Kant zu lernen?," *Kant-Studien* **72**, 1981.

C.L. Becker, *The Heavenly City of the Eighteenth Century Philosophers,* Yale U.P., 1932.

F.C. Beiser, *The Fate of Reason: German Philosophy from Kant to Fichte*, Harvard U. P., 1987.

E. Bencivenga, *Kant's Copernican Revolution*, O.U.P., 1987.

R.J. Benton, *Kant's Second Critique and the Problem of Transcendental Arguments*, Martinus Nijhoff, 1977.

J.A. Bernstein, *Shaftesbury, Rousseau and Kant,* Associated University Presses Inc., 1980.

E. Bloch, *The Principle of Hope*, transl. N. Plaice et. al., Basil Blackwell, 1986.

A. Boboc, "Kants Kritizismus und die neue Bedeutung der Metaphysik," *Kant-Studien* **74**, 1983.

J. Bohatec, *Die Religionsphilosophie Kants in der "Religion innerhalb der Grenzen der bloßen Vernunft,"* Hildesheim, 1966.

W.J. Booth, *Interpreting the World*, Toronto U.P., 1986.

J.L. Bruch, *Kant: Lettres Sur La Morale et La Religion,* Aubier 1969.

J.L. Bruch, *La Philosophie religieuse de Kant,* Aubier, 1968.

P. Byrne, "Kant's Moral Proof of the Existence of God," *Scottish Journal of Theology* **32**, 1979.

B. Carnois, *The Coherence of Kant's Doctrine of Freedom*, transl. D. Booth, Chicago U.P., 1987.

E. Cassirer, *Kant's Life and Thought,* transl. J. Haden, Yale U.P., 1981.

E. Cassirer, *Rousseau, Kant, Goethe: Two Essays,* transl. J. Gutman et. al., Harper Torchbook, 1963.

H.W. Cassirer, *Grace and Law*, Wm.B. Eerdmans Publishing Co., 1988.

G. Clive, *The Romantic Enlightenment*, Meridian Books, 1960.

R.G. Collingwood, "Reason is Faith Cultivating Itself," *The Hibbert Journal* **26**, 1927.

J. Collins, *The Emergence of the Philosophy of Religion*, Yale U. P., 1986.

F.C. Copleston, *A History of Philosophy, Vol. VI,* Burns and Oates, 1960.

A. Cortina, "Die Auflösung des religiösen Gottesbegriffs im Opus postumum Kants," *Kant-Studien* **75**, 1984.

J.G. Cox, *The Will at the Crossroads*, University Press of America, 1984.

K.H. Crumbach, *Theologie in kritische Öffentlichkeit,* München, 1977.

D. Cupitt, *Taking Leave of God*, S.C.M., 1980.

D. Cupitt, *The Nature of Man*, Sheldon, 1979.

D. Cupitt, *The New Christian Ethics*, S.C.M., 1988.

F. Delekat, *Immanuel Kant*, Heidelberg, 1963.

G. Deleuze, *Kant's Critical Philosophy*, transl. H. Tomlinson, Athlone, 1984.

R.L. DeMolen, ed., *Erasmus Symposium of 1971*, Twayne, 1971.

A. Deneffe, *Kant und die katholische Wahrheit,* Freiburg, 1922.

M. Despland, *Kant on History and Religion*, McGill U.P., 1973.

A.R.C. Duncan, *Practical Reason and Morality,* T. Nelson and Sons, 1957.

L. Dupré, *A Dubious Heritage, Studies in the Philosophy of Religion After Kant*, Paulist Press, 1977.

K. Düsing, "Das Problem des höchsten Gutes in Kants praktischer Philosophie," *Kant-Studien* **62**, 1971.

K. Düsing, *Die Teleologie in Kant's Weltbegriff*, Bonn, 1968.

R. Eisler, *Kant-Lexikon*, Hildesheim, 1961.

A.E.A.E. Elschazli, *Kants kritische Philosophie und das Problem der Offenbarung,* Hamburg, 1970.

F.E. England, *Kant's Conception of God*, Allen and Unwin, 1929.

D. Erasmus, *Enchiridion*, transl. and ed., R Himelick, Indiana U.P. 1963.

D. Erasmus, *The Education of a Christian Prince*, transl. and ed., L.K. Born, Columbia U.P., 1963.

C.S. Evans, *Subjectivity and Religious Belief*, Christian U.P., 1978.

E.L. Fackenheim, "Immanuel Kant," in *Nineteenth Century Religious Thought in the West, Vol.I,* ed., N. Smart et al., C.U.P., 1985.

E.L. Fackenheim, "Kant and Radical Evil," *University of Toronto Quarterly* **23,** 1954.

E.L. Fackenheim, "Kant's Concept of History," *Kant-Studien* **48,** 1956-57.

J.N. Findlay, *Kant and the Transcendental Object*, O.U.P., 1981.

A. Flew, ed., *New Essays in Philosophical Theology*, S.C.M., 1955.

E. Förster, ed., *Kant's Transcendental Deductions*, Stanford U.P., 1989.

H. Frankenberger, *Kant und die Frage nach der göttlichen Allgenugsamkeit,* Frankfurt, 1984.

R.Z. Friedman, "Hypocrisy and the Highest Good, Hegel on Kant's Transition from Morality to Religion," *Journal of the History of Philosophy* **24**, 1986.

J.A. Froude, *Life and Letters of Erasmus*, Longmans and Green & Co., 1899.

G. Funke, *Akten des 4. Internationalen Kant-Kongress*, Berlin, 1974.

G. Funke, *Von der Aktualität Kants*, Bonn, 1979.

G.U. Gabel, "Canadian Theses on Kant 1976-1985," *Kant-Studien* **80**, 1989.

G.U.Gabel, *Eine Verzeichnis der. Dissertationen aus deutschland 1900-1980,* Köln, 1987.

G.U. Gabel, *Hegel, Kant: Eine Bibliographie der Dissertationen aus den deutschsprachigen Ländern 1900-1975*, Hamburg, 1980.

G.U. Gabel, *Kant. An Index to Theses and Dissertations Accepted by Universities in Canada and the United States 1976-1985*, Köln, 1989.

G.U. Gabel, "Theses on Kant Accepted by Universities in Australia and New-Zealand 1918-1987," *Kant-Studien* **81**, 1990.

W.A. Galston, *Kant and the Problem of History*, Chicago U.P., 1975.

B.A. Gerrish, *Grace and Reason*, O.U.P., 1962.

C.F. Geyer, "Das Jahrhundert der Theodizee," *Kant-Studien* **73**, 1982.

C.F. Geyer, *Leid und Böses*, Freiburg, 1983.

J.H. Gill, "Kant, Analogy, and Natural Theology," *International Journal for Philosophy of Religion* **16**, 1984.

F. Gniffke, "Die gegenwärtigkeit des mythos in Kants mutmaßungen über den anfang der menschheits geschichte," *Zeitschrift fur philosophische Forschung* **38**, 1984.

J.J. Godfrey, *A Philosophy of Human Hope,* Martinus Nijhoff, 1987.

T.F. Godlove, *Religion, interpretation, and diversity of belief*, C.U.P., 1989.

A.H. Goldman, *Moral Knowledge*, Routledge, 1988.

L. Goldmann, *Immanuel Kant,* transl. R. Black, N.L.B., *1971.*

M.Goulder, ed., *Incarnation and Myth: The Debate Continued*, S.C.M., 1979.

M.Green, ed., *The Truth of God Incarnate*, Hodder and Stoughton, 1977.

R.M. Green, *Religion and Moral Reason,* O.U.P., 1988.

R.M. Green, *Religious Reason,* O.U.P., 1978.

M.J. Gregor, *Laws of Freedom,* Basil Blackwell, 1963.

N. Grimaldi, "Espoir et desespoir de la raison chez Kant," *Kant-Studien* **82**, 1991.

F. Groß, ed., *Immanuel Kant, sein Leben in Darstellung von Zeitgenossen*, *Die Biographien von*

L.E. Borowski, R.B. Jachmann und A.Ch. Wasianski, German Library in Berlin, 1912.

P. Guillamaud, "La Negatif chez Kant," *Etudes Philosophiques* **2**, 1990.

A.Gulyga, *Kant: His Life and Thought,* transl. M. Despalatovic, Birkhäuser, 1987.

C. Gunton, *Enlightenment and Alienation,* Marshall Morgan and Scott, 1985.

E. Haenssler, "Die Philosophie im Bild und Urteil der Theologie," *Studia Philosophica* **26**, 1966.

D. Hampson, *Theology and Feminism,* Basil Blackwell, 1990.

W.L. Harper et. al., eds., *Kant on Causality, Freedom, and Objectivity*, Minnesota U.P., 1984.

K. Hart, *The Trespass of the Sign,* C.U.P., 1989.

L. Hauser, *Religion als Prinzip und Faktum*, Frankfurt am Main, 1983.

B.L. Hebblethwaite and S. Sutherland, eds., *The Philosophical Frontiers of Christian Theology*, C.U.P., 1982.

B.L. Hebblethwaite, *The Problems of Theology,* C.U.P., 1980.

G.W.F. Hegel, *Faith and Knowledge*, transl. W. Cerf and H.S. Harris, State University of New York Press, 1977.

M. Heidegger, *Kant and the Problem of Metaphysics,* transl. J.S. Churchill, Indiana U.P., 1962.

H. Heimsoeth, *Astronomisches und Theologisches in Kants Weltverständnis,* Wiesbaden, 1963.

J. Hick, *An Interpretation of Religion,* Macmillan, 1989.

J. Hick and P.F. Knitter, eds., *The Myth of Christian Uniqueness*, S.C.M., 1987.

J. Hick, ed., *The Myth of God Incarnate*, S.C.M., 1977.

J. Hick, *The Philosophy of Religion,* Prentice-Hall Inc., 1963.

J. Hick, *The Second Christinaity*, S.C.M., 1983.

T.E. Hill, "Moral Purity and the Lesser Evil," *Monist* **66**, 1983.

H. Hofmeister, "' Etsi Deus Non Daretur': Zum Verhältnis von Philosophie und Theologie," *Neue Zeitschrift für systematische Theologie und Religionsphilosophie* **21**, 1979.

H. Hofmeister, "Philosophische und theologische Ethik," *Wiener Jahrbuch für Philosophie* **11**, 1978.

P. Hutchings, *Kant on Absolute Value*, George Allen and Unwin, 1972.

R.B. Jachmann, *Prüfung der kantischen Religionsphilosophie in hinsicht auf die ihr beygelegte Aehnlichkeit mit dem reinen Mystizism*, Königsberg, 1800.

K. Jaspers, "Das radikal Böse bei Kant," *Aneigung und Polemik*, ed., H. Saner, München, 1968.

K. Jaspers, *Kant: Leben, Werk, Wirkung,* R. Piper and Co., 1975.

H.E. Jones, *Kant's Principle of Personality*, Wisconsin U.P., 1971.

W.T. Jones, *Morality and Freedom in Kant,* O.U.P., 1940.

T. Kadowaki, *Das radikal Böse bei Kant*, Dissertation, Bonn, 1960.

I. Kaftan, *Kant, der Philosoph des Protestantismus*, Berlin, 1904.

E. Katzer, *Luther und Kant*, Gießen, 1910.

F. Kaulbach, *Immanuel Kant*, Berlin, 1969.

C. Keller, *Das Theologische in der Moraltheologie*, Dissertation, Tübingen, 1973.

J. Kemp, *The Philosophy of Kant*, O.U.P., 1968.

A. Kenny, *Reason and Religion,* Basil Blackwell, 1987.

G.E. Kerford and D.E. Walford, transl. and intro., *Selected Pre-Critical Writings and Correspondence with Beck*, Manchester U.P., 1968.

G.C. Kerner, *Three Philosophical Moralists, Mill, Kant, and Sartre*, Martinus Nijhoff, 1983.

H. Köhl, *Kants Gesinnungsethik*, Berlin, 1990.

E.W. Kohls, *Luther oder Erasmus*, Basel, 1978.

K. Konhardt, "Die Unbegreiflichkeit der Freiheitüberlegungen zu Kants Lehre vom Bösen," *Zeitschrift für Philosophische Forschung* **42**, 1988.

J. Kopper, "Quelques remarques sur la doctrine du mal chez Kant," *Etudes Philosophiques* **1**, 1990.

R. Koppers, *Zum Begriff des Bosen bei Kant*, Bamberg, 1986.

A. Koutsouvilis, "Kant and the Christian Command," *Heythrop Journal* **14**, 1973.

L. Kreimendahl, "Kants Kolleg über Rationaltheologie—Fragmente einer bislang unbekannten Vorlesungsnachschrift," *Kant-Studien* **79**, 1988.

R. Kroner, *Kant's Weltanschauung,* Chicago U.P., 1956.

G.W. Leibniz, *Theodicy*, Routledge and Kegan Paul, 1951.

O. Lempp, *Das Problem der Theodizee in der Philosophie und Literatur des 18. Jahrhunderts bis auf Kant und Schiller*, Hildesheim, 1976.

A. Lichtigfeld, "A Kantian Contribution to the Problem of Evil," *Kant-Studien* **58**, 1967.

H. Linden (van der), *Kantian Ethics and Socialism*, Hackett Publishing Co., 1988.

A.L. Loades, *Kant and Job's Comforters*, Avero, 1985.

J.B. Lotz, *Kant und die Scholastik heute,* München, 1955.

F. Lötzsch, *Kritik der Autorität,* Köln, 1974.

F. Lötzsch, *Vernunft und Religion im Denken Kants*, Köln, 1976.

K. Löwith, *Zur Kritik der christlichen Überlieferung*, Stuttgart, 1966.

V.A. McCarthy, *Quest for a Philosophical Jesus: Christianity and Philosophy in Rousseau, Kant, Hegel, and Schelling,* Mercer U.P., 1986.

J.D. McFarland, *Kant's Concept of Teleology*, Edinburgh U.P., 1970.

D. McKenzie, "A Kantian Theodicy," *Faith and Philosophy* **1**, 1984.

D. McKenzie, "Kant and Protestant Theology," *Encounter* **43**, 1982.

A. MacIntyre, *After Virtue*, Duckworth, 1981.

A. MacIntyre, *A Short History of Ethics*, Routledge and Kegan Paul, 1967.

D.M. MacKinnon, *A Study in Ethical Theory*, Adam and Charles Black, 1957.

D.M. MacKinnon, *Borderlands of Theology*, Lutterworth, 1968.

D.M. MacKinnon, "Coleridge and Kant," in J. Beer, ed.,*Coleridge's Variety,* Macmillan, 1974.

D.M. MacKinnon, "Kant's Agnosticism," *Blackfriars* **28**, 1947.

D.M. MacKinnon, *Themes in Theology*, T. and T. Clark, 1987.

D.M. MacKinnon, *The Problem of Metaphysics*, C.U.P., 1974.

J. Macquarrie, *Jesus Christ in Modern Thought*, S.C.M. Press, 1990.

B. Magee, *The Philosophy of Schopenhauer,* O.U.P., 1983.

R. Malter, "A Kant Bibliography 1976-1978," *Kant-Studien* **72**, 1981.

R. Malter, "Gott is doch kein Wahn, Bemerkungen zur transzendentalen Freiheitslehre von Hermann Krings," *Philosophisches Jahrbuch* **90**, 1983.

R. Malter, "Kant Bibliography 1987," *Kant-Studien* **80**, 1989.

R. Malter, "Kant Bibliography 1989," *Kant-Studien* **82**, 1991.

R. Malter, "Neue Bücher zu Kants Rationaltheologie und Philosophie der Religion," *Akten* **I**, pp.155-177, 1974.

G. Marcel, *Being and Having*, A. and C. Black, 1949.

J. Maritain, *Moral Philosophy*, Geoffrey Bles, 1964.

F. Marty, *La naissance de la metaphysique chez Kant*, Beauchesne, 1980.

F. Marty, "L'analogie chez Kant," *Les Études Philosophiques* **Juillet-Decembre**, 1989.

V. Mathieu, *Kants Opus Postumum*, Frankfurt am Main, 1989.

G. Meckenstock, *Deterministische Ethik und kritische Theologie*, Berlin, 1988.

W. Metz, *"Christologie bei Immanuel Kant?," Theologisches Zeitschrift* **27**, 1971.

G.E. Michalson, *Fallen Freedom*, C.U.P., 1990.

G.E. Michalson, "Moral Regeneration and Divine Aid in Kant," *Religious Studies* **25**, 1989.

G.E. Michalson, "The Non-Moral Element in Kant's Moral Proof of the Existence of God," *Scottish Journal of Theology* **39**, 1986.

K.H. Michel, *Immanuel Kant und die Frage der Erkennbarkeit Gottes*, Wuppertal, 1987.

M. Midgley, *Heart and Mind*, Harvester, 1981.

F. Mildenberger, "Das Glaube als Voraussetzungen für ein wahres Denken Gottes," *Neue Zeitschrift für systematische Theologie und religionsphilosophie* **32**, 1990.

B. Mitchell, *Morality, Religious and Secular,* Clarendon, 1980.

J. Moltmann, *Theology of Hope*, transl. J.W. Leitch, SCM, 1967.

J. Moltmann, *The Trinity and the Kingdom of God,* transl. M. Kohl, S.C.M., 1981.

I. Murdoch, *The Sovereignty of Good,* Routledge and Kegan Paul, 1971 edition.

J.G. Murphy, *Kant: The Philosophy of Right,* Macmillan, 1970.

D. Nineham, *The Use and Abuse of the Bible,* Unwin and Brothers, 1976.

G. Norburn, "Kant's Philosophy of Religion; a Preface to Christology?," *Scottish Journal of Theology* **26**, 1973.

W. Oelmüller, "Kants Beitrag zur Grundlegung einer praktischen Philosophie in der Moderne," *Philosophisches Jahrbuch* **75,** 1967-8.

J.C. Olin, ed., *A Catholic Protestant Reappraisal*, Fordham U.P., 1969.

J.C. Olin, *Desiderius Erasmus: Christian Humanism and The Reformation*, Fordham U.P., 1975.

O. Oneill, *Constructions of Reason*, C.U.P., 1989.

P.R. Ostermeyer, *Kants Lehre von dem bösen und guten Prinzip im Vergleich mit der christlichen Lehre von der Sünde und Erlösung,* Königsberg, 1905.

R. Otto, *The Idea of the Holy*, O.U.P., 1950.

R. Otto, *The Philosophy of Religion based on Kant and Fries*, William and Norgate, 1931.

S. Palmquist, "Faith as the Key to the Justification of Transcendental Reflection," *The Heythrop Journal* **25**, 1984.

S. Palmquist, "Immanuel Kant: A Christian Philosopher?," *Faith and Philosophy* **6**, 1989.

H.J. Paton, *The Categorical Imperative*; *A Study in Kant's Moral Philosophy,* Chicago U.P., 1948.

L. Paul, *Kant's Lehre vom radikalen Bösen. Ein Vergleich mit der Lehre der Kirche,* Halle, 1865.

F. Paulsen, *Immanuel Kant, His Life and Doctrine,* transl. and ed., J.E. Creighton and A. Léfevre, Nimmo, 1902.

F. Paulsen, "Kant, der Philosoph des Protestantismus," *Kant-Studien* **4**, 1900.

J. Payne, *Erasmus, His Theology of the Sacraments*, M.E. Bratcher, 1970.

D. Pears, *Wittgenstein*, Fontana, 1971.

M. Mann Phillips, *Erasmus and The Northern Renaissance*, Collier Books, 1965.

M. Mann Phillips, *The Adages of Erasmus: A Study with Translations*, C.U.P., 1964.

G. Picht, *Kants Religionsphilosophie,* Stuttgart, 1985.

F. Pitschl, *Das Verhältnis vom Ding an sich und den Ideen des Übersinnlichen in Kants Kritischer Philosophie*, München, 1979.

G. Prauss, *Kant über Freiheit als Autonomie,* Frankfurt am Main, 1983.

G. Prauss, *Kant und das Problem der Dinge an sich,* Bonn, 1977.

S. Priest, ed., *Hegel's Critique of Kant*, O.U.P., 1987.

D.P. Quinn, *An Examination of Kant's Treatment of Transcendental Freedom*, University Press of America, 1988.

P.L. Quinn, "Christian Atonement and Kantian Justification," *Faith and Philosophy* **3**, 1986.

P.L. Quinn, "Original Sin, Radical Evil and Moral Identity," *Faith and Philosophy* **1**, 1984.

G. Rabel, *Kant: A Study,* O.U.P., 1963.

C.A. Raschke, *Moral Action, God and History in the Thought of Immanuel Kant,* A.A.R.and Scholars Press, 1975.

B. Reardon, *Kant as Philosophical Theologian*, Macmillan, 1988.

O. Reboul, "Kant et la Religion," *Revue D'histoire et de Philosophie Religieuses* **50**, 1970.

O. Reboul, *Kant et le Probleme du Mal*, Montreal, 1971.

H. Reiner, *Duty and Inclination,* Martinus Nijhoff, 1983.

H. Renz, *Geschichtsgedanke und Christusfrage*, Göttingen, 1973.

W. Ritzel, *Immanuel Kant—Eine Biographie*, Berlin, 1985.

J. Roberts, *German Philosophy: An Introduction,* Polity Press, 1988.

J.A.T. Robinson, *Honest to God,* S.C.M., 1963.

K. Roettgers, *Kritik und Praxis*, Berlin, 1975.

G. Rohrmoser, *Emancipation und Freiheit*, München, 1970.

G. MacDonald Ross, ed., *Kant and His Influence,* Thoemmes, 1990.

P. Rossi, "Kant as a Christian Philosopher—Hope and the Symbols of Christian Faith," *Philosophy Today* **25**, 1981.

P. Rossi, "Kant's Doctrine of Hope—Reason's Interest and the Things of Faith," *New Scholasticism* **56**, 1982.

P. Rossi, *Together Towards Hope: A Journey to Moral Theology*, Notre Dame U.P., 1983.

N. Rotenstreich, *Practice and Realization,* Martinus Nijhoff, 1979.

E.G. Rupp et al., transl. and ed., *Luther and Erasmus: Free Will and Salvation*, Westminster Press, 1986.

H. Rust, *Kant und das Erbe des Protestantismus,* Gotha, 1928.

G.B. Sala, *Kant und die Frage nach Gott, Gottesbeweiskritik in den Schriften Kants*, Berlin, 1990.

G.B. Sala, "Kant und die Theologie der Hoffnung," *Theologie und Philosophie* **56**, 1981.

J. Sallis, *The Gathering of Reason,* Ohio U.P., 1980.

R. Schaeffler, *Die Wechselbeziehungen zwischen Philosophisches und Katholischer Theologie,* Darmstadt, 1980.

R. Schaeffler, "Philosophie der Hoffnung als socratik der praktischen Vernunft," *Philosophisches Jahrbuch* **88**, 1981.

R. Schaeffler, *Religionsphilosophie*, Freiburg, 1983.

R. Schaeffler, *Was Dürfen Wir Hoffen?,* Darmstadt, 1979.

R.M. Schott, *Cognition and Eros: A Critique of the Kantian Paradigm*, Beacon Press, 1988.

G. Schrader, "Kant's Presumed Repudiation of the 'Moral Argument' in the Opus Postumum: an Examination of Adickes' Interpretation," *Philosophy* **26**, 1951.

N.O. Schroll-Fleischer, *Der Gottesgedanke in der Philosophie Kants*, Odense U.P., 1981.

H. Schülke, *Kants und Luthers Ethik*, Greifswald, 1937.

C. Schulte, "Zweckwidriges in der Erfahrung zur Genese des Mißlingens aller philosophischen Versuchen in der Theodizee bei Kant," *Kant-Studien* **82**, 1991.

W.A. Schulze, "Das Johannesevangelium im Deutschen Idealismus," *Zeitschrift für Philosophische Forschung* **18**, 1964.

J.G. Schütz, *Der Individualitäts—und Sozietätscharakter der Reich-Gottes-Idee Immanuel Kants,* Bamberg, 1977.

A. Schweitzer, *Die Religionsphilosophie Kants von der Kritik der reinen Vernunft bis zur Religion innerhalb der grenzen der blossen Vernunft,* Freiburg, 1899.

G.C. Scot, "The Practical Theology of Martin Luther," *Religious Humanism* **18**, 1984.

R. Selbach, "Eine bisher unbeachtete Quelle des 'Streits der Fakultäten,'" *Kant-Studien* **82**, 1991.

W.L. Sessions, "Kant and Religious Belief," *Kant-Studien* **71**, 1980.

T. Siegfried "Luther und Kant," *Lutherjahrbuch* **9**, 1927.

T. Siegfried, *Luther und Kant: Ein geistesgeschichtlicher Vergleich im Anschluß an den Gewissensbegriff*, Gießen, 1930.

E. Simons, "Hoffnung als elementare Kategorie praktischer Vernunft," *Philosophisches Jahrbuch* **88**, 1981.

N. Kemp Smith, *A Commentary to Kant's Critique of Pure Reason*, Macmillan and Co., 1923.

P. Smith, *Erasmus: A Study of his Life, Ideals and Place in History*, Harper and Brothers, 1923.

W. Soffer, "Kant on the Tutelage of God and Nature," *Thomist* **45**, 1981.

C.F. Stäudlin, *Beitrage zur Philosophie und Geschichte der Religion und Sittenlehre*, Lübeck, 1797.

R.P. Stevens, "The Impact of Theodicy on Kant's Conception of Moral Practice," *Theoria* **47**, 1981.

P.F. Strawson, *The Bounds of Sense*, Methuen and Co., 1966.

J. Stuckenberg, *The Life of Immanuel Kant,* Thoemmes, 1990 edition.

R.J. Sullivan, "The Kantian Model of Moral Practical Reason," *The Monist* **66**, 1983.

R.J. Sullivan, *Immanuel Kant's Moral Theory,* C.U.P., 1989.

K. Surin, *Theology and the Problem of Evil,* Basil Blackwell, 1986.

S.R. Sutherland, *God Jesus and Belief,* Basil Blackwell, 1984.

S.R. Sutherland and T.A. Roberts, eds., *Religion, Reason and the Self, Essays in honour of H.D.Lewis,* Cardiff U. of Wales, 1989.

R. Swinburne, *Responsibility and Atonement*, O.U.P., 1989.

T.G. Tappert, ed., *Selected Writings of Martin Luther, 1520-1523,* Fortress U. P., 1967.

A.E. Teale, *Kantian Ethics,* O.U.P., 1951.

H. d'Aviau de Ternay, *Traces Bibliques Dans La Loi Morale Chez Kant*, Beauchesne, 1986.

R. Theis, "La sens de la metaphysique dans la Critique de la Raison Pure," *Revue Philosophique de Louvain* **83**, 1985

P. Tillich, *Systematic Theology,* W. Clowes and Sons, 1953.

G. Uphues, *Kant und seine Vorgänger,* Berlin, 1906.

H. Vaihinger, *The Philosophy of 'As-If,'* transl. C.K. Ogden, Kegan Paul, 1924.

R.L. Velkley, *Freedom and the End of Reason*, Chicago U.P., 1989.

G. Vesey, ed., *The Philosophy in Christianity,* C.U.P., 1989.

H. de Vos, *Kant als Theoloog*, Baarn, 1968.

W. Vossenkuhl, "The Paradox in Kant's Rational Religion," *Proceedings of the Aristotelian Society* **88**, 1987-8.

F. Wagner, "Aspekte der Rezeption Kantischer Metaphysik-Kritik in der evangelischen Theologie des 19. und 20. Jahrhunderts," *Neue Zeitschrift für systematische Theologie und religionsphilosophie* **27**, 1985.

F. Wagner, "Religionsphilosophie und philosophische Theologie," *Philosophische Rundschau* **37**, 1990.

R.C.S. Walker, *A Selective Bibliography on Kant,* Study Aids Vol. V.,Oxford, 1978.

R.C.S. Walker, *The Coherence Theory of Truth,* Routledge, 1989.

W.H. Walsh, *Kant's Criticism of Metaphysics,* Edinburgh U.P., 1975.

W.H. Walsh, "Kant's Moral theology," *Proceedings of the British Academy* **49**, 1963.

B. Wand, "Religious Concepts and Moral Theory: Luther and Kant," *Journal of the History of Philosophy* **9**, 1971.

K. Ward, *The Development of Kant's View of Ethics,* Basil Blackwell, 1972.

K. Ward, *Rational Theology and the Creativity of God,* Basil Blackwell, 1982.

M. Warner, *Philosophical Finesse*, O.U.P., 1989.

E.I. Watkin, *Theism, Agnosticism and Atheism,* Unicorn, 1936.

J.R. Watson, ed., *An Infinite Complexity*, Edinburgh U. P., 1983.

J. Watson, *The Philosophy of Kant Explained,* J. Maclehose and Sons, 1908.

C.C.J. Webb, *Kant's Philosophy of Religion*, O.U.P., 1926.

C. Webster, *The Ethics of Bishop Butler and Immanuel Kant,* Ann Arbor, 1888.

D. Wiebe, "The Ambiguous Revolution: Kant on the Nature of Faith," *Scottish Journal of Theology* **33**, 1980.

T.E. Wilkerson, *Kant's Critique of Pure Reason,* O.U.P., 1976.

T.E. Willey, *Back to Kant,* Wayne State U.P., 1978.

R. Wimmer, *Kants kritische Religionsphilosophie,* Berlin, 1990.

A. Winter, "Gebet und Gottesdienst bei Kant," *Theologie und Philosophie* **52**, 1977.

A. Winter, "Kant zwischen den Konfessionen," *Theologie und Philosophie* **50**, 1975.

A. Winter, "Theologische Hintergründe der Philosophie Kants," *Theologie und Philosophie* **51**, 1976.

D. Witschen, *Kant und die Idee einer christlichen Ethik,* Dissertation, Münster, 1984.

K. Wojtyla, *Collected Plays and Writings on Theatre*, transl. B. Taborski, California U.P., 1987.

A.W. Wood, "Kant's Deism," in *Kant's Philosophy of Religion Reconsidered*, ed., P. Rossi and M. Green, Indiana U.P., 1991.

A.W. Wood, *Kant's Moral Religion.*, Cornell U. P., 1970.

A.W. Wood, *Kant's Rational Theology*, Cornell U.P., 1978.

A.W. Wood, ed., *Self and Nature in Kant's Philosophy,* Cornell U.P., 1984.

M. Wundt, *Kant als Metaphysiker*, Hildesheim, 1984.

Y.Yovel, *Kant and the Philosophy of History*, Princeton U.P., 1980.

Y. Yovel, ed., *Kant's Practical Philosophy Reconsidered*, Klüwer Academic Publishers, 1989.

G. Yule, *Luther: Theologian for Catholics and Protestants*, T and T. Clark, 1985.

S. Zac, "Religion naturelle et religions révélées selon Kant," *Revue de Metaphysique et de Morale* **73**, 1968.

M-B. Zeldin, "The Summum Bonum, the Moral Law, and the Existence of God," *Kant-Studien* **62**, 1971.

A. Zweig, ed., *Immanuel Kant: Philosophical Correspondence, 1759-1799*, Chicago U.P., 1967.

A. Zweig, ed., *The Essential Kant*, Chicago U.P., 1970.

AUTHOR INDEX

SUBJECT INDEX